MW01601919

Runaway Train

H.R. Johnson

KWE Publishing

Johnson, Heather. *Runaway Train*

Copyright © 2024 by Heather all rights reserved.

ISBNs: 979-8-9865705-4-9 (paperback), 979-8-9865705-5-6 (e-book)

Library of Congress Catalog Number: 0000000000

Second Edition. All rights reserved. No portion of this book may be reproduced, stored in a retrieval system, or transmitted in any form or by any means - including but not limited to electronic, mechanical, digital, photocopy, recording, scanning, blogging or other - except for brief quotations in critical reviews, blogs, or articles, without the prior written permission of the publisher, KWE Publishing.

For my beautiful mother, L.B. ~
Your darkest days lit a fire in me so bright
it will continue to glow for generations to come.

In Memory of Marialena "Maria" Coco Ward

Maria, my dedicated, compassionate book coach and an author herself, helped me bring *Runaway Train* to life. Over months of writing, Maria was always there to offer me encouragement, answer my questions, and give me advice and support. She made sure I never felt alone as I wrote about some of the most challenging times of my life.

Maria, thank you for helping make these books a reality. I couldn't have asked for a better book coach, confidant, and mentor You are loved and missed.

Preface

Runaway Train is a true story about my family's struggle to survive the severely flawed foster care system, and the cycles of family abuse that led us there. I tell my story in present time where you will come alongside me through over 40 different foster care placements in a seven-year period with countless caseworkers, counselors, etc.

The facts are:

In 2019, 672,000 kids spent time in foster care, 71,000 of which were waiting to be adopted. More than 20,000 kids aged out of the foster care system that year without permanent families. According to research, those who age out of the system are more likely to become homeless, unemployed, or incarcerated. Only 4% of the youth that aged out of foster care earned a four-year college degree, whereas 36% of their peers in the general population had done so (childrensrights.org).

At the age of nineteen, I told myself that someday I would tell my story with the hope of helping someone else that may be going through similar circumstances. I spent years making excuses not to do it; I'm not smart enough; I never finished college; people will judge me; my family will be angry. Growing up in the system poisoned my way of thinking. The thought that I could ever do it seemed ridiculous. It wasn't until the age of thirty-two that I finally sat down and wrote it. And now, at almost forty, after wasting more time on fear and self-doubt, I feel compelled to finish what I started.

Writing my story in the present time came with many challenges. I felt the only way to tell the story honestly was to become that lost little girl again. I needed to relive all the trauma and feel all the emotions as if I were going through them for the first time. There were times I wanted to give up from the mental exhaustion of it all. In the end, I gained far more from it than I could have ever imagined. I had to recognize and face the cycles I was unknowingly repeating. I knew I couldn't help another person if I did not at first help myself. To call it therapeutic would be an understatement. It was an awakening. I knew I had to make major changes in my life if I ever wanted that happy ending, and I did. It didn't fall into my lap as soon as I left the system. I had to fight my ass off for it. I still continue to fight for it. No matter what the outcome is of telling my story, it is worth it. Even if the only person it saves is me.

My reasons for writing my story are so much bigger than any of the excuses I can come up with not to. After all of these years, it still amazes me how incognizant people are of the system and the voiceless children who are trapped in it. While all of our stories differ in many ways, one thing remains the same: we are the forgotten children that very few fight for. My hope is to help give a voice to those children. I know there are a lot of kindhearted people out there who would want to do more if only they knew.

Names and identifying details have been changed to protect the privacy of individuals. However, the story, the experiences, and the words are mine alone.

WARNING - This book contains explicit content and language.

Introduction

To the adults reading this:

If you are working in the system, fostering, or going to school to work with these kids in any capacity, my hope is that you gain knowledge from reading my story. I want to give you a glimpse of what goes on inside the minds of the children you will work with. Most importantly, I hope you learn to have compassion and the immeasurable amount of patience it's going to take. During my journey, I met a lot of people who seemed to simply not care at all. But a lot of times, some were just burned out. There may be times you will have to fight like hell to not allow that to happen to you. If you start to feel defeated by it all, remember why you started doing it in the first place. We need you, even when we're difficult and act like we don't. We learned at a young age not to get too close. People leave, so we unintentionally push them away to avoid the pain. If you stay and fight, you will make all the difference in a child's life. Stay and show them that they are not broken or damaged goods unworthy of love. Throughout all of my time in the system, there were only a few who stayed and fought for me. But that's all it took; one would have been enough. Those people are my heroes, and I am thankful for them every day.

To the young people reading this:

If you are in the shoes I once was, you are my soulmate. I want you to know that you are worthy; you are loved; you are strong; you are fierce; and you matter! If you keep going and never give up, I promise, you will be a force to be reckoned with. Don't let yourself get stuck because of self-doubt. I'm here to tell you, it's all *bullshit!* Those things you tell yourself are lies. You are just as smart and capable as anyone else. Don't let anyone tell you otherwise. Most importantly, be kind to yourself; love yourself; and don't give up on yourself. I'm not going to lie and tell you that it will always be easy. The challenges don't end the day you turn 18 and leave the system. You will have to continue to do the work. What I can promise you is that every day you keep fighting, it's so incredibly worth it! You have a power within yourself that a lot don't. You have the knowledge, courage, and strength it will take to break all of those generational curses that came before you. My mother once said something to me in a dream that was so incredibly real I could feel her hair and smell her perfume. It never made more sense to me than it does right now. So I will give you the same advice she gave me: "You know what you need to do, now go into the world and do it!"

Runaway Train
Derailed

Part One

Chapter One

"Heather! Heather! Wake up! Mom and Dad are fighting again. I think he's really going to hurt her this time!"

I wake up from my comatose sleep to see my eleven-year-old sister, Malory, standing above me, her long, bleach-blonde hair tickling my face as she's shaking me to get up.

"Leave me alone, I'm sleeping!" I groan, pushing her hair out of my face.

She continues to shake me, and I open my eyes, ready to punch her in the face for ruining my dream about a life where Mom and Dad don't get drunk and beat each other up. When I see the fear in her hazel-green eyes, I suddenly snap out of it and jump out of bed. "What happened? What's going on?" I ask in a panic, rubbing the sleep out of my eyes.

I hear the crashing of dishes and shattering of glass as Mom screams out in her slurred, drunken voice, "I'll kill you, you sorry son of a bitch! You coward! You think you're better than me? You think your shit doesn't stink?"

I hear the pounding of what must be Dad's footsteps on the floor as he runs after Mom like a bull charging his target. I poke my head out of the bedroom door to get a better look, and I see my little brother, Theo, running down the stairs towards Dad so fast that nothing could stop him. He leaps and lunges himself onto Dad's back. *Oh, shit!*

"Heather! What's going on?" asks Mal, who's sitting on the bed behind me, terrified.

"Get off her! Leave my mom alone you asshole or I'll kill you!" Theo screams.

Dad flings Theo off his back. "Get off me and go back to your room!" he shouts.

I have to call the police. Get to the damn phone, Heather, and call the police before he kills her!

I run as fast as I can to my parents' bedroom to the bedside phone and dial 911. "My dad is going to kill my mom. Please come right now!" I blurt out, in a panic.

I hear a female voice on the other end of the phone. "Ok, try to calm down. What's your name?" she asks, concerned.

"Did you not hear what I said, lady? Who the hell cares what my name is! Come right now!" I shout, and then quickly ramble off my address, breathing so heavy that my words sound like a jumbled mess.

"Ok, honey, officers are on the way. Now please, tell me, what is your name?" she asks again.

"My name is Heather. How soon will they be here?"

"How old are you, Heather?"

"I'm nine. How much longer is it going to take them to get here?"

Panic is starting to set in, and I'm growing tired of all these silly questions when I hear what sounds like the kitchen table being overturned.

"Knock it off, you damn drunk!" Dad screams. Mom is really tearing up the house. She always does this when she's drunk. *God, I really hate her sometimes!* I hear a big bang from what sounds like Dad wrestling Mom to the floor.

"Where are you in the house, Heather?" the stranger on the phone asks.

"I'm in my mom and dad's bedroom hiding next to the bed."

"Where are your mom and dad now?" she asks.

"I think they're downstairs in the kitchen."

"Ok, you stay where you are. Ok, Heather? Do they have any weapons?" The glow from the moon is shining a light through the curtains onto the table, and I can see Dad's cigarettes so I take a few for later. "Heather, are you still there? Does your dad have a weapon?"

"No, I don't think so. Please just hurry up! My brother is down there!" I plead.

"Is your brother hurt?" she asks.

"I don't know. I can go check."

"No!" she cries out. "Heather, I want you to stay right where you are. The officers are outside of your house now. I want you to tell me as soon as they're inside, ok?"

"Ok," I whisper, feeling a sense of relief.

"Now you're going to jail, you son of a bitch! They're coming to get your sorry ass!" screams Mom.

I hear banging on the door and a loud voice. "POLICE! OPEN UP!"

Mom runs across the room and swings the door open with such force it smashes into the closet door behind it. The picture frames from the shelf by the door hit the floor with a big crash.

"Get him! Take him to jail! He was beating me again!" Mom yells.

Great! I think to myself, *another show for the neighbors.*

"Ok, ma'am, I'm going to need you to back away from the door and let me in," says the officer.

"Heather, are they in the house now?" asks the dispatcher on the phone.

"Yes," I reply.

"Ok, I'm going to hang up now. You stay where you are, ok?" she adds.

"Yeah, ok," I say quickly, hanging up the phone so I can crawl over to the bedroom door to get a better look.

As I slowly open the door, I see my five-year-old brother, Johnny, sitting in his bedroom doorway a few feet away, watching and crying.

3

"Johnny, come in here with me," I say, holding out my hand. He crawls over to the bedroom door, and I grab him and pull him close to me. I squeeze him as tight as I can. "Stop crying, ok? Everything is going to be alright. Mom's just drunk again. She'll pass out soon, and everything will be ok tomorrow," I assure him as I usher him into Mom and Dad's bed. I pull the covers tightly over him. "Try to go back to sleep."

"Ok," he says, wiping the tears from his eyes.

I go back to the bedroom door and crawl out into the hallway to watch through the staircase banister. I see a very tall, muscular Black officer standing right outside the door. He's been to our house before. Mom's standing in front of him, rambling on in her drunken tone, and I can tell he's losing his cool. I don't like him; he seems like a real mean prick. He never talks to us and doesn't have much patience with Mom's drunken rages. Some of the other cops that come over are really nice to us, especially Paul. He's my favorite. I wish he was the one that came tonight.

"I said to back the fuck away from the door so I can get in!" he yells out in his big, mean voice.

"Geesh! What the hell did I do?" Mom yells back as she opens the door further and stumbles to the side to let him in. "You don't have to talk to me that way, I didn't do anything! He's the one beating me up!" she yells, pointing her finger at Dad.

Oh my God, Mom, please just shut up!

"Hey, lady, close your mouth right now! You speak when I tell you to speak, and if I have to keep warning you, I'm gonna take your drunken ass to jail!" he snaps at her as he walks past her through the front door.

"Hey! Screw you, buddy! I have rights too!" Mom yells, walking around him and going toward the kitchen where Dad is.

Uh-oh! There she goes running her mouth as usual. When she's drunk, she thinks she can say whatever she wants to whoever she wants. It's so embarrassing.

"Alright that's it! Put your hands behind your back, I'm taking your mouthy ass in! I told you the last time we were here I wasn't gonna take your shit anymore!" the officer snaps.

Theo, who's sitting on the couch, jumps up and yells out, "Leave her alone! She didn't do anything!"

The officer shoots a look at Theo. "You just sit down, little man, and keep quiet!"

Dad walks over to Theo and puts his hand on his shoulder. "Hey, why don't you go upstairs and try to go back to bed, ok? I'm going to take care of everything."

"Get your hands off me! You never take care of anything!" he replies, pulling away from Dad. He turns and races up the stairs without even looking and stumbles over me.

"Hey! Watch where you're going, Theo!" I snap.

"Shut up, Heather! It's your fault anyway for calling the cops!" he yells back as he slams his door.

Jerk! He's always sticking up for Mom no matter what she does. Only eight years old, but he walks around with his chest pumped out like nothing in the world scares him and anyone who messes with his mom is going to get it.

I turn to look back as Mom tries to make a break for it but trips over some shoes by the front door and falls flat on her face.

The officer cuffs her and stands her up. "Stop resisting!" he yells as he picks her up off the floor. She's yelling and cussing the whole way out the door and through the front yard.

Great! Everyone on the block can probably hear her. I was hoping when we moved here a couple months ago that we would get a fresh start, and no one would find out how screwed up we really are.

I go to my bedroom and open the door to find Malory lying across her bed, crying.

"They're taking Mom to jail," I say calmly as if this is the most normal occurrence in the world. In our world, though, it is normal.

Malory rolls over and looks at me with her tear-filled eyes. "Good!" she says angrily. "I hope she stays there forever!"

"C'mon, let's go downstairs and see what's going on, they're still out front," I say with a bit of excitement in my voice. *I think I'm happy she's getting arrested, at least we won't have to deal with her tonight.*

We head downstairs and kneel on the couch, where we can peek out the living room window. I look over at Dad, who is sitting on the front step, and I see him rubbing his eyes. I think he's crying. I look back toward the street where the officer is wrestling with Mom trying to get her in the car as she's screaming at him and carrying on like a drunken fool.

"I'll have you fired, you stupid n*****!" she screams out and then she spits right in his face.

Oh, no! Mom, what are you doing? I can't believe she just said that! She just said the worst word any person could say!

I'm terrified of what's coming next when the officer hauls off and punches Mom so hard in the face that she falls to the ground. Dad jumps to his feet and starts to sprint toward the street.

"Get in the house or I'll arrest your ass too!" the officer screams, pointing his finger at Dad while lifting Mom back off the ground with his free hand.

Malory jumps off the couch and runs out the front door, screaming, "You can't do that! You can't hit my mom in the face!"

Dad catches Mal in the middle of the yard and fights her back toward the house as she continues screaming and crying out. The officer barely looks up as he throws Mom in the back seat and shuts the door. With the interior light still on, I can see her thrashing around, banging her head off the divider and the window next to her. The officer jumps in the squad car and pulls off.

I can't believe what I just saw; he can't be allowed to do that, right? I can't blame him for being angry at what she said. At the same time, I am worried about her. She is my mother, but I am disgusted by her.

Dad and Mal walk through the front door. Dad looks over at me with fear and sorrow in his eyes. The happiness I felt about her leaving minutes before is now gone.

"Dad, what's going to happen to her?" I ask, my voice shaking.

"I don't know, Heth. You guys go back to your room to get some sleep, and we'll figure everything out tomorrow," he replies quietly. I can tell he's holding back his tears.

"But Dad, he hit her! Can he do that?" I ask, barely containing my tears.

"No, Heather, he can't, but your mom needs to learn to keep her mouth shut."

"Dad, you should call the police and tell them! He can't just get away with that!" cries Malory.

"It's useless, Mal. They're not going to believe us, anyway. Now, you girls need to stop worrying about everything and get to bed, you got school in the morning," he replies.

Stop worrying about everything? Is he crazy? We just saw a man three times the size of Mom, punch her in the face! How can we not worry?

We head back up to our room and close the door. Malory plops down onto her bed, buries her head into her pillow, and starts bawling. I walk over to her bed and sit down. I can feel the stinging in my eyes as my pent up tears start to roll down my face.

Malory sits up and grabs me to hug me. "I hate our life, Heather, I wanna run away!"

"I know, Mal, me too. Let's promise each other that we will never turn out like Mom and Dad, ok?"

"I promise with all my heart, Heather!" she assures me. "Let's just try to go to sleep now so we can get up in time for school in the morning," she adds, climbing under her covers.

After turning out the light and climbing into bed, I whisper, "Hey, Mal, I stole a couple cigs from Dad. Wanna smoke one with me?"

"No, Heather! You are so stupid for smoking! I should go tell Dad. You need to stop!" she says in a huff.

"If you tell on me, I'll tell all your friends you still suck your thumb like a little baby!" I snap back at her.

"And if you do that, I'll tell everyone you pee the bed, and then I'll beat your ass, you little brat!"

"Whatever, Mal, you're such a little goody two-shoes!" I snort.

"Shut your face, brat, I wanna go to sleep!"

Knowing my sister will pummel me if I don't shut up, I roll over and face the wall. There's been enough fighting for one night, so I close my eyes. I can't fall asleep, so I lie there, wondering what's going to happen to Mom and if he hurt her. I wish she would quit drinking. Life would be so much better if she would just stop. She's not a bad mom when she's not drunk, but she's drunk a lot. I feel kind of bad for Dad. I know he was probably just trying to protect himself from her during the fight; it happens all the time. She goes out drinking, comes home in a rage, and fights with him. Without Mom, we spend time playing games with Dad. He's a drinker, too, but he mostly drinks at home. The only time he really interacts with us is when he is drinking. Any other time, he's gone, working midnights on the railroad or sleeping when he is home. Mom stays at home and drinks sometimes, but she doesn't want to play games with us. When she drinks at home, she sits in the kitchen, all alone in the dark, talking to herself. I don't know if it's because she is crazy or drunk—maybe a little of both. She gets mean when she wants to be left alone. We're better off when she goes out to drink.

Maybe Dad will go to bed soon so I can go sneak my cig down in the basement. I better wait for the goody two-shoes to be asleep before I even try to sneak out or she will probably tell on me.

While waiting for the coast to be clear, I start to worry about school the next day. I wonder if my new backstabber friend, Bobbi, who lives across the street, saw what happened and if she will blab her mouth to the whole class about it tomorrow. *Mom is probably right about her, and I should stay away from her, but I don't have anyone else to talk to here.*

I don't understand the girls I'm around at my new school. They're so much different than the girls at my old school. One day, they act like my friends. The next day, they are saying things about me behind my back and wanting to beat me up on the walk home from school. Goody Two-Shoes can teach me how to fight; she's so tough she can teach me how to take them all down at once. I think about what Mal said about running away. I swear one of these days, I'm going to do it and never come back to this hell. This can't possibly be my life or my family.

Something inside of me is so different from any of them. I know it. I can feel it so strongly sometimes. I think it's going to burst out of me.

Mal and Theo are always telling me I must be adopted because I'm fat, ugly, and stupid, while they are all so perfect. *Ha! Perfect? What a joke!* "Adopted Freak" is what they call me. I'm not fat, ugly, or stupid. I know that, but I still think they must be right. *Yes! That's it! I must be adopted! Why else would I feel so different from the rest of them? My real parents are going to come find me someday, and my life will finally be normal. My real, perfect parents wouldn't have given me away on purpose, so I must have been switched at birth or stolen from the hospital. I've read that it really can happen.*

Reality sinks in, and I realize how much I look like my parents. I know I'm dreaming. My fantasies are much better than my reality. I'll keep dreaming until the real nightmare is finally over.

I think it's safe now. Mal is asleep, so I creep to the door and slowly open it. *Maybe I'll sneak across the street to Bobbi's and knock on her bedroom window. I'll see if she wants to smoke with me. She's the one that got me hooked on it in the first place.* I tiptoe down the hall and turn to go down the stairs only to find Dad standing at the bottom.

"What do you think you're doing?" he asks curiously, raising an eyebrow.

"Uhhh, nothing," I reply, lying through my teeth. *Shit! Think fast, Heather. He's caught me smoking before, and I got whacked good for it.* "Uhhh, I'm thirsty, so I was gonna get something to drink," I reply quickly.

"Go get water from the bathroom and get your ass back in bed!" he snaps back at me. He knows I'm up to something. I can hear it in his tone, so I turn to get the hell out of his sight before he gets angrier. I pretend to get some water from the bathroom sink, knowing that if I really drink any, I might pee the bed. Then, I head back to my room and slide under the covers.

Oh well, I'll just hide under the big pine tree on my way to school tomorrow and smoke there. I slowly drift off into a deep sleep.

Chapter Two

On the fifteen-minute walk to school the next day, I trail behind Mal, deeply lost in thought about the events from the night before and all the nights that have ended that way. I think about running away again, but where would I go?

Maybe I could run away and go back to Indiana. That's where we lived before we came to this crappy old place. I could stay with our friend, Laura, and her mom. I definitely don't want to go back to the foster homes we lived in when we were there, though.

Laura is my sister's age but I always tagged along with them, even though they were mean as hell to me. I really miss Laura's mom, Bridget. When she was around, she made sure they were nice to me. Laura is a bully like my sister, but I love her just as much as my sister anyway. Bridget watched us a lot when my parents went out, and I didn't mind at all. I used to wish she was our real mom. I wonder why we couldn't live with them instead of going into foster homes. It's probably because Bridget takes care of Laura and her older brother, Luke, by herself. And she has to work a lot to pay the bills.

Now, we live in Illinois. We were born in Ohio. That's where all my family is. Mom's family is supposed to come visit us around Christmas time. Maybe I can get one of my aunts or uncles to take me home with them and drop me off at Grams' house, Dad's mom; she's my favorite. *I really miss her.* We've spent a lot of time with Grams. We lived with Dad at her house for almost a year before we moved to Indiana. Mom didn't live with us when we were there, and I don't even know where she was most of the time.

Once, I overheard them saying that Mom and Dad needed to get help. *Get help for what?* I thought. I think there was more to it than just their drinking, but they never talked loud enough for me to hear everything. They were always whispering, but I know a lot more than they think I do.

Before we moved in with Grams, we used to live in a downstairs apartment of a big brick house in Ohio. I used to peek out my bedroom door at night when my parents would have parties and watch them pass around a mirror that had white powder-looking stuff on it that they would sniff up their noses with a rolled-up dollar bill.

Why would anyone ever want to sniff anything up their nose? Surely, it must hurt. I'm not sure what it's called, but I'm no dummy; I know it's some kind of drug. They always tried to be so secretive about it. Well, they were not as secretive as they thought. They would also smoke the funny-smelling stuff, kind of like a cigarette, but they used a little clip that had a feather hanging on it to hold it. I've smelled them smoking it plenty of times.

When we were moving here, I rode with Dad in the big moving truck while everyone else was in the car with Mom. I felt special being alone with Dad driving the big truck. He kept stopping on the way here, and I knew he was smoking the funny stuff because the smell was coming through the truck window. *He really must think I'm dumb.*

Mom and Dad fought a lot when we lived in the apartment. The cops were there often, but mostly because Mom used to leave us at home alone at night when Dad was at work so she could go out and party. She would even leave Johnny, and he was only a baby.

Malory was only six or seven and supposed to be in charge, but she couldn't watch all of us. God, what was Mom thinking?

She would wait until we were asleep and then sneak out. The cop who always came to our house knew Dad from high school, so he tried to help us out and not arrest Mom. He would call Grams to come get us, and she would, every time. However, the last time, they finally did arrest Mom. Mal was going to have to go to court and talk in front of everyone to tell them how Mom left us alone, but for some reason, she didn't have to. I think Mom agreed with them on something so Mal wouldn't have to talk to everyone. I'm not sure what she agreed to, though.

All of that aside, I have a couple of good memories from living in that apartment. I know as many bad memories as I have, a few isn't nearly enough. When the weather was nice and Mom was a normal mom for the day, she would take us out in the backyard for little picnics. She would lay out a blanket and we would eat PB&Js with the crunchy peanut butter because that was our favorite. We would pick dandelions, and she would show us how to make curly qs out of the stems by peeling them down the middle and dropping them into a cup of water. We would watch excitedly, "oohing" and "ahhing" as they would curl up into little spiral shapes. We'd laugh and play all afternoon. As childish as it seems now, I really miss those picnics. We don't get to do that with Mom anymore. I'd give anything to have every day be like those days.

In the winter, Dad would help us build snow forts in the backyard, and we would have snowball wars with the stinky neighbor boys that we never got along with. With Dad helping us, we were unbeatable. Their dad didn't help them, so they didn't stand a chance against us. Days that Malory was at school, I would sit on Dad's lap in the living room and watch *The Three Stooges'* with him. We would pretend to be the stooges and play fight, making all these silly noises. *Dad can be so funny sometimes.* I wish I could see that side of him more. He's mostly tired from work, and I think he's sad a lot because of Mom.

Mom wasn't supposed to come with us when we moved to Indiana. I love Mom, but sometimes I wish she wouldn't have. I know we wouldn't have lived in those foster homes if she didn't come. Dad had everything figured out, and he planned to find a live-in nanny for us so he could work. He even had an ad in the newspaper looking for one. I believe he was trying to break free and start a better life for us. *Why didn't he?* I know he loves Mom, and I suppose he thought it was best if we had her with us. He can't seem to resist her beauty and her promises to change. He wants to believe that she'll change as much as the rest of us do. Maybe someday, she really will change. I wonder where she is right now and if they have her locked away in a tiny cell. I'm worried that they might be hurting her like that cop did last night. I really hope she's home when I get back from school.

"Heather, stop dragging your feet and let's go or we're going to be late!" Malory yells, breaking me free from my thoughts. I look up at her and nod. She's ahead of me, walking with her friend, Molly.

I still don't know if anyone saw anything last night. We usually take the bus but I insisted on walking today so I could avoid Bobbi for as long as possible.

"Hey, Mal," I call out, "do you think Mom will be home when we get back from school today?"

"I don't know, Heather, stop talking about it and let's go!" she calls back through gritted teeth. She's probably embarrassed for Molly to find out, but she's nice, so she won't care or tell anyone else.

We already passed the big pine tree, so I can't sneak my cig. Besides, I couldn't find any matches or a lighter to bring with me. Dad was up when we were getting ready for school and eating our generic cereal with our powdered milk.

What happened to all the money he said he was supposed to be making working downtown? That's why we moved here, so he says. *Oh well, Malory is probably right, I need to stop smoking. She says I don't do it right, anyway, and I look stupid because I don't inhale it the way everyone else does. What does she expect? I'm only in third grade.*

The rest of the way to school, I think about the foster homes we were in when we lived in Indiana and wonder if we will have to live in foster homes here, too. One day while Dad was at work, Mom drove us to this place to talk to these people and then just left us there. We met a woman who said she would be our caseworker. *Whatever the hell that is.* Mom said that we would have to go live with another family for a little while because she was going to get help so she could be a better mom. I was afraid and hoped it wouldn't be like the place with the nuns that she dropped us off at for a weekend when we lived in Ohio.

Everyone was so mad at her when she did that. *Did Dad know where she was taking us? Mom promised us that we would all be together when she left us there that day, but she lied just like she always does.*

Theo and Johnny went to live with an Amish family while me and Malory went and lived somewhere else. Malory got along ok there, but I didn't like the new family too much. The foster mom would make me stand in the corner for what seemed like hours and the foster dad would hit me on top of the head with his fork for having my elbows on the dinner table. On another occasion, he forced me into a bath of pure hot water. The water was so hot that my body must have been shocked because it took me a few seconds to realize how hot it was. Then, he kept calling me a baby when I tried to tell him it was too hot. *Asshole!*

The grandparents seemed nice enough, though. Sometimes, we used to go to their house and swim. The grandpa taught me how to read and spell better, which I'm thankful for because I love to read books now. When I read, I like to get lost in the stories and pretend I'm in another place, living another life. It's my escape away; I would read all day long if I could.

The foster mom was as big as a house because she was pregnant. One day, she tried to spank me with a paddle. For what, I don't remember. I didn't mean to do it, but when I was trying to squirm away from her she claimed that I kicked her in the stomach. The caseworker came and got us that day to take us to live somewhere else. Malory was really mad at me for getting us moved, especially after we got to the next place. The caseworker took us to an old woman's house who was at least in her seventies. She was a real mean bitch, almost evil in a way. We had to sleep in her basement, and it was every bit of a basement—cement floors and walls, spiders, and I swear it was haunted. There were four of us sleeping down there: me, Mal, a girl named Angela, and a boy named Tommy. Tommy was tucked away into a corner by himself on a cot behind the water heater and the furnace. *At least us girls had real beds to sleep on.*

Almost every night, I would wake up in terror. I could be dreaming about ponies, it didn't matter how good or bad my dreams were. Something would wake me up, and I would feel like I couldn't move. It felt like something was sitting on me, holding me down to the bed, and I was convinced that whatever it was wanted me dead. I couldn't move my arms, legs, or even my head. I was stuck. In complete horror, I would scream out for Mal to help me because I thought I was dying. Something or someone was trying to kill me. She would wake up every night and save me. As soon as she would pull me off my bed, I could move again. On the nights that it happened, I was too afraid to go back to sleep in my own bed, so I would crawl into bed with her. She would let me, even though she knew she was bound to wake up drenched in my urine. As a good sister trying to protect me, I know it scared her almost as much as it scared me.

One night, I refused to go back to sleep in the basement at all. So, we woke up the mean old bitch, and she made me a bed on the dining room floor in the corner of the room next to the table. *Maybe she was afraid I would drench her couch?* There was a TV in the dining room that was turned on that night, and I was so delirious from the night terror that I actually tried to take grapes I saw on a commercial out of the television screen. I think that scared my poor sister more than anything. Even now, it scares the shit out of me when I think about it.

After that night, I decided I didn't want to live in that haunted place anymore with the mean old lady, so I begged her to let me call the caseworker. The old bitch wouldn't let me, so I terrorized her until she finally gave in. After pulling my hair and slapping me in the face, she called my caseworker and handed me the phone. I told the worker what had been going on there, and then, she was on her way to get me. Not my sister, though; I had to leave without her, the one who always protected me. I was happy to leave but terrified to go alone. Off to my third foster home in less than a year and I was only eight. *Wow!*

The next home wasn't like the other two at all. I was grateful given that I was there all alone. The mom was sweet and nice. She paid more attention to me than anyone ever has. She didn't have a husband or kids of her own, so everything was all about me, and I liked it. She liked to read and took me to the library every day so we could read together. I missed my family, but I really liked living there. I didn't stay with her long before it was time to go home.

I don't know why, but for some reason, I got to go home first. I spent a few weeks alone with Mom and Dad before the others came home. I liked getting to spend the time alone with them, but I wondered about Mal and the boys all the time. *Was Mal ok with that mean old lady? Mal is tough, though, she can handle almost anything.* I was excited when she and my brothers finally came home and we could be a family again.

I snap out of my thoughts as we approach the school. *Great! I wish I could have just stayed home today.* I say goodbye to Mal because she goes to another school down the street, and I head into the building. As I walk to class, I see my friend, Crystal, and wave "hi" but she doesn't wave back. Instead, she looks at me with disgust, rolls her eyes, and keeps walking.

Damn it! Bobbi snitched. That little backstabber! I'm gonna show her someday! Bobbi thinks her life is so perfect, but her dad was just sent to prison. She's the youngest of seven kids and has six older brothers, most of which are troublemakers. You don't see me walking around the school bad-mouthing her family.

I decide to hide in the bathroom so I don't have to face the class. Maybe I can stay there all day and no one will know I even came to school. I go into the bathroom and lock myself into a stall. Tucking my feet up onto the toilet seat, I pull my *Baby-Sitters Club* book out of my book bag. *I'll just sit here and read and sneak out at the end of the day when the halls are crowded.*

I only read through one chapter when there is a light knock on the bathroom door. *Oh, shit!* Crystal probably told the teacher she saw me in the hall. I didn't consider that until now. *How could I have been so stupid?*

The door slowly opens. "Heather, are you in here?" It's my teacher, Mr. Becker. He's a nice man, only in his mid-twenties but already going bald. I sit quietly, pretending not to be here, hoping he goes away.

"Heather, I know you're in here. Can you please come out so we can talk about what's going on, honey?" he says in a soft, concerned voice.

I feel my face flush a little from the sound of him calling me "honey." He knows I'm here. There's no point in trying to hide anymore, so I put my book away and get up and go out into the hall. I feel the tears of embarrassment coming, and I try to fight them because I don't want my new teacher to see me cry. There's no use though; I can't hold it back, and I suddenly start bawling.

Mr. Becker kneels down in front of me and grabs both of my hands. "Heather, what's wrong? Did something happen with one of the other girls?" he asks with concern in his eyes.

I shake my head and quickly blubber out what happened the night before with tears and snot running down my face. I tell him how I just know Bobbi must have told the other girls.

"Please don't make me go in there, Mr. Becker," I beg.

"Here's what we're going to do. I'm going to take you down to the nurse's office, and you can sit there for a little while and maybe read your book or take a nap. I'm sure you're exhausted. Don't you worry about the other girls; I'm going to take care of them so that they don't bother you anymore. How does that sound?" he asks.

I quickly shake my head in agreement.

He walks me down to the nurse's office, and I know he not only means what he says, but he has the best of intentions. I know that as long as I'm in his class, he will protect me. Maybe this is why I admire him so much; he makes me feel safe. This is something I don't feel from Dad when I'm at home. Dad doesn't protect me the way Mr. Becker does, but oh, how I wish he would. Only, Mr. Becker can't protect me from what I know is in store for me when I get off the bus this afternoon.

Chapter Three

On my way home from school, Bobbi pulls my hair and shoves my face in the snow. She punches, slaps, and kicks me. When I swing my purse as hard as I can, I get one hit in and whack Bobbi across her nappy head. *I wish I could hit the bitch again for making me break all the crayons that are in my purse.*

I run home as fast as I can. After snooping through Dad's car and finding a lighter, I decide to hide between the house and the garage to have a smoke before I go in. As I reach inside the secret pocket in my purse where they have been hiding since I stole them last night, I see that they're all broken. *Fuck! That bitch made me break my cigs too!*

But then I remember that I know how to fix them because Bobbi's older brother taught us how. Carefully breaking it the rest of the way off at the filter, I flip it around to fit the smooth end tightly back into the filter. I light it and take a long drag in. It's not as strong as it normally is, but it'll do for now. I quickly finish, knowing that if I don't get inside soon, Dad is going to wonder where I am. *Thank God it's Friday and I don't have to go to school with a fat lip tomorrow.*

As I walk in the door, I'm greeted by Dad, who is standing at the bottom of the stairs. "What the hell happened to you?" he asks immediately.

Shit!

"Nothing," I reply, lowering my head, trying to avoid eye contact.

"Don't give me that bullshit! I know you're lying! What happened to your lip?" he asks, sounding angry.

Why is he mad at me? Exhausted and unable to hold it in any longer, I suddenly lose it and start sobbing uncontrollably. I don't know if it's the embarrassment of being beat up or the events from last night—probably both.

"Dad, she beat me up!" I say through my sobs with my head lowered in shame. I'm surprised when I see Malory appear at the top of the stairs because she usually gets home after me.

"Who beat you up? Did Bobbi do this?" she asks, walking down the stairs toward me. I shake my head "yes," and it's as if there's been a fire lit under my sister. "That's it!" she yells. "I'm going over there and kicking the crap out of her!"

Dad grabs Mal by the arm as she tries to pass him, heading toward the door. "You aren't going anywhere! Get back in your room, NOW!" he yells.

She obeys with a huff and stomps back up the stairs, slamming the bedroom door behind her. Dad turns, looks at me, and with anger in his voice says, "Knock off your crying right now! I told you to stay away from her. We don't start fights in this family, but we finish them, damn it! If you ever come home crying again, I'll be the one beating your ass! You better never let me hear about you throwing the first punch, either!"

God! Why is he so mad at me? I can't do anything right! I think he wishes I was more like Mal, stronger and more athletic, just like him. She's always been his favorite, and I think that's why. He has boxes full of trophies in the garage from all the sports he played and perfected growing up. Being really popular in school, he had it all: good looks, muscles, and the prettiest girl in school at his side.

I think Mom is just as pretty, if not prettier, than his high school girlfriend. Dad's still good-looking, but not as muscular as he was when he was younger. His gut is starting to stick out a little from all the beer.

Dad doesn't understand me. I like sports and I'm pretty good at softball, but I don't live for it like my sister does. I like to do other things, too. Someday, I'll try harder to make him proud, even if it's not because of sports. Right now, I have bigger things to worry about.

I go up to my room and open the door, where Malory is pacing back and forth. "I swear to God, Heather, I'm going to get her for you! I swear to it, and I don't give a shit what Dad says!"

"It's ok, Malory. I don't want you to get her for me. I want you to teach me how to fight like you so I can stick up for myself," I say, exhausted, plopping down onto my bed.

"I'll teach you how to fight, but I'm still going to kick her ass!"

Oh, geez! "Malory, please don't do anything, it will just make me look like a bigger wimp. I don't need my older sister fighting all my battles." *Who is she? Mike Tyson?*

"Fine, but later, we're going down to the basement, and I'm going to teach you. Then, you're going to go over there and beat the shit out of her as soon as she opens the door! Got it?" she says with her nostrils flared. She looks like a bull, ready to charge, and I kind of want to laugh.

"Ok," I respond, holding in my sudden urge to giggle.

I can't help but think that I'll probably just get beat up again. Besides, she's got all those older brothers over there that will probably hold me down while she beats on me. *Hmm, maybe I can get her to meet me in the middle of the street.*

I quickly change the subject. "Why are you home from school so early anyway?"

"Because I told them that I was sick, but I lied. I just wanted to come home and see what was going on with Mom. She's home, by the way," she says, her voice softening.

"WHAT? She is? Where is she?" I ask, barely able to contain my emotions.

"She's in her room sleeping."

Instantly, I feel happy and sad at the same time. I want to run to her, hug her, and cry. I want to tell her how glad I am that she's home, beg her to never drink again, and have her console me for what happened the night before and the beating I took after school.

Why can't she be a real mom and wipe away all my tears?

I go to her room and slowly open the door. The blinds are closed, and the room is really dark for being the middle of the day. It smells of stale cigarettes and last night's booze. I go into the room and quietly close the door behind me. I know she's sleeping because I can hear her lightly snoring. Tiptoeing over to the bed, I gently lay down next to her, careful not to wake her. I lay there for a while just watching her. *She's so pretty...wonder if she knows just how pretty she is?* I love her hair; it's finally starting to grow back from when she cut it off when we lived in Indiana. I remember waking up one morning to find her asleep on the couch with all her dish-water-colored, beautiful, long, curly hair chopped off up to her ears. I was so devastated; I cried as if I lost my best friend. Later that day, I overheard her telling her sister, Aunt Phoebe, over the phone that she must have been having a nervous breakdown or something. *How could being nervous make you cut your hair off?* I wondered. I didn't understand what Mom was talking about, but I knew it was probably because she was drunk.

Aunt Phoebe has the same long curly hair, only hers is red. Mom's hair is mostly blonde now from hair dye, and it crinkles when you touch it. It's not the same as it used to be, but the smell is always the same. I lean closer to smell her hair. It smells like her White Diamonds perfume and cigarette smoke. She always smells that way, and there's something comforting about it.

Mom opens her eyes, and after blinking a few times, looks at me and says, "Heather, what happened to your lip?"

I begin to cry as I tell her what happened that day, trying to hide in the bathroom at school and then getting beat up on the way home. I tell her what Dad said and how I tried to tell him I didn't do anything but he wouldn't listen. And now, how I think he's mad at me.

"Mom?" I ask with a sniffle.

"Yes, honey?"

"Why does it matter so much if I know how to fight or if I like sports as much as Malory does? Why can't people just leave me alone?"

"Heather, you don't need to know how to fight, and your dad shouldn't have said that. I don't like you guys hitting each other the way you do." I can hear how annoyed she is with Dad by the tone in her voice. *I hope it isn't going to cause another fight later.*

Mom is the opposite of Dad. I think the only sport she played in high school was tennis. She liked to paint and read. She was very artistic in a lot of ways and still is. Sometimes, she goes downstairs and works on her craft projects. She says she's going to open a craft store someday. *I can't wait!* Maybe if she did that, she wouldn't want to drink so much, and I could help her in the shop. She could teach me how to make all those crafty things she likes to make, and we can spend every day together being happy.

She wasn't popular like Dad was in high school, but she was so beautiful. I don't think she was ever considered a nerd for being quiet and smart. Aunt Phoebe was the popular one.

Mom always says Aunt Phoebe has to be the center of attention all the time. "Oh, Phoebe, Phoebe, Phoebe, everything is always about Phoebe."

Mom and Aunt Phoebe talk on the phone all the time, sometimes for hours. As close as they are, they fight just as much. Sometimes, they go months without speaking to each other. Dad says that Malory and I are just like Mom and Aunt Phoebe.

I hope we never go months without talking. She drives me crazy, but I love her too much to be without her.

As violent as Mom can be when she's drinking, sober, she's nothing like that. I don't know what it is about alcohol that makes her act that way. When she's sober, she acts like a real mom, like she is right now, hugging me and letting me cry, telling me everything is going to be ok. One of these days, I hope she will mean it, and everything will *really* be ok. I know that I probably shouldn't believe her because she's said it so many times before. I hang on to her every word because, right now, that's all I have. Mom knows she's different when she's drunk, so I don't understand why she keeps drinking. I don't think she likes to be that way. She's always extra nice on days after, like she is today.

"Heather, you're going to have to learn to try to ignore these girls and walk away from them as much as you can," she says, interrupting my thoughts. "They are just jealous of you because you are beautiful, and they are threatened by you."

Beautiful? Yeah, right!

"You're going to come across girls like that the rest of your life. It's time to build a tough shell, little girl, because you're gorgeous just like your momma, and there's nothing you can do about it!" she says, smiling, tucking my hair behind my ear.

I know she's just saying these things to make me feel better, but I'll take all I can get from her right now. I don't see what she's talking about when I look in the mirror.

I take after Mom and Dad, not looking more like one than the other. My eyes are hazel-green, and I have dirty blonde hair like Mom's natural color. It is straight and fine like Dad's. I hate my hair and wish it were curly like Mom's. It's so fine, and I always have static. I hate my nose, too. It's long and pointy from Dad's side. *It's a family curse!*

One thing for sure—I hope Mom is wrong about dealing with girls like them my whole life. I can't imagine having to walk around always fighting everyone. I better learn how to fight now, or I'm not going to last until my tenth birthday.

Later that night, Mom makes dinner, and we sit around the table, eating in silence. Eating together is one thing I know that is normal about my family. Every time I go to Bobbi or Crystal's house, they eat while sitting in front of the TV. Mom says it's important to eat as a family, and I guess she's right, but there's always a lot of arguing at the table, so I don't really see the point. Mom loves to cook, just like her mother. I like most things she makes, but there are a few things I don't care for. I try to sneak those things to our dog, Mindy, under the table when no one is looking.

We got Mindy when we lived in Indiana from Mom's mom,

Grandma Torres. She is a Shih Tzu, and she's funny-looking. Most of the time, she doesn't really want to be around us unless we're giving free food away under the table. She's Mom's dog. If she's sitting by her and we go near her, she will try to bite us. *The little bitch!* I still love her, though. Tonight, Mom made tacos, our favorite, probably because she's feeling bad. I won't be sharing my dinner tonight, so Mindy is wasting her time sniffing at my ankles.

The next morning, I wake up and go downstairs to get some generic cereal and powdered milk to find Dad standing over the stove cooking breakfast. *Yum!* I love when Dad makes breakfast. He makes the best scrambled eggs I've ever tasted.

Now I know for sure Mom and Dad made up. I had a feeling they did last night from the sounds I heard coming down the hall. Mom is never quiet about it. *Doesn't she know or care that we can hear her? It's so disgusting!* I'll never let my kids hear me like that because I'm never going to do it. *That's gross!*

"Dad, where's Mom?" I ask, taking in the smell of his scrumptious cooking.

"She's in the bathtub," he replies, not taking his eyes off the eggs he's scrambling.

Geez, what's he trying to do? Beat them to death?

I run up the stairs and knock on the door without waiting for an answer before walking in.

"Damn it Heather, can't you kids ever knock?"

"Sorry," I mutter. "Can I come in?" I ask.

"I guess," she says, sighing and moving out of the way so I can get in.

I sit down on the toilet seat and watch her, standing in front of the mirror with a towel wrapped tightly around her. She's putting her makeup on, and I can tell she's trying hard to cover the small bruise and scratch she has under her eye. It doesn't look like it's working too well. It's only ten in the morning, so I wonder why she's putting makeup on already.

"Where are you going, Mom?"

27

"Crazy," she replies, with her mouth half-way open, as she applies her mascara. She always says that.

"Can I go with you?" I ask excitedly.

"No. Not today, Heather."

"But Mom, why not?" I ask, feeling disappointed.

"Because I said so!" she snaps.

Another famous Mom line!

"Well, where are you *really* going?"

She's growing impatient with all my questions. "To the store, Heather," she says, and she lets out another sigh, a longer one this time.

"Then why can't I go with you?" I persist.

"Because I said so, damn it, now get out of here and shut the door!" she yells.

"FINE! You don't have to yell at me!" I snap back as I push my way around her and slam the door behind me. I storm into my room and slam the door so hard I hear a crack.

Uh-oh! Seconds later, I hear footsteps pounding on the stairs. *Shit!* Here comes Dad to beat my ass for slamming the door. I jump under my bed as fast as I can. He throws the door open and comes over to my bed. He knows I'm hiding under here. I hide here every time I'm in for it.

"God fucking damn it, Heather!" he screams. "How many fucking times do I have to tell you about slamming the goddamn fucking doors?"

Please don't hit me!

He gets down on the floor and looks under my bed. I'm squeezed up against the wall so tight I'm hoping he can't reach me. He tries a couple of times to slap at me, but he misses; I'm just out of his reach. This just angers him even more, so he pulls the bed away from the wall and grabs me up by my hair to pull me out. He starts slapping me in the side of the head, back, and wherever else he can while screaming profanities at me. I'm crying, begging him to stop, and I keep saying I'm sorry, but to no avail. I think the more I beg and cry, the angrier he gets.

Just when I think I can't take any more, Mom comes running into the room. "Theodore, stop it right now! That's enough!"

Thank God!

Mom doesn't like it when he hits us. She never hits us. But when we've pushed her too far, she will say while clenching her teeth, "That's it! You just wait until your dad gets home!" That's when we know we better be hiding when he walks in the door. Mom says her step-father used to beat on her and Aunt Phoebe badly when they were growing up, so she doesn't agree with hitting us. For that reason, she has always promised us she will never hit us. So far, she's kept that promise.

There was one time that she chased me with a wooden spoon, threatening to beat me with it for cursing at her but she couldn't catch me. By the time she did, she was exhausted, out of breath, and just started crying. She never did hit me. Then, I felt really bad when I saw her crying because I was laughing the whole time she was chasing me. I knew she wasn't really going to hit me, and at the time, the idea of her chasing me was funny.

Mom wasn't raised by her real dad, and I don't think she had a relationship with him at all growing up. He started coming around when we lived in Indiana. Once, he came to visit us there. He says he's going to come here to see us, too. I don't really think much of him because I don't know him. The only grandpa I've known is my mom's step-father. I don't really think too much of him, either, because we're never around Mom's family. Even when we lived in Ohio, we were always with Dad's family. Mom is always fighting with her family, and I have a feeling they didn't want us around when we were little because Mom never left us with them the way she left us with Grams.

Her step-father adopted her when she was a newborn and Aunt Phoebe was two years old. I have two more aunts and two more uncles from my grandma's marriage to him. Mom says he never beat on his own kids the way he did to her and my aunt, though. *I wonder why?* When she's drunk, she rambles on about it being because he's Mexican. She says it makes him meaner. I can't see how the color of someone's skin would make them beat you. *That's just weird!* I wonder why he only hit them and not his own kids. *Maybe that's why my mom didn't leave me and my sister alone there? Maybe she thinks he will beat on us, too.* He doesn't seem mean to me because he barely ever talks. He does seem shy, yet he smiles and laughs a lot. Maybe he's different now that he's older.

After sitting in my room for a while after my beating, I poke my head out of the door to see if it's safe to come out. I see Dad sitting on the couch downstairs in the living room, watching TV.

"Dad, can I come out now?" I ask quietly.

"I don't care," he mumbles.

I go downstairs and sit on the opposite couch from him, feeling embarrassed and still a little bit afraid. I sit quietly for a bit and then finally break the awkward silence. "Did Mom already leave?" I ask nervously.

"Yeah," he says without looking up from the TV.

"Do you think she's going to come back this time?"

"I don't know, Heth," he says with defeat in his voice.

That's why he was beating the eggs to death. He knew she was going to leave!

Mom does this a lot. I know when she's getting ready to go somewhere. I always try to get her to take me with her so I know she will come home. Whenever she says she's going "crazy" and I can't come with her, it's not a good sign. She leaves for days at a time, sometimes weeks. Dad has to work, so we are home alone to fend for ourselves a lot.

Maybe that's why he got so mad about me slamming the door.

Maybe he knows she's not going to come back too, and he's sad about it.

I don't know what she does when she's gone for that long. Bobbi's older brother called her a crackhead once. I'm not sure what crack is exactly, but I know it's a bad drug. She's still my mom, so it makes me mad when people talk about her that way.

I can feel the rage starting to boil inside of me over the thought of what she's going to do. I loved her so much yesterday after our talk, and now I hate her all over again. *Why is she doing this to us? Why doesn't she love us enough to stay home?* I think she wishes she never had us. She acts like she can't wait to get away from us every chance she gets. *Fuck it!* I don't care if she comes home this time or if I ever see her again. My plan is to run away from this crappy life and this crappy family once and for all. I'm never coming back to this hell!

Chapter Four

I open my eyes and there's a nurse standing above me. "Heather, Heather, it's time to wake up now. I have to draw some blood."

Crap! I wasn't dreaming. How did I get here? How could Mom give up on me and dump me off like this? If I could give up on her when she screwed up, I would have had a new mom years ago.

"You're going to feel a little pinch, ok?" says the nurse after wrapping a rubber band looking thing tightly around my arm.

"Ok," I reply.

As she sticks the needle in my arm, I wonder why they need to take my blood. I'm not sick or anything. Mom brought me here in the middle of the night after we had a big fight. I destroyed my room and the rest of the house. Dad was at work when it happened. I don't see what the big deal is; she does it all the time when she's drunk and mad. We don't make her go live in the hospital.

This is so unfair!

Once the nurse is gone, I inspect the room. I couldn't see much last night; it was too dark. It has a funny smell and the room is gloomy and cold. There's a bathroom in the room. *Wow! My own bathroom? Cool!* The bed is hard and the pillow is flat. There's another bed in the room but no sign that anyone else is staying in the room with me. I'm glad about that. I'd rather be alone.

Thinking back to three months ago when Mom left the house to go "crazy," she was gone for over three weeks. When she did come home, she came home in hospital clothes but she only stayed there one night.

I wonder how long I will be here? Maybe I'll go home later today and this is just some scare tactic. I heard Mom telling Aunt Phoebe over the phone that three men took her in their van into the clay pits near our house and raped her. That's why she was in the hospital. I asked Bobbi's older brother what rape was a few days later, and I was horrified when he told me. He said that it probably had something to do with drugs and that's what she's probably doing when she leaves for weeks at a time. We play in the clay pits all the time; I don't know if I'll ever be able to go back there without thinking about what happened to my mom in that van.

Then, Mom's family came for a visit right after Christmas, so we got to have a second Christmas with them. It was nice to have them here since we never get to see them. I could tell it made Mom happy that they all came. She acted somewhat normal while they were here. They always drink together, but it was ok because Mom was happy and there was no fighting. I was sad when they left because I knew things would go back to the way they always are. I got some cool gifts—mostly clothes. Grandma always gets me and Mal the worst clothes but Mom took us to exchange them later. The clothes she gets are so girly and frilly. Mal and I aren't into that. We're total tomboys who like climbing trees, playing sports, and causing fights. Girls like us don't do ribbons and bows. Uncle Gabriel got me a cool sweatshirt. He's my godfather, and he always makes sure that I know I'm his special to him. I love my Uncle Gabriel; he's so funny. He always makes me laugh when he talks like Donald Duck. Maybe someday, I can go live with him.

Grams came for a visit after Christmas, too, but not at the same time. Mom and Dad's families don't get along very well. Grams doesn't like all the drinking. She let me stay up all night with her in the basement, watching all the old shows like *Patty Duke, I Love Lucy,* and the *Dick Van Dyke* show. *ME, watching TV that's in black and white? Who would have thought?* She stayed with us for three whole weeks. Her visit ended suddenly when Mom came home drunk one night and said a lot of really mean, nasty things to her. I was so mad at Mom for treating her that way. I don't know how she could do that. Grams has always been there for us, more than Mom's family ever has been. I was so sad when we dropped her off at the bus station. I could tell she was, too. She says maybe I can come stay with her in the summer sometime. I would really love that! *Man, I wish I were with her right now.*

After the holidays, Bobbi and I became best friends again. She doesn't mess with me anymore, and I don't think she ever will again. A couple of weeks after she beat me up, I got my revenge. I kicked the crap out of her using the new fighting techniques Mal taught me. I didn't get into trouble for it, either. I tormented her until she pushed me first. Then, I proceeded to give her a beating I know she would never forget. *Serves her right for backstabbing me!* She ran home, crying and with a bloody nose, and her family threatened to call the cops on me. You didn't see me calling the cops when she beat me up. *Coward!* "She can dish it out, but she can't take it," is what Dad said.

I've sort of become one of the bullies in the neighborhood since then. I chase this girl Kim home every day just because I feel like it. She hasn't really done anything to me to deserve it. I guess I just want people to know that I won't be messed with anymore. There's only one girl I'm still afraid of. Her name is Samira, and she looks exactly how her name sounds. She's big and scary. Almost every day at the bus stop, she walks up and slaps me across the face for no reason. I suppose just because she can, like I do to Kim. There are at least ten of us at the bus stop, and I'm the only one she ever messes with. Mal doesn't stick up for me, either. She just lets her do it. I think she might be afraid of her, too. *Or maybe she's just happy that someone else is doing the job for her.*

One day, I got tired of it so I walked straight up to Samira and asked, "Why do you always slap me?"

Without saying a word, she slapped me so hard with her big hand that my ear started ringing. Again, I asked, "Why do you keep slapping me?"

WHACK! She smacked me again. I kept persisting. "I am not going away until you tell me why you keep slapping me, Samira!"

WHACK! Every slap got harder until my face was on fire. Malory yelled out at one point for me to leave her alone before she really gave me a beating. But I was determined and didn't take her advice. I scowled at Samira and wouldn't let the tears fall because she was going to know how tough I was. I was no longer going to be afraid of her. She looked at me as if she were a rabid dog about to tear into a juicy steak and said, "You better get your pretty little honky ass away from me before I hit you again!"

I finally decided I had enough and walked away.

Her words still ring in my ears. "Pretty little honky ass." I know Mom was right when she said girls would be jealous. *Why else would she call me that?* I got the answer I was looking for that day. She hasn't hit me since. I guess standing up for myself really does work, or maybe I made her feel bad. *Who knows!* Mom was wrong about walking away, though; I've tried that, and it doesn't always work. I knew I had to face her head-on eventually, and I'm glad I finally did.

Even though Mom came back after leaving us for three weeks, I really started to hate her and hate my life. I'm angry all the time now. I feel like I have no control over my temper. Unless, of course, Dad is in the room because I know he'll whack me good if I talk back or act up. Sometimes, the fear of him doesn't even stop me anymore. I get kicked out of school all the time for fighting and even got suspended once for hitting Mr. Becker. I feel bad about doing it, but he was squeezing my arm so tight while pulling me into the hall. It hurt, and I wanted him to let me go, so I punched him in the stomach. He's a man, so I'm sure I didn't hurt him much. I think it shocked him more than anything. *I hope he doesn't hate me now.*

I've run away at least ten times since then, too. I don't go very far. Most of the time, I just leave for the day and come back late at night when I can't stand being outside in the dark anymore. A few times, I've snuck into Bobbi's house, and she'll hide me out in her room all night. It's easier to get away with stuff now that her dad isn't there watching her every move. Most of her brothers are older and live in their own houses, so I don't have to worry about them. Her brother, Charlie, knows when I'm there, but he doesn't care.

Mom talks about me all the time when she's on the phone. She says I'm out of control, and she doesn't know what to do with me anymore. I hate it when she talks about me like I can't even hear her. I don't do anything she tells me to do. If she tells me I'm grounded, I tell her to piss off. I don't listen to her, and I run out the door. She sends Malory after me sometimes, and I hate it when she does that. Malory runs track, so I can't outrun her. When she catches me, she beats on me while she drags me back to the house by my hair. I'm tough now, but I don't think I'll ever be tough enough to fight Mal back. She scares the crap out of me.

I'm really starting to hate Miss Goody Two-Shoes. *Shouldn't she be on my side and not Mom's?* All we ever do is fight. She tells on me for everything. She's constantly telling on me for smoking, and I smoke all the time now, too. Every chance I get, I'm stealing cigs from Mom and Dad and anywhere else I can steal them from. I'll even smoke their cigarette butts; I don't care as long as I can smoke. Bobbi taught me how to inhale, so I do it the right way now and don't look like such an amateur. It hurt at first, but I'm used to it now.

A couple of months ago, I almost got caught stealing. There's a flower shop on the busy street outside of our neighborhood. They sell lots of other things besides flowers. Nothing that really interests me, but Bobbi says she steals all the time and wanted me to try it with her. We got away with it the first time I ever stole with her. I stole a crystal that had a fish imprinted on it and gave it to Mr. Becker as a peace offering for punching him. He had other fish things on his desk, so I knew he would like it. I knew by the doubtful look he gave me when I gave it to him that he questioned where I got it. I told him Mom helped me pay for it, so he took it with a smile and thanked me. I felt guilty for stealing it and really did not want to do it. But I wanted to stay friends with Bobbi, so I went along with it.

The next time we went into the store to steal, we stuffed our book bags so full of meaningless stuff; we could barely zip them shut. On our way out, the cashier was standing in the way, blocking the door, demanding to see what we had in our bags. I was so scared and speechless that I couldn't move or respond. I just stood there, staring at him like a deer in headlights. He gave us an out when he told us we could take a walk back around the store and then show him our bags. I quickly agreed, knowing exactly what he meant by it. I had to yank Bobbi away. She wanted to stand there and argue with him, saying things like, "My dad will get you!" Knowing damn well her dad wasn't going to get anyone from prison, I pulled her toward the back of the store, explaining what he was giving us the chance to do.

I felt so ashamed of what I had done, and I promised myself I'd never steal again. My only exception is cigarettes since I'm too young to get them the right way. Bobbi must not have felt ashamed because she still steals all the time. I've even caught her stealing from me. Now that I know what it feels like to have something stolen from me, I'm positive I've learned my lesson and will never steal again. Thank God my parents never found out, or Mr. Becker, who would be so disappointed if he knew I stole that pretty crystal fish that sits on his desk.

Now, as I sit on the bed, I am wondering what's waiting for me outside the bedroom door. No one has come in to tell me I should come out, so I'll just sit here until they do. When I came in, all the other kids that are patients here were asleep. I hope I don't have to fight any of them. I'm really getting tired of always having to fight.

Last night, when Mom brought me in, she had to call Dad home from work to bring me here. There was no way I was letting her bring me. Mom isn't very big and she has a hard time controlling me. She's only about five feet, three inches tall and only weighs about 100 or so pounds. I know I can't fight Dad, so I didn't even bother resisting once he got home. I expected him to be extra upset when he had to come home early from work and see what I did to the house. I was hiding under my bed, waiting to get it for what I had done. When he came to my room, he was quiet and calm. Then, he asked me nicely to get dressed and come downstairs. That made me even more nervous.

I was scared to death of where they might be taking me. I tell them all the time how much I hate them and want to live somewhere else. I don't really mean it, and I don't want to live in another foster home. I just want my parents to be normal.

Mom did all the talking when we got here. I was too afraid and exhausted from the tantrum I threw to say anything. Dad sat quietly with a look of sorrow on his face the whole time. *I wonder what he was thinking about.* Mom told the nurse in the emergency room all the bad things I've been doing lately. She said she didn't know why I could be acting that way or what's wrong with me. She also told them that she thinks I might need medication. *Medication for what? I'm not sick!* The things she was saying and the way she was saying them just made me even madder at her. *Is she kidding? She doesn't know why I'm acting this way? How about because I hate her for not being a normal mom! I hate her for leaving us for weeks at a time! I hate her for drinking and using drugs, and I hate her for being raped by those men! I don't need medication! I need a new mother! Why didn't Dad say anything? Why didn't he tell them why I'm so angry? Probably because he's almost just as bad as her! Why can't he just protect me from this crazy person I have to call Mom? Why does he always let her do all the talking? He never talks, and she never shuts up! I hate him, too! I hate them both!*

The door suddenly opens, and it startles me from my thoughts. I turn to look toward the door and see a short, red-haired woman with a funny-looking nose that reminds me of Miss Piggy. She walks toward me. "Hi, Heather, my name is Tina. Can we talk for a little bit?" she asks with a very soft, quiet voice.

"Ok," I reply shyly.

She sits down on the bed across from me. "Do you know why you're here, honey?"

"I guess because I'm always getting in trouble."

"Why do you think you're always into trouble?" she asks, her voice still soft.

I just shrug my shoulders at her and lower my head. She can't expect me to open up to her about everything already. I don't even know her. *I'm not telling this lady anything.* As far as I'm concerned, she's on my parents' side, so why should I tell her?

"Ok, well, if you don't want to talk about it now, then that's ok. You don't have to. Would you like to come out for breakfast and meet all the other kids? We're all happy that you're here, and everyone is excited to meet you."

I'm starving from not eating dinner last night, so I say ok and stand up.

She stands up in front of me, and I realize how short she really is. We are almost the same height. Taking after Mom in that department, I'm not tall, either. She reaches out and hugs me gently. *Whoa! This is unexpected, and if she doesn't let go, I might start crying.*

"I know that you're scared, Heather, and you're in a new place, but everything is going to be ok, I promise. We are all here to help you honey," she says in a voice that comforts me.

I want to believe her, so I walk with her toward the door even though I am terrified of what's waiting for me on the other side.

Chapter Five

I'm surprised when I get out to the dining area and find only boys. *No girls at all?* I can't believe I'm the only girl. *How can I be the only girl who ever gets in trouble?* Maybe it's not as easy for people to give their daughters away even when they're bad. My parents certainly didn't have a problem with it. After Tina introduces me to everyone, I sit down and dig in. This might not be such a bad place after all. There are ten of us, five seated at each table. The food isn't so bad for being hospital food, either.

I look at the boys around me and wonder why they're all here. One of the little boys at the other table looks like he's around Johnny's age. *How could a boy so small need to be in here?* A few minutes later, I find out why when, out of nowhere, he starts chanting unknown words and banging his spoon on the table over and over while rocking back and forth in his chair.

A man named Eddie who works here yells out, "Nicky, that's enough! You don't want to go to the time-out room again, do you?"

What's the time out room? I wonder. We don't have one of those at home. We don't get time-outs; we get our butts beat.

Suddenly, Nicky screams out in an ear-piercing yell, "I don't fucking care! I'm not going to the time-out room, and you can't fucking make me, you asshole!" and he picks up his tray of food and smashes it onto the floor.

Holy crap! I sit there in shock with my mouth dropped open. *How could a boy so little talk like that?* I talk like that, but I'm almost ten. He looks to be five, maybe six at the oldest. Eddie and Tina jump to their feet and walk quickly toward him. He jumps out of his seat and takes off running, still screaming at the top of his lungs. I watch as he traps himself in the dead-end hallway as they follow quickly behind him.

This place isn't very big. There's only the one hallway where our rooms are and where Nicky is currently terrorizing the staff. The small dining area is connected to the living room. It's just one big open area— nowhere to go. *Trapped!* I see five doors from where I'm sitting. One is off the living room, which I know is the classroom because it says it on the outside of the door. There's another door that leads to a hallway because I can see through the small glass window on it. It looks like it leads to another hallway with more rooms. *I wonder who sleeps over there.* One of the doors leads out of here; it's where I came in last night. The other one looks like it might be an office. The fifth door is not too far away from where I'm sitting. There's one small plastic-looking window at the top of the door. It's too high off the floor for me to see through it. *Hmmm, I wonder if that's the time-out room.* All the doors have keypads and heavy-duty locks on them. There's no way to run away from here. I *am* trapped, like a caged animal.

I watch Tina and Eddie trying to calm Nicky down as he's screaming and banging on the window at the end of the hall. They try to talk him out of his "t, but it's not working. They look at each other and say something that I can't understand from here. Suddenly, Eddie wrestles Nicky to the floor.

Tina quickly walks back toward us from the hall. "It's ok, everyone, Nicky is going to be fine. He just needs a little time-out. Finish eating your breakfast," she says as calmly as possible but is visibly shaken.

I can't rip my eyes away from what's going on. I've never seen anything like this before. Tina walks over to the counter, grabs a big set of keys, walks over to the fifth door, and opens it up. *I was right! It is the time-out room.* I lean forward a little in my chair so I can see inside. The walls are all white and look cushioned. Charlie has joked with me before that I need to be locked inside a padded room, but I never knew what that was. *This must be it.* I can tell by the floor and the walls that there is no way anyone could hurt themselves in there. The room is empty and about as big as a shoe box. *Charlie was wrong.* I don't need to be in a room like that. If Mom and Dad ever put me in a room like that when I throw my tantrums, I think I would probably stop. I wish we could put Mom in that room when she comes home drunk. Then we wouldn't have the cops at our house so much. We could make her sleep in there all night, and then we could forget about everything in the morning.

While holding Nicky's arms in front of him tightly, Eddie lifts him off the floor and starts walking toward the room. He's so little that Eddie is carrying him with the small boy's feet no longer touching the floor. Nicky continues to scream at the top of his lungs, thrashing his feet and head all over, determined to make contact with Eddie.

"You can come out when you have calmed down!" yells Eddie with authority, locking the door behind him.

I'm surprised at how much noise it drowns out. We can't hear him at all now, only the very faint sound of his screams and banging on the door. I can barely believe what I just witnessed. I'm in shock but also a little afraid. I don't understand what made him so angry. No one did or said anything to him; he just did it for no reason at all. When I act up at home, it's not for no reason. I guess Nicky probably has his reasons, too, even though none of us can tell what they are.

A little later after Nicky gets out of time-out and everything is calm again, Tina and Eddie announce that it's time for group. *What the hell is group?* Hopefully, it's a fun game. By the sounds of the moans all of the boys let out, I'm guessing if it is a game, it must not be a very fun one. Aside from Nicky's fit, it's been a boring day. I'm starting to feel homesick, and I wonder what they're all doing while I'm stuck here.

They're probably celebrating that they finally got rid of me, the bad one, the "adopted freak."

"Ok, everyone. It's been an exciting day. We have a new girl. Has everyone had a chance to get to know Heather a little?" Tina asks, and they all nod their heads.

The truth is, I haven't really talked to any of them that much so far. *What am I supposed to say to a bunch of dumb boys?* I think one of them has a crush on me because he won't stop staring at me with this dumb grin on his face. His name is Jack, just like a boy from Indiana I beat up. If he doesn't watch it, I'll punch his lights out, too.

"Heather, every day, twice a day, we get together as a group, and we share our feelings," Eddie says.

Oh, God! This is not a game after all, this is dumb, and I don't want to do it! Why should I want to share my feelings with a bunch of people I don't know? I feel my face starting to turn red with embarrassment at the thought of having to talk in front of everyone.

Group isn't so bad. After all, I don't say much, and they aren't making me. It's kind of nice to hear all the boys talk about their families and why they're in here. It makes me feel like my life isn't so bad. One eleven-year-old boy is talking about how his father molests him and beats the crap out of him all the time. *Thank God, Dad isn't like that!* He would never in a million years do those things to us. He does spank me sometimes when I'm bad. Sometimes, he even leaves bruises on my legs and back when he misses my butt because I'm trying to squirm away, but it's nothing in comparison to what this boy is talking about.

Part of me knows I deserve to be spanked, but the other part of me knows he shouldn't be leaving marks on me either. I have a newfound respect for Dad after hearing that boy's horror story, and it makes me miss home even more. I didn't know fathers could be so sick in the head. I've seen stuff in movies, but I thought it was all pretend. At least, that's what Mom always tells me. *Maybe it is my fault I'm here. If I was a better kid, maybe Mom and Dad wouldn't drink so much.*

A couple days later, Tina comes into my room and tells me I have to go see the psychiatrist. She says everyone must go see him and have tests done when they are first brought here. She says Mom is coming, too. This makes me happy and gives me hope. I can't wait to see her. Maybe this psychiatrist will let me go home with her today. Tina walks me through the door that I came in when I first arrived, and I become even more excited. *The door to freedom!* As we walk down the long hall-way, we pass adults that I can tell are patients here, too. Some of them are really scary looking. Their faces remind me of the zombies from *Night of the Living Dead. Yikes!* I'm glad that I don't have to be around these scary people in my unit.

We come to a door that's partially open. Tina knocks lightly. "Dr. C?" she calls as she pushes the door open.

I see an older, heavyset man with gray hair and a gray mustache and beard sitting on the other side of a desk.

He looks up with a big grin on his face. "Well, hello, young lady. You must be Heather?" he asks with a funny accent I don't recognize.

I smile shyly and nod.

He points to a chair in front of his desk, gesturing for me to have a seat. "I'm glad to finally meet you. Have a seat and we'll get started," he says looking down at a file.

I wonder where Mom is.

"Is my mom coming?" I ask curiously.

"Yes, she's here in the waiting room. I've already had a chance to speak to her, so after we're all done here, I will have her come back so we can all talk," he answers with a smile.

Tina puts her hand on my shoulder, and I turn to look up at her. "Heather, I'm going to go back to the unit now. Everything is going to be fine; I promise. Dr. C is a nice man. You will like him a lot. I'll be back to get you when you're done, ok?"

"Ok," I say quietly. *I wish she could stay.* I really like her a lot, and I'm starting to trust her. I'm unsure about this man with the funny voice, but he has a nice, friendly smile that makes me feel better.

"My name is Dr. Cucamunga," he begins. "All the kids call me Dr. C." *Cuca what? I can see why they call him Dr. C. What a funny name.* "I'm going to start by asking you some questions. I want you to answer as honestly as you can. After that, I'm going to show you some pictures, and I want you to tell me what you see," he continues. "That doesn't seem so bad, does it?" he asks with a smile and kindness in his voice.

I'm not blind, why would he need to show me pictures? It seems easy enough, so I nod with approval.

He begins by asking me all kinds of silly questions. "Do I see things that aren't there? Do I hear voices? Have I ever hurt myself? Do I ever want to hurt myself? Do I hurt animals?" A whole series of questions that are equally as strange. *Do I hurt animals? What kind of question is that?* They are very weird questions, but the answers are easy enough. *NO, NO, and NO!*

Now, onto the pictures, this should be less weird. *I hope!* When he holds up the first picture, I'm a little confused because it's a funny-looking picture. It's not a normal looking picture like I thought it would be. It's black and white and blotchy looking.

"Heather, these are ink blot pictures. There are no right or wrong answers to what they look like to you. You just tell me the first thing that comes to your mind when you look at the picture," he explains.

"Ok," I reply hesitantly.

"What do you see?" he asks, holding up the first picture.

"A Dorito," I say, but my reply sounds more like a question.

"That's ok," he says, smiling. "You're doing great. How about this one?" he asks, holding up another one.

"Uhhh, that looks like a butterfly," I reply. *Hmmm, this is easy.*

"Ok, good, how about this one?"

"A house," I reply quickly.

I'm just starting to get the hang of it when he holds one up that throws me off my guard. It looks like a skull, but I am afraid if I tell him that then it means something is wrong with me.

He must sense my hesitation because he lowers the picture and says softly, "Heather, remember what I said, there is no right or wrong answer just tell me what you see."

I quickly tell him what I see but wonder what it means that I see that. *Am I crazy?* I wish I could see something else, but it just looks like a skull. I can tell by how this is going with the questions he's asking and the pictures he's showing me that he's trying to figure out more about me. I'm not sure what he's going to find out with all these silly pictures and crazy questions.

After we're done, he has me sit outside of his office in a chair across the hall. He walks to a nearby glass door that leads toward the elevators. *The elevators to freedom!* I watch as he punches a code into the dial pad next to the door, it buzzes, and he walks through it. He then disappears into a room on the opposite side. It feels like he's been in there forever as I wait impatiently, biting my fingernails down so low they are starting to hurt. Mom's voice rings in my ears. "Quit biting your nails, Heather!" *I definitely can't quit biting them now.* I wonder if I passed his tests, and if I'm going to get to go home today.

I quickly pull my hands away from my mouth when I see him come out of the room from the corner of my eye. Mom is following behind him. I'm instantly overcome with joy and excitement to see her pretty face. I spring to my feet as they walk through the glass door. Mom's walking toward me with a slight smile on her face, but there are tears in her eyes. *Oh, no! Why is she crying?* My hopes are quickly diminished, and I wonder if I have to stay here. As she approaches me, she bends down, and I hug her as tight as I can and start crying. I bury my nose in her hair and take in the smell of cigarettes and White Diamonds perfume. It makes me cry even harder.

"I'm sorry, Mom! Please let me come home. I promise I'll never be bad again; I swear!" I beg through my sobs.

She pulls away and holds my face gently with both hands. "Look at me, Heather." I look into her eyes. She's crying, too. "You're going to have to stay here for a little while so we can figure out how to fix everything, ok?"

WHAT? My heart sinks. *How could she just leave me here like this? Doesn't she love me at all?* I can smell the faint hint of last night's party on her breath as she talks, and I start to feel the anger and hatred towards her build up again.

"Heather, I can't stay. I'm going to have to leave," she says softly.

47

"FINE!" I shout. "Just leave me here then! I don't care anymore! You're a liar, Mom! That's all you ever do is lie and leave us all the time! I know you've been drinking. I can smell it!" I scream, and she looks at me as if I've just broken her heart into tiny pieces, but I don't care. How does she think this makes me feel? *She's so selfish! She doesn't care about me at all!*

"Heather, please don't start," she says through gritted teeth.

I look at her feeling nothing but hate, "I hate you, Mom!" I say with my voice cold and firm.

Devastated, I watch as she turns around and walks away from me without even turning back before Dr. C. buzzes her through the doors. Once she's out of sight completely, Dr C. puts his hand on my shoulder.

"Heather, it's going to be ok. We're going to take care of you here, and we're going to get you back to your family soon, I promise."

Promises, promises! Overcome by the sudden feeling of total abandonment, I start crying so hard I begin to shake, and I sink back down into the chair.

"Do I have to stay because I answered your questions wrong? Is it because I saw a skull instead of something pretty in that picture?" I ask desperately.

"No, Heather, not at all! You answered all the questions just fine," he says, kneeling to make eye contact with me.

"Then why do I have to stay?" I ask.

"Sometimes, families just need a little help getting along better. While you're here, we're going to get your family some counseling and try to teach you all better ways to handle things. We don't want you to feel like you have to run away anymore," he says softly.

"But you heard me, Dr. C.! I could smell alcohol on her. It's her fault I run away!" I cry out.

"I know, honey, and we're going to work on that, too. Something very bad could happen to you when you're out there alone, and we don't want that," he says with concern in his brown eyes.

48

"Well then, my mom should be the one in here, not me! She's the one with the problem. This is so unfair," I say, still sobbing.

As he walks me back to the unit with his arm around my shoulder, I continue to cry, and I know Tina was right. He is a nice man, and I can tell I'm really going to like him.

Chapter Six

Dear Diary,

   Tina gave me this diary last night and told me I should start writing in it every day. She thinks if I start writing about my feelings and what's going on in my life, it will help me deal with things better. Unless this diary has some sort of magic power that will make my parents suddenly different people, I don't see what the point is. It seems kind of stupid to me, but I guess I'll give it a try. I've been here for a month now, and I'm going home tomorrow. I can't believe it's been a month since I've slept in my own bed. I miss my friends, my toys, and my dog. As much as I really hate them sometimes, I miss my family. Being here hasn't been bad. I kind of like it.

   I'm afraid of what's going to happen once I get home. I know nothing has really changed. My family comes to see me once a week for visits on Tuesday nights, and on Thursday nights, they come for family counseling with Dr. C. I can use the phone in the day room every day to call them, but I can't call anyone else. I wonder if my friends know where I am or if any of my family back in Ohio knows.

   I smell alcohol on Mom sometimes when she comes, so I know she *hasn't stopped drinking. I don't feel like my anger towards her has changed, so how can things be different? I guess I was supposed to learn how to tolerate things better instead of running away all the time. But why should I have to tolerate my parents being that way? It seems so unfair; they should have to change, too.*

I don't think the people here really get what I am dealing with at home. If they do, they don't say so. They just look at me like they feel sorry for me. Mom only tells them what she feels like telling them...which is half of the truth. She tells them all the bad things I do, but she doesn't tell them why. She never tells them the bad things she does. She pretends like she doesn't know why I act up.

She got into an argument with Dr. C last week right in front of me about why they haven't put me on any meds. She keeps insisting to anyone who will listen that I need them. I'm not sure what she thinks medication will do for me. Maybe turn me into the perfect child she's always wanted instead of the devil that she insists I am. I've been here long enough to know what medication is for because almost all the kids here take meds. Dr. C told her that I'm a perfectly normal, healthy child, and he's not going to put me on medication when I don't need it. I wonder if that has something to do with all those silly questions and the pictures. She kept arguing with him that I'm faking it, that I'm not showing them the real me. She says I'm pretending so I can get out of here. I never hated her more in my life than I did when she said that about me. How dare her talk about me like that, and right in front of me, as if I'm too young and stupid to know what she's saying. She must really hate me to say something so mean about me. I haven't done anything to fake who I am since I've been here.

How do you fake who you are? I don't even know what that means. If anyone is fake, it's her! It made me feel good when Dr. C stuck up for me. I wish he would always be there to stick up for me. I haven't gotten into any trouble here because there is nothing to get in trouble over, so how does that make me fake? Maybe it's because I don't have to deal with her crap while I'm here. I wonder if she's considered that!

I get along with all the boys and all of the people who work here. I've gotten close to Tina and Eddie; they are my favorites. Every night that Tina works, she comes into my room at bedtime to read me a story and rubs my back. I'm really going to miss her when I leave. I wish Mom could be more like her.

I'll be going back to school when I get home. I'm nervous about it. I'm going to miss the teacher here; she's nice. We get to work on computers here, too, and I really like them. We don't get to do that at my regular school. All the boys here tease me and say that I'm the staff's favorite because I'm the only girl. They're probably right, but I'm enjoying the attention anyway. It's not something I'm used to getting at home.

They do lots of fun stuff with us here. There's an art room where we go a couple times a week to paint and make ceramics. There are all kinds of cool things to do in the art room. They also take us on bike rides through the trails that are nearby and have even taken us bowling a few times. When I talk to my mom about all the things I get to do, she says it sounds like they're paying for me to be at a day camp instead of getting me help. Whatever that means! She doesn't like it when I act up, but now she acts like it makes her mad that I'm happy and being good. I wish I did more fun stuff at home like I do here.

Maybe if we spent more time together as a family, we wouldn't fight so much. We barely ever do things together at home, except on birthdays. I don't think I'm learning the things here that my mom thought I would. I've learned more about what's wrong with her and my dad and less about what's wrong with me. I've learned that it's not my fault she leaves and drinks the way she does. And that it's ok for me to be angry about all of it, but to find different ways to deal with my anger. So, I'm going to try really hard to take their advice and write in this diary when I get upset instead of running away or breaking things.

I'm nervous about going home, but I'm really excited, too. I'm hopeful that things will be better since I haven't gotten in any trouble for a month. I've also decided that I'm going to try hard to never smoke again. I know they say it isn't my fault, but when Mom leaves, she says it's because we are all driving her crazy. I can't help but wonder if she'll stay home more now since I'm not getting into so much trouble.

Well, that's all I'm going to write for now. I have to finish packing before I go to bed. I'm sure I will be writing again soon.

Heather

Chapter Seven

My heart is beating so fast it feels like it's going to pop out of my chest. I don't think I've ever run this fast before. My side is starting to cramp up bad, and I need to find a place to hide soon before they catch me. It's dark outside, so it'll be easier to hide from them. I just rounded the corner, and they're still on the other block. So, before they see me, I jump into the nearest bush and stay as still as I can.

I just want to last long enough to make it to the tunnel; they'll never find me in there. I can hide there for a few hours until they stop looking. Then, I can walk the rest of the way to my friend Brandy's house.

I'm trying so hard to quiet my heavy breathing when I hear one of them turn the corner and stop. *Damn it, I shouldn't have smoked all those cigarettes.* I hear a click as I watch the police officer turn on the flashlight he just pulled from his belt. *Shit, he's going to shine it over here and see me.*

I hear the sound of Officer Paul's boots pounding on the ground and the jingle of the keys that are hanging from his belt as I watch him turn the corner. "Do you see her anywhere?" he asks, out of breath.

"No, but she's gotta be hiding around here somewhere," the other officer replies.

Paul clicks on his flashlight, and I watch as they walk around the houses across the street and shine their lights into the bushes. *Crap, they're going to find me.* I close my eyes, stay as still as I can and pray, they just go away.

"Heather, I see you. It's time to come out now," says Paul.

"Paul, why can't you just let me go? You see what I have to deal with at home. Why do you make me go back there?" I beg.

"Because we can't have you running the streets, Heather. You're only eleven years old. Now come out here and talk to me," he demands. I love Paul, but right now, I hate him for making me go back there.

I don't want to go back, but I know I can't argue with him. So, I crawl out of the bushes and stand up. I brush the dirt off my legs and pull the twigs out of my matted hair.

Paul looks at me with a smirk on his face. "You know I should take you to jail just for making me run like that, right?"

I'm not in the mood to joke around with him tonight so I just stare off in the other direction. "I wish you would take me to jail, Paul. I would rather be there than at my house," I pout.

"Look, Heather, I know you have it rough at home." He pauses. "Please look at me while I'm talking to you."

I turn and look at him.

"We've had this talk a million times before. You can't run away. You have to stay put for a little longer. The day you turn seventeen, you can go anywhere you want, and they can't stop you," he adds.

"I know, Paul, but I can't wait that long! I have to get out of there now!" I plead.

"You will soon enough, trust me. You just need to hold tight for now, ok?" he says looking down at me with sympathy.

I nod and follow as we start on the short walk back to my house.

During the walk, Paul and the other cop are busy talking about something, and I consider running again when they're not looking. It's useless, though; they'll probably just catch me anyway. And I don't want to make Paul angry. He's always good to me. He comes to my house all the time. If he's on shift and the cops get called over, he's there.

I think he likes to come to my house. He cares about us, but I don't know why. Most of them treat me like the delinquent runaway that I am, but not him; he's different. I know I can trust him. He's given me his card more than once and has told me to call him if something is going on. I probably should, but I know he'll just make me go home, and that's not what I want.

The fight I had with Mom tonight was stupid. She wanted me to do the dishes, and since Dad's not home to *really* make me, I refused. When he's at work, I know I can get away with murder. It was a normal night for the most part. She made dinner, and we sat around the table to eat together. Everything was fine. I don't know why I just didn't do what she asked.

When I refused, it turned into a big, huge fight, and she pulled the "you just wait until your dad gets home, little girl" routine. I know what that means, and I knew I had to get the hell out of there. It doesn't matter how nice she is when she asks, I never do anything she asks me to do. I just don't want to listen to her. Maybe if she acted like a real mom more than once a week, I would care more about her and what she wants. She doesn't care about what I need and want. *Screw her!*

As we get closer to my house, Paul interrupts my thoughts. "Heather?"

"Yeah?" I respond.

"Did you hear what I said tonight?" he asks.

"Yeah, I heard you," I reply in a huff.

"Heather, I mean it! No more running! We don't want to find you in a ditch somewhere. A lot of bad things can happen to you out here, so you need to stay home, ok?" he says with concern in his voice.

"Yeah, ok, Paul."

What bad things? Nothing is going to happen to me. People know better than to mess with me. If some weirdo tries to get me, I'll just run. I'm more worried about what's going to happen to me when my dad gets home from work in the morning than I am of being outside all night by myself.

Mom is sitting on the front porch, smoking a cigarette when we walk up. She looks like she's been crying, and I feel bad. But at the same time, I wonder what she could have to cry about because she acts like she doesn't want me here anyway. I'm not going to let her know it bothers me that I made her cry, so I brush right past her, walk straight up to my room, and slam the door. I've learned my lesson in the past by trusting her and letting her see my real feelings. I'm not going to do that anymore.

"Heather, why do you have to be such a little bitch all the time? Why can't you just do what Mom tells you to do?" asks Malory as I walk into the room.

"Shut up, Malory! You don't get it and you never will! You're such a little daddy's girl book worm. You will never understand," I shout, grabbing my pjs on my way to the bathroom to change.

Mom is still outside talking to the cops, so I walk down to the kitchen. I see her cigs on the counter and take a few. I head down to the basement bathroom to change so I can get a few puffs before bed. The basement bathroom is not even really a bathroom. It's a big utility room with a toilet in it.

I hate it down here, and it's kind of scary. It's the easiest place to smoke, but there are spiders down here. The basement is our place to hang out. My parents don't come down here a lot unless mom is doing laundry or working on her crafts. She only does that during the day and never comes down here at night.

All that's down here is some ratty old furniture, a small TV, our video games, and random toys that there isn't any room for upstairs. Mom has an old wooden picnic table down here that she repainted and put in the corner. That's where she sits and does all her crafts. The carpet down here is some ugly old red stuff that turns our socks pink. *Who the hell has red carpet, anyway?* I hear the upstairs door shut and quickly flush my cig down the toilet and head back upstairs.

On the way up, Mom is standing at the top of the basement stairs.

"What were you doing down there?" she asks, but she already knows the answer.

I roll my eyes. "Nothing!" I say as I try to pass by her quickly, but she grabs me by the arm and pulls me back.

"Let me smell your fingers then!" she demands, holding my arm tightly. She knows I've been smoking, or she wouldn't have even asked.

"NO! Let me go right now or I'm gonna leave again!" I yell.

"You're not going anywhere, and if you do it, Heather I swear to God..." she says, her voice trailing off. The look on her face tells me that she means something by that. *What's SHE going to do?*

"You swear to God what, Mom? Are you gonna drop me off at the hospital for a third time? I don't care! Do it! Take me anywhere you want to. As long as I'm not here, I'll be happy!" I yell, trying to squirm away from her tight grip.

She lets go of my arm, suddenly falls to the kitchen floor, and starts crying so hard she can barely catch her breath. She looks up at me with the saddest eyes I've probably ever seen. "Why can't you just stop, Heather? Why do you always fight me on everything? Why do you always have to make everything so difficult?" she asks through her sobs.

I look at her coldly. "Because I hate you, Mom! You make me sick, and I wish you were dead!" I say calmly, as if it's the most normal thing in the world to say. I run back up to my room slamming the door behind me.

The next morning, I wake up before anyone else, so I sneak out of the house through the sliding glass door in the kitchen to make my way down to the end of the street where the bridge is. It's a good place to hide to avoid trouble or hide out and smoke. Maybe if I sit under the bridge long enough, Dad won't be as mad when I go home later. I'll still be grounded for sure, but at least I can avoid getting whipped.

I have a knot in my stomach from the things I said to Mom. I've said those same things a million times before, but not like that. The other times, it was in the middle of a screaming match. This time, I was calm, and it seemed so much meaner because she was so upset. I've never seen her like that before. She's usually yelling at me.

Maybe she does really care after all. The guilt I feel is overwhelming. Maybe if I go home and tell her I'm sorry, we can forget it ever happened. I know I should tell her that I didn't mean it, but I don't think I can. I can't talk to her about anything anymore.

I wonder if she's really thinking about taking me back to the hospital. *Oh well!* I like it better there, anyway. I still have the diary Tina gave me the first time I was there, but I barely write in it. It doesn't help. It's not like I can ask my sister to stop kicking my ass so I can go write in my diary real quick or tell Mom to stop destroying the house when she's in a drunken rampage so I can take notes. When bad things are happening, all I can think about is getting away from it. Writing in a stupid diary doesn't take me away from everything like running does.

The last time I went to the hospital was about six months ago, almost exactly a year after the first time. I was only there for two weeks that time. Doctor C told Mom there was nothing they could do for me because when I'm there, I appear normal. I had to go through all the testing again and saw the same skull I saw the first time. It must be normal to see a skull in the middle of Doritos, houses, and butterflies because he still thinks I'm normal.

Mom went on with her same argument to him about how I'm faking it. But I'm really not; I was honest with him and everyone else. I tell them the truth about what happens at home. Not that I don't do anything wrong, I just don't act that way while I'm there. *Why should I? None of them are ruining my life like my parents are.*

When I came home from the hospital, I knew things weren't going to change. I daydreamed that everything would be perfect even though I knew better. It seemed to work for a little while. My parents got a membership at the sportsman's club in a small town not far from home. There is a lake there with a small beach, and we started going there on the weekends to camp, swim, and fish.

I love going there, but it hasn't made us any closer. They just get drunk and fight while we're there, which embarrasses us around the other camping families. It's easier to get away from them there because

I can just run off and fish for hours by myself or go hang out at the beach.

Mom's real dad came to see us at the beginning of the summer, and we went camping while Dad was working. It was nice to have him here, but I still don't really know him. He's not very talkative with us, and he drinks a lot like Mom. They drank together the whole weekend while we were off doing our own things.

It's not always bad; Mom and I get along sometimes. I'll never forget one weekend when we were at the lake last summer, Mom and I had a good laugh together at Mal's expense. Mal met a boy who she had a crush on. She demanded that I not leave her side because she was too shy to be alone with him.

While sitting on a bench with them in dead silence, I whispered to her that I wanted to go do something else. Because Miss Goody Goody was too shy to talk, she refused to let me leave, grabbing me by the elbow and giving me the look of death. I knew it meant, "leave me, and I'll pummel you."

During the silence, out of nowhere, she ripped the biggest fart I had ever heard! I could even feel the vibration underneath me. If I didn't feel so embarrassed for her, I could have dropped to the ground in laughter right there. She didn't know how to react, so she just got up and ran away as fast as she could.

I was speechless and didn't know what to say to him. All he did was look at me, smile, and say, "I don't know what the big deal is, it's just a fart."

I walked back to the blanket where she was with Mom. She was crying her eyes out with her head buried in the blanket Mom was tanning on. Mom was initially frantic, asking what the heck was going on.

I couldn't hold it in anymore and fell to the ground, laughing so hard I couldn't breathe.

The whole time, Mom was bursting to know what happened. "What? What? Oh my God, someone please tell me what's going on!"

She didn't know whether to laugh or worry. Malory was screaming at me the entire time to shut up before she beat me up.

When I finally stopped laughing long enough to tell Mom what happened, Malory ran off again in embarrassment while Mom and I laughed our butts off together on the blanket. I felt bad for Mal, but it was by far one of the funniest moments we have ever had.

I'm suddenly laughing so hard at the memory of it that if someone saw me right now, they would think I was completely nuts. Holy crap...that was funny!

When my laughter subsides, I become saddened and suddenly want to cry. I wish Mom and I laughed together that way more often. I start to think that I can go back home and say, "Hey, Mal, remember when?" and we can all get a good laugh to forget all about everything else. She still doesn't think it's funny, so I better not risk it and cause another fight.

Dad finally taught me how to swim that summer at the lake. I could swim short distances, but I was too afraid of the water to swim any farther. There's a dock at the beach that has a diving board on it, but you have to swim out kind of far to get to. I used to always float there and back on a raft. One day, Dad came out there with us. It was late in the day, so the beach was going to close soon.

When the lifeguards blew their whistles for the few people that were left to pack it up for the day, Dad looked at me and said, "Well, Heather, today's the day you swim back on your own." I begged him not to make me, but he wouldn't listen. He took my raft, and everyone left without me.

He said either I get over my fear, or I would be sleeping out there that night. I really thought he would come back if I sat out there long enough. But after I watched them walk out of the gates and down the trail back to camp, I knew I had to do it. I swam most of the way on my back. It worked. I was never afraid again and haven't used the raft since. At first, I was mad at Dad, but now I'm glad. I cannot stay scared of the water forever.

What if I would have drowned? The thought sickens me, but surely Dad knew I could do it or he wouldn't have left me there. *Would he?*

The thought brings me back to a memory I have from living in Indiana when I almost drowned. There was a creek behind our house that we always played in that had a fast current. The older kids would go in the creek on tubes and let it take them all the way around the city until it brought them back.

I was tired of always being left behind because I was too afraid to swim. So, I decided that I was going to teach myself. I jumped right into an undertow, and I couldn't bring myself back above the water. With no one around, I thought for sure I was going to die that day. A man, who had been fishing nearby, saw me thrashing around and pulled me out. *God, what was I thinking? I was only seven. Where were my parents while we were playing in that dangerous creek?* I shudder at the thought of what could have happened and quickly turn my thoughts to something else.

Malory is an even bigger bully than before. I try not to make her angry too much. I'm smart enough to know that I can't beat her, so I keep my mouth closed as much as possible. When I am brave enough to run my mouth, I make sure I'm close enough to the upstairs bathroom where I can run and lock myself inside until she has calmed down. The bathroom is so small. If I sit with my back against the door, I can press my feet tight against the toilet bowl. She doesn't have a chance of getting in that way. It's my favorite place to hide from her.

Sometimes, she hits me for no reason, and I'm too scared to hit her back. Before I was put in the hospital the second time, she was picking on me and beating me up so much. I couldn't take it anymore, and I snapped. I went into a rage, grabbed a couple small steak knives from the kitchen, and chased her through the house with them.

When I couldn't catch Daddy's little track star bully, I started flinging them at her while chasing her down the basement stairs. One of them missed, but the other one hit her right in the back. It didn't stick in her back, but the tip of the knife got her and left a small cut. That day, I needed to be locked in the padded room, but I was so sick of

63

her beating me up; I lost it. She didn't mess with me for a while after that...but it did not take long before she was back to being the same old bully.

All the sudden, I realize how loud it is under the bridge with the sound of the tractor-trailers and cars passing down below on the highway and I am jerked out of my memories. Mom hates that we hang out under here. She says it's too dangerous. I don't think so. I stay up at the top where the ground is flat and safe. Some other kids that come under here like to slide down on the rocks toward the bottom and then throw the rocks at the semi-trucks that pass. I think it's stupid. They call me a chicken because I won't do it with them, but I don't care. I don't want to hurt anyone.

Our backyard faces the highway, too, and I used to throw the tomatoes from Mom's garden over the fence at the trucks. It's funny when they splat against the side of them, and all the others on the road start honking their horns. I quit doing that when Mom explained how it could cause a bad accident and people could get killed. Plus, she was really pissed that we were ruining all of her tomatoes.

I start to doze off with my head propped up against the cement wall when, out of nowhere, Malory appears and startles me. "Mal, you scared me! Don't do that!" I say, catching my breath.

"Shut up, you big baby," she replies, laughing. "I knew you would be down here. Mom is worried about you. She thinks you might have run away last night after she went to bed. She was going to call the police again, but I told her I'd try to find you first," she explains.

I roll my eyes. "Well, maybe I should stay gone for a couple weeks, and then she would know how we feel when she leaves."

"Hey, Mal?" I ask, after minutes of silence.

"What?"

"Do you think what Mom said about Grandpa Torres that one night when she came home drunk is true?" I ask.

Malory seems startled by the question and quits fumbling with the rocks. As she looks at me with serious eyes, she says, "I don't know,

Heather. I try not to think about it too much. It's hard to forget when we see them. I can't look at him the same way anymore."

I stand and start to walk closer to my sister. I have a bad headache. Probably from all the screaming I did. "I know, Mal, me too. I wish she would have never told us. I wonder if that's why she and Aunt Phoebe are so messed up compared to the rest of their siblings. It must be true then, right, because they're so different?"

"I think so, Heather. I don't think Mom would lie about something like that," she says, as she turns to walk towards the way out. "Come on, Heather, let's go home. Dad doesn't know about all of this yet. If you get home and start kissing Mom's butt before he wakes up, maybe she won't tell him."

She might be right, I think as I follow her out and head back home to face the music.

Chapter Eight

It's been a few weeks since that night, and Mom hasn't taken me back to the hospital. *Thank God.* I don't want to be here most of the time, but I don't want to be locked away like a wild animal, either. She never told Dad what happened. I don't know why she didn't. This is the first time she has ever stayed quiet about the cops being at our house. It happens so much that it wouldn't be a normal week if they didn't come at least once. Maybe she just didn't want him to hit me.

We have actually been extra nice to each other since then. Malory says she wants to gag, and keeps calling me a brown-nosing butt-kisser. I'm not trying to be a butt-kisser. I really feel bad about what I said to her.

Today is Johnny's birthday. That's probably why Mom didn't send me back to the hospital or tell Dad. I'm sure she didn't want me to ruin Johnny's day. He's turning seven. It's June, the first day of summer, and it's hot outside. I don't want to be stuck in the house all day, so I'm going to see if I can hang out with Bobbi.

Mom is in a good mood today; she always is on our birthdays. I don't want to ruin her good mood by asking if I can leave right away, so

I'll wait for a little bit. She doesn't like me hanging out with Bobbi that much, but there's nothing else to do. Unfortunately, she doesn't really like any of my friends

The best days of the year in our house are birthdays and holidays. Mom never messes them up, no matter what. We always get to pick what we want for dinner, and we always have parties. They haven't always been big parties, especially when Mom and Dad don't have a lot of money, but they are always fun.

Mom always wakes us up in the morning at the time we were born, telling us happy birthday, smothering us with kisses and hugs. She always makes us feel extra special on our day.

I got to have my last two birthday parties at the roller rink, and all my friends were there. It's my favorite place to go. I'd go there every weekend if they would let me. When things are going good at home, that's where we are hanging out.

Malory and Theo's birthdays are both in April, only four days apart from each other. On their last birthdays, when Mal turned thirteen and Theo turned ten, we were in Ohio visiting family. Mom thought it would be a good idea to do both of their birthdays together since everyone could be there. We had it at Grams' house. She bought a big cake and split it down the middle. One side was decorated with a baseball field, and the other side was decorated with flowers. Mom learned her lesson to never do that again because Mal and Theo were furious about it. I guess I would be too if I had to share my special day with anyone else.

Christmas at our house is always the best. I don't know how they do it, but even when Dad is laid-off from work, we always have a ton of Christmas presents to open. Johnny still believes in Santa, but the rest of us know he isn't real. I found out when I was only six years old and I caught Dad putting the presents under the tree. He and Mom were being loud in a drunken rant and woke Malory and me up. Shortly after, not knowing any better, we told Theo. They never knew we caught them.

Mom and Dad have known for a while that we know there is no

Santa, so every year, Mom tells us to pick what we want out of the shopping catalogs and write it down but make sure it doesn't go over a certain amount.

I can never sleep on Christmas Eve. We always wake up around four in the morning and lay by the tree, trying to guess what everything is until Dad gets up. Meanwhile, Mom takes pictures and drinks her morning pot of coffee.

Malory tries to ruin Christmas every year, and I hate it. She and Theo always go snooping for the presents when Mom and Dad aren't home. Malory is so mean. She will tell me what I got when she finds them.

Last Christmas, I covered my ears and yelled really loud so I couldn't hear her. When she finally shut up, I told her that I would tell Mom and Dad that she was snooping if she kept trying to tell me what I was getting. I don't understand why she and Theo go looking for them; I like to be surprised. I've tried to warn them before they find them that it won't be as much fun opening them, but they don't care—they go looking anyway. Mom and Dad need to find better hiding spots. Our house isn't very big, so they don't have to look very far.

With Mom's love for cooking, she always cooks a lot of food on holidays, and I love to watch her. I get to help her sometimes, but most of the time all I hear from her in an irritated groan is, "Get out of the kitchen and out from under me!" She lets Johnny be with her. He gets to be with her for everything. He's her baby and is always attached to her hip. If he wasn't so cute and I didn't love him so much, I'd probably be more jealous.

Johnny's not a brat like Mal and Theo, so I don't mind him. He's always so sweet to everyone. He has bleach blonde hair like Mom and Mal, and the same hazel-green eyes as the rest of us. He's the only innocent one in our family. I hope he never changes.

After breakfast, I take a shower and do my hair and makeup. Mom doesn't mind that we're into doing our hair and putting on makeup already, but Dad always complains about how much hairspray we go through.

I'm standing in the mirror finishing up when Dad appears in the doorway, waving his hand in front of his face and says, "Geeez, Heth! Do you think you have enough hairspray in your hair? I don't know why you girls think you need all that junk in your hair and on your face. You look fine without it."

Is that supposed to be a compliment?

"Whatever, Dad! You don't know what you're talking about," I reply with sarcasm.

He acts like such a hippie sometimes. If it were up to him, we would be walking around with no makeup and hair long enough to sweep the floors. Mom cut mine and Mal's hair once when we lived in Ohio, and he almost had a heart attack. In his defense, though, she did make us look like boys. I think she did it because she was tired of us coming home from school with lice all the time.

"Dad, do you think I can go to Bobbi's today? Charlie's girlfriend, Heidi, has a softball game later, and Bobbi wants to know if I can go with her," I ask in the most innocent tone possible, hoping he'll say yes.

"I don't know, Heth. You're going to have to ask your mom," he replies.

I hate when he says that.

"But Dad, she always says no. She never lets me do anything!" I plead.

"Well, today is Johnny's birthday, Heather. You can't just take off all day," he snaps back.

"I know, but I'll come back when it's time for cake and ice cream, I promise!" I beg, changing back to my innocent tone.

"I don't know. We'll have to see what your mom says. Now, get out of here, I gotta use it," he says, tapping his newspaper against his leg. He's starting to do his little potty dance and lets out a big fart. "GEEEZ, Heather, ya pig!" he says smiling.

"Ewww...Dad! You are so disgusting!" I cry out, holding my nose and laughing. *God he's so gross!*

I grab my stuff and make a break for it before he starts stinking up the bathroom with me in here. "Dad you're such a dork!" I say, heading toward my room.

I don't know what to do to pass the time until I'm brave enough to ask mom if I can go. I sit down on my bed, look around my room, and spot my diary on the shelf with all my other books in the corner. Maybe I will write in it for a while or maybe read one of my books. I read all of those already, and I need new ones. I hate reading the same books over and over.

I walk over to the shelf, grab my diary, and lay across my bed on my stomach. Just as I open it Theo walks into the room.

"What are you doing, ya adopted freak?" he asks in his usual annoying tone of voice.

"Ughh! Theo, get out of here! Go play with your friends or something, and leave me alone, you little jerk!" I snap back at him.

"Hey! What have I told you about talking like that?" screams Mom from the bottom of the stairs.

I look at Theo and smile. "Haha! You got yelled at! Now, get out before I pound your face in!"

He sticks out his tongue and makes a grunting noise as he leaves the room.

Idiot!

I turn my attention back to what I was doing and decide I don't want to write today. I'm not sure what to write about since it's been so long since I've written, so I start reading my old entries. When I come to the one about Mom coming home smashed and telling us about Grandpa Torres, I read...

Dear Diary,

Mom came home in a drunken rage again last night. I hate her so much. Sometimes, I wish I were never born, then I wouldn't have to deal with her crap. Dad was at work, so he wasn't home to save us from hearing the things that came out of her mouth. When he's home, he keeps her out of our bedrooms, so she doesn't start in with us. I wish he was home, so I didn't have to hear it. If only there were a way to go back in time, I would have run away before she got home. Hell, I would have even chopped my own ears off to avoid hearing it.

I don't know if I should believe her because she was so drunk. I've never known my mom to tell lies before though, drunk or sober. I'm not sure what to think right now. I'm just so angry I could scream. I feel so sick to my stomach because I can't stop picturing it in my head over and over. Her words keep repeating in my ears, and I can't make it stop. It all feels like a bad dream. She has told us plenty of times before that Grandpa used to beat her and Aunt Phoebe really badly. I didn't know how bad it truly was until last night. I don't really want to know, either. It may seem selfish of me, but I don't care! I just want Mom to stop thinking about herself so much and take care of us for a change. The things that she said last night will be forever burned into my memory.

This is how it all went down, Diary;

We had school today, so we were sound asleep. Mal and I were startled awake to Mom turning on the light and slamming the bedroom door into the wall. When I sat up and realized what was going on, I quickly became irritated and yelled at her to get out of our room and leave us alone. I laid back down and covered my head with my pillow when she refused to go away. She stumbled to my bed and ripped my pillow and blankets off me. I begged her to leave me alone and reached out to grab my pillow and blanket from her. When I pulled on them, she fell forward onto my bed face first. Serves her right for being such a horrible mother! Malory cried out for her to stop, but nothing was stopping her. Mom was so close to me I could smell the alcohol, and I just wanted to get away from her, so I stood up on my bed and backed myself into the corner. Mom got up on my bed and stood right in my face, breathing her nasty liquor breath all over me. I squeezed my eyes shut as tight as I could and tried to turn away from her to avoid the disgusting smell.

Then, Mom said, "You think your life is so bad, little girl?"

Ughh...I hate when she says that! Of course I think my life is bad, I have to deal with her drunken craziness!!! Her smell and her slurred speech was enough to make me go crazy. On top of it, she was spitting on me as she was talking! I never wanted to hit her so bad in my life. Mal *and I both kept begging her to get out of our room, both of us yelling at one point, but she just wouldn't stop.*

She finally got out of my face and started to leave the room. Just when I thought it was finally over, she turned around and said, "Listen to me, you little spoiled brats! You think your life is so bad, don't you? You think your shit don't stink? Well, let me tell you something!" Then, after a brief pause, Mom said it. The worst thing a little girl could ever hear about the man she always called Grandpa. The man who took Mom in as his own when her real dad left, "At least you don't have your stepfather coming into your room in the middle of the night and standing over your bed, telling you to suck his dick!"

As soon as she said it, I wanted to scream out in horror, but I couldn't. I was speechless, but at the same time didn't want to hear any more, so I screamed for her to get out and shut up. I plugged my ears as if that was somehow going to take back what I already heard her say.

So now what, Diary? How do I forget about that? How does writing in you make that go away or make anything better? I'll never be able to look at him again without knowing what he did to her and my aunt. I have so many questions I want to ask Mom right now, but I also want to tape her mouth shut so I don't have to hear those disgusting things ever again. I hate him now, I hate him more than I hate her. How could he do that to them? Now, she's ruining our lives the same way he ruined hers. It's all his fault she's so screwed up! Where was Grandma when he was doing that to her? She has to know, doesn't she? Why is she still married to him after what he did to them? Why do they always pretend like everything is so perfect in their family all the time when it's all so messed up? They've always tried to say it's Dad's fault that she drinks so much, and they blame him for everything she does, but now, I know the truth. I see what goes on; they don't. They have never been around enough to really see anything she does.

Oh my God, that's it! That's why Mom never took us over there and dropped us off like she did at Grams' house. She was afraid he would do it to me and Mal, too. I want to scream at the top of my lungs so bad right now, but all I can do is cry. I love Mom, but I hate her so much for dumping all her problems on us. Why does she keep trying to be close to people who did such awful things to her? I'll never understand her. I can't wait to grow up so I can get as far away from these crazy people as I can. I swear to God, I'll never be anything like Mom!

Signed,

The Pissed Off One!

I'm surprised at how reading that made a lot of those old feelings come back. I'm starting to feel angry and sad all over again. Maybe reading my diary wasn't such a good idea. Most of the time, I try to force the thoughts out of my head, but sometimes, I can't think of anything else. And then, I have a hard time looking Mom in the eyes.

Everything has changed since then. Mal was right that day under the bridge. I can't look at him the same, either. I can't look at any of them the same way. Visits to Ohio to see Mom's family will be ruined forever.

My grandparents still live in the same house Mom grew up in, and every time I go there, I can't help but think about it. I picture it when I go into her old room, and it makes me sick to my stomach. I still hug him and tell him I love him because I have to, and they can't know that Mom told us. The truth is...I don't love him. I hate him now.

I try really hard not to think about it when I see them, but it's impossible. I know too much, and I was never close to them anyway, so I don't feel bad about hating him. They don't care about us, anyway. They only came to see us the one time since we moved away. If they cared, wouldn't they come visit more or want us to come stay summers with them the way Grams does?

All they ever do is fight with Mom. Sometimes, they go months without talking to her. She gets so sad when they fight and then she drinks more. If I were her, I would be happy they didn't want to talk to me. I don't know why she isn't.

Dad's father is the only real grandpa we have. I know he's not a perfect man, but he is nothing like Mom's stepdad. Grams divorced him when Dad was only a toddler. They both remarried and had more children.

I'm not really close to his wife, who is also the woman he cheated on Grams with. *Maybe I don't want to be close to her because of my loyalty to Grams, who knows.* Sometimes, I get the idea that Grams still loves Grandpa. I can tell by the way she talks about him.

Grams' second husband cheated on her, too. Recently, he picked up and moved to New Mexico with the new woman and hasn't spoken to anyone since. How can a dad leave their kids behind like that? As I sit here thinking about it, I start to feel bad for Grams. I really miss her, and I can't wait to see her again. She's been through a lot, and you don't see her drinking like my parents do.

I have to try to stop thinking about all of this. It's time to make my move on Mom and try to get out of the house before I drive myself crazy with all my thoughts.

Chapter Nine

Mom is in the kitchen, making Johnny's cake when I approach her. "Mom, is it ok if I go to Bobbi's today?"

"Why can't you just stay home today, Heather?" she replies with a sigh.

"Because I'm bored and there's nothing to do," I huff.

"Well, you know I don't like you hanging out with her, Heather. Today is Johnny's birthday. We all need to be together as a family."

Yeah, now she wants to be a family.

"Please, Mom? I'll come back when it's time to sing to him and do his cake," I beg.

"No, Heather. Just stay home!" she growls.

"Come on, Mom! Why not?"

"Because I said so, damn it. Now quit asking!" she yells, giving me that, "don't push it!" look.

"Ughh...it's so unfair! You never let me do anything!" I bark back, then turn to stomp out of the room.

"What's the big deal? Why can't you just let her go?" asks Dad, appearing in the kitchen doorway.

Yes! Dad to the rescue. Mom hates when Dad questions her decisions, and I can tell before she even speaks that she's furious.

"Because, Theodore! She doesn't need to go over there every single day!"

"Well, I don't see what the big deal is, Lorynn. Just let her go," Dad replies.

I don't get it, why didn't he just tell me yes in the first place? We could have avoided this whole awkward argument.

"FINE, just go! I don't know why I bother saying anything in this house when no one listens to me anyway! Do whatever the hell you want!" she screams.

Oh, boy, she's really mad! Time to get out now before she changes her mind.

Usually, if Dad is home and we want something that Mom says no to, he steps in, and they argue until we get what we want. I don't know why he bothers telling us to ask her. We know to go to Dad first when we want something. He always says yes. If it were up to Mom, we would never leave the front yard. I don't know what she's so worried about.

As I make my way across the street, I see that there aren't any cars in the driveway at Bobbi's. *Awesome!* Her parents aren't home, so we'll have the house to ourselves. Hopefully, Mom doesn't look over here and notice, or she might make me come home. She's always worried about what I'm doing over here.

I know I do terrible things at Bobbi's house sometimes, but she's my closest friend. We have become more like sisters than me and Mal. Her family treats me like I'm one of them. Her mom is nothing like my mom, and even though her family isn't perfect either, I'd rather be there than at home most of the time.

Walking up the driveway, I hear, "Freeze, bitch!"

I look up and see Charlie hunched over the top of the roof, pointing his BB gun at me. I duck under the archway of the door as fast as I can and just miss being hit by one of his BBs as it goes whizzing past my head.

"Charlie, knock it o!!" I shout, covering my head. "Watch it, guys, he's gonna shoot someone with that stupid thing," I yell, seeing Bobbi and Charlie's girlfriend, Heidi, walking toward me from the side of the garage.

Just as Bobbi turns to look up at him, he shoots and plants one right in the side of her head. *Oh my God!*

"Charlie, you asshole! I'm telling Dad!" she screams out, holding her head and dropping to the ground in tears.

God, I hate the way she cries. It's more like a wailing sound than a cry.

Their dad is out of prison now, and he's a mean old man. I wouldn't want to mess with him. Once, I saw him beat Bobbi with his belt. He was hitting her in the face, head, and anywhere else he could. He looked at me while he was doing it and threatened to hit me with it, too. I was so scared. I never told my parents because I knew I would never be able to come to her house again.

It was all because we were up late when I was sleeping over, and we couldn't stop laughing. Her dad scares the crap out of me. I avoid him as much as possible. I wonder if he was that mean before he went to prison. I didn't really know him then. I'm glad my dad isn't *that* mean.

I run over to Bobbi to see if she's ok and see the metal BB lodged into her skin by her temple. "Charlie! It's stuck in her head!" I yell.

"Quit being such a baby!" he calls out, laughing as he climbs down from the roof.

I grab Bobbi by the arm, help her off the ground, and start to walk towards the house.

"Charlie, why did you do that? You could have shot her in the eye!" says Heidi, slapping him in the arm.

"You'll shoot your eye out! You'll shoot your eye out!" he chants, laughing.

Once in the house, Heidi goes to get rubbing alcohol and tweezers to get the BB out of Bobbi's temple. It's not really bleeding, so I think she'll be fine. She's still crying like a baby. Charlie yells at her to knock off her crying before he beats her up. He will too, he's done it plenty of times.

I'm glad I don't have six older brothers. I only have to worry about one person bullying me at my house.

A while later after Bobbi is cleaned up and no longer crying, we're sitting around watching TV, smoking cig after cig, when Charlie asks us if we want to go to the basement and smoke a joint. Bobbi and Heidi say ok, but there's no way I'm doing that again.

"Nah, I don't feel like it," I say.

"What's the matter, Heather, you got knocked on your ass last time and now you don't like it?" teases Charlie.

"Yup! I'm never touching that crap again!" I say with confidence.

"Don't be a wuss, Heather. Come on, let's go," says Bobbi.

"No way! I don't like it. You guys go ahead, I'll stay up here and keep watch."

"Fine, you big sissy!" laughs Charlie.

The three of them leave the room and head toward the basement. I sit in the chair by the window and light another cig. Their mom is at work and their dad is probably fishing, so they won't be coming home anytime soon. Their older brother, Josh, who lives here, is who we really need to worry about. He's mean, too, and also a trouble-maker. He just got out of jail not that long ago. That's where they get their pot. They steal it from his stash when he's not home.

Bobbi takes it from her other brother, Sam, when we go to his house too. I don't know why she takes it; we never smoke it. I think she just likes to see if she can get away with stealing it. He almost caught her once and told her if he ever finds out she's taking it, it'll be the last thing she ever does. I like Sam; he's the nicest to me. He is always teasing me and telling me how pretty I am. He says he can tell I'm going to be a little knockout when I get older. He jokes that I better call him the day I turn eighteen. *Whatever that means.*

We go to Sam's as much as possible because his wife, Harmony, lets us smoke. Sam doesn't want Harmony smoking, so she hides it from him. Bobbi threatened to tell Sam about her smoking if she didn't let us smoke too. I thought that was kind of mean, but I'm not going to argue with her when she asks me if I want a cigarette.

I've tried smoking pot with them a few times. The first couple of times I tried it, I was ten, and it wasn't a big deal. It didn't make me feel any different than normal, so I really didn't understand why people made such a big deal out of it.

One night, Bobbi and Charlie came knocking on the sliding glass door with a joint when Mom and Dad were out at the bar. I smoked it, thinking it would be like the other times, no big deal. It took a little bit to hit me, but once it did, I hated it. It was the worst feeling ever, and I don't want to ever feel it again. Everything was in slow motion, and my heart was beating so fast I thought I was going to die. *Why do people think that's fun? I don't get it.*

When the three of them come back into the room, they're laughing so hard they can barely talk.

"What's so funny?" I ask.

Charlie is laid out across the couch laughing and holding his stomach.

"Shut up, Charlie!" laughs Bobbi.

"Come on, guys, tell me! What's so funny?" I ask, smiling.

Charlie sits up and points at Bobbi, still laughing. "She had a BB stuck in her head!" he says, cracking up, barely able to get the words out.

I chuckle but it's not *that* funny. *I guess I have to be high to get it.*

"Hey, I have an idea," says Charlie, walking toward the kitchen. Moments later, he returns, holding a glass and a bottle of his mom's Boones Farm. "Let's play quarters," he says with a big cheesy smile on his face. Bobbi and Heidi don't hesitate to say yes.

"What the hell is quarters?" I ask, dumbfounded.

Heidi shoots a look at Charlie. "I don't know. It's probably not a good idea to get your little sister and her friend drunk."

I know what being drunk is, and I definitely don't want to do that.

"Oh, come on, Heidi! Bobbi just got high. What's the big deal? It's

81

only Boones Farm. They won't get drunk. Bobbi has played it before," he adds.

"Quarters is a game where you have to bounce the quarter into the cup. If you miss, you have to drink what's in the cup. Just don't miss it and you won't have to drink it," he explains.

This actually sounds like fun, and I'm pretty confident I can get a little quarter into a cup. *I'm a softball player, I got this!*

Thirty minutes later, after hearing, "Drink it! Drink it! Drink it!" I realize it's not so easy to bounce a quarter into a cup. The room is starting to spin, and I'm starting to feel nauseous when the bottle is finally gone. *Thank God it's over and I don't have to drink anymore.* It tasted good but I don't like the way I feel right now. I can't believe this is how Mom and Dad feel when they drink. *Why the hell do they like this? Another thing I don't understand.*

I laugh and joke with the rest of them for the next hour, pretending I'm having a good time. But the truth is, I just want to go to sleep and pretend this never happened. The phone suddenly rings. Charlie answers it and then quickly hangs up.

"Heather, you have to go home and sing happy birthday to your brother."

"Oh, no!" I shout with a hint of a slur, jumping to my feet, stumbling over the dog, and almost falling flat on my face. "What am I going to do, you guys? I can't go home like this!" I cry out.

They're laughing at me. They think it's funny that I'm a stumbling drunk idiot right now, but I hate it. I wish I wouldn't have done it. My parents are going to know I'm drunk as soon as they see me. I have to find a way to play it cool so they don't find out.

The walk across the street never seemed shorter. *Just be normal Heather. Be normal and everything will be fine. If I don't talk to anyone, they won't smell it on my breath. Sing, watch him open his presents, and then get the hell out of there until you're not drunk anymore.*

I walk in the front door and Dad is standing right there in front of me. *God! Can you be any closer?* "Hey!" he says, smiling.

I look up at him and smile really quick, trying to avoid eye contact and go straight to the couch to sit down. I need to be as far away from him as possible.

He sits down on the couch opposite me, "Look what's on TV, Heth! It's *Back to the Future, Part One*," he says, somewhat excited.

Dad always tells us when something old is on TV, like he thinks we're going to jump up and down with excitement or something.

"Uh-huh," I say, barely opening my mouth, afraid the smell will somehow cross the room. I'm careful not to make eye contact.

"So, Heth, are you going to practice for your softball games at all this summer, or are you just gonna run the neighborhood and not care how good you play?"

Is he kidding me right now?

He never wants to lecture me about anything unless he's been drinking, much less talk to me about softball. *Now at this very moment, when I'm so drunk I can barely see because my world is spinning and all I want to do is hurl, he decides to talk about softball?! This must be that karma thing Mom is always talking about.*

In a quiet voice, my lips pursed so I'm barely opening my mouth to talk, I quickly say, "I don't know," still avoiding all eye contact.

"Hey, what's with you? Why are you acting weird?" he asks with his eyebrows raised.

Crap! I'm not being normal at all.

He's sitting far enough away that he shouldn't be able to smell it on my breath, so I look at him as normal as possible and say, "Shut up, Dad! I'm not being weird. I'll practice, ok?" as I let out a little chuckle.

He gives me a look as if he's trying to figure me out. His eyebrows are still raised, and he's got a funny look on his face.

Uh-oh, I'm busted!

He continues to stare at me for what seems like forever.

"What, Dad? You're the one being weird. Stop staring at me like that!" I say, smiling as he finally looks away. *Whoa! That was a close call.* I get up and quickly head toward the bathroom. I think I might be sick.

After singing to Johnny, watching him open his gifts, and posing for pictures, I ask my dad if I can leave to go to Heidi's softball game.

"Yeah, go ahead, but come right home after," he says, giving me that look again.

I wonder if he knows. If he does, he's not saying anything. Mom definitely doesn't know. She's too busy with Johnny and has barely even looked in my direction except to take the pictures. I'd hate to see what those pictures look like later.

After the game, Bobbi and I go walking around the neighborhood. I don't go right home like I'm supposed to. As long as I'm home before dark, they won't care. I'm starting to feel normal again, but I have the worst headache in the world. My head is pounding so hard that it hurts to have my eyes open, and I'm still feeling a little nauseous.

What did I do? I can't wait to go to sleep tonight.

"Bobbi, I'm never drinking again. I hate it! Have you ever gotten drunk before?" I ask.

"Yeah, a few times with Charlie. It's not that bad, Heather," she snorts.

"You do what you want, but I'm never touching it again!"

Bobbi turns to say something else when a gold car pulls up and stops. We stop to look, thinking we might know who is inside. As soon as I get a closer look, I back away. It's a bald, older Black man wearing square-shaped glasses with gold rims.

I don't know this creep.

"Hey, ladies, what are y'all out doing on this fine summer day?" he asks, flashing a big smile.

Weirdo!

"Nothing, just walking around," Bobbi says, giggling, leaning into the passenger side of his car window.

Is she stupid? Why is she talking to this guy? Why does he want to talk to us anyway? He's got to be one of those freaks Mom's always warning me about.

I'm starting to get a really bad vibe and a sick feeling in my stomach when he asks Bobbi where we live. She starts to tell him, but before she can get a word out, I grab her by the arm, and pull her back towards the curb. "Bobbi! Don't tell him where we live! Are you crazy? Why are you even talking to him?" I ask in a rushed, furious whisper.

She just stares at me, pale-faced, not knowing what to say.

"I'll take care of this. You stay right here and don't say another word," I demand, letting go of her arm.

I walk around her to face him, being careful not to get too close to his car. "That's my house right there, and I can see my dad watching us through the window. You better leave before he comes outside," I say pointing to the house on the corner, lying through my teeth.

His smile quickly fades. "Well, ok then. You girls have a nice day," he says, sounding worried, and he quickly drives off.

I'm sick to my stomach from drinking, and now I'm angry and scared. I'm pretty sure Bobbi almost got us kidnapped. All I want to do is get out of here before he comes back and realizes I lied to him.

"Come on, Bobbi, time to go home!" I snap at her, walking away. "Geez, Heather, what's wrong with you?" she asks, completely dumbfounded by what just could have happened.

Wow!

"What's wrong with me? Are you really that stupid, Bobbi? Don't you pay attention at school when they try to teach us about strangers? I just want to go home and go to bed. It's almost dark out, anyway," I call out, walking quickly in front of her.

We walk the rest of the way home in silence with her trailing behind me. We're only a short distance away, but I don't think I could have outrun that man's car. I don't know how I thought up that lie so quickly, but I'm glad I did. Bobbi better be glad I was with her, or she might be dead by now. I think I'm going to start listening to Mom more. She really does know what she's talking about sometimes.

Chapter Ten

Dear Diary,

Mom sucks!!! I woke up this morning and went to her room and found her in bed asleep with a man that wasn't my dad! Can you believe that, Diary? My mom is not just a drunk, she's also a cheater and a liar! As if it couldn't get any worse, he's one of the cops that's always at our house, AND he's Black!!! I don't have anything against Black people. I have lots of Black friends at school. I just don't understand because Mom always acts like such a racist. She's always saying the "n" word, and I hate her for it. So, what is she doing? I don't think I have ever been so confused and pissed off. Where the hell is Dad? Why isn't he home? Why doesn't he just take us and run away from her crazy ass?!?!?!

When I left her bedroom, I slammed the door shut as hard as I could and screamed, "I fucking hate you, Mom! You make me sick!" I wanted them to wake up, but more than that, I wanted to run away from what I was seeing as fast as I could. After I came back to my room to wake Mal up and tell her, I heard the bastard sneaking out. What a scumbag! He's lucky my dad isn't here 'cause I know he would beat his ass! I am so disgusted with her right now. I hate her so much!!!

I have to go. I hear Malory coming back to the room. Life sucks!!
Heather

"I hate her, Malory! I wish she were dead!" I cry out after Mal closes the door.

"Heather, don't say that about Mom! I know she's messed up, and I'm really starting to hate her too, but I don't want her to die!" she says, her lips pursed.

I'm clenching my teeth together so hard that it feels like my jaw is about to break. I don't know if I should scream or if I should cry. Maybe both would make me feel better. The only thing that could ever make me feel better is not having to see that.

"I know, Mal. I don't really want her to die either, I just don't know how else to say how I feel. Why does Dad stay with her? I wish they would get divorced so I could just live with him. I can't stand living with her anymore. I have to get out of here."

Mal is pacing the room, and I can tell by how angry she is that she's starting to feel the same way.

"Do you wanna come with me this time, Mal? Just come with me! Let's get away from her for good. We can go to Jessica and Carla's house!" I beg.

Carla is my new best friend. I met her not long after I quit hanging out with Bobbi as much. I've been spending a lot of time at her house this summer. Her sister, Jessica, is Mal's age. They go to school together. Mal and I have been getting along a lot better because she quit acting like such a goody-goody.

I knew that one day she would finally get sick of Mom and stop sticking up for her. I think the hate has been building up for a while. She just doesn't let it out the way I do. Mom has been coming and going a lot lately. She's been arrested a bunch of times for drinking and driving. And she was raped again. *Now this!*

"Ok, Heather. I'm coming with you!" says Mal.

"REALLY? You're really going to come with me?" I ask, surprised.

My heart starts beating faster from the anticipation or fear—I don't know which.

"Yes, Heather, screw Mom! Let's get the hell out of here!" she says angrily, still pacing the room.

"Hey, Mal. You know what I've been thinking?"

"What, Heather?"

"When that guy broke into our house last year in the middle of the night, I wondered if Mom owed him money for drugs and that's what he came here to get."

"Duh, Heather! I've always known that!" she says matter-of-factly.

"What? How do you know that?" *I'm always the last to know everything!*

"Because I heard her whispering about it on the phone a couple days after it happened," she explains.

"No way! Why didn't you tell me?" I ask, starting to feel angry and stupid for not knowing sooner.

"Because I didn't want you to be scared," she replies sympathetically. She finally quits pacing and sits down on the bed beside me.

"Mal, do you think if the cops wouldn't have come he would have shot Mom?" I ask, feeling a lump starting to form in my throat from the thought of what could have been. *He could have shot us!*

"I don't know, Heather, maybe. Why else would he have a gun with him?"

There is no way I could have been more scared than I was when that happened. Even thinking about it now, I get scared. He broke in through our basement window while Dad was working one night, and we were all in bed. Mom heard the window break, so she quickly made her way down to the kitchen. Before he came up the basement stairs, she was able to hide in the corner and call 911.

The house was pitch-black, but she watched his shadow move slowly up the stairs toward our bedrooms. Thank God the police made it here as fast as they did or who knows what would have happened. When they got here, they found him in our room with a gun in his hand.

I had made a tent under my bed that night and was sleeping under it. I slept through the entire thing. Mom made Mal promise she wouldn't wake me up and tell me what happened. She told me every-thing as soon as I woke up the next morning.

She said there were around ten cops in our room, pointing their guns at him, screaming at him to get down on the ground and drop his weapon. I can't believe I slept through the whole thing. I'm really glad I did, though. Mal also told me that she heard the man telling the cops that he was a friend of Mom's, and she called him asking for help. He said she told him that Dad was beating her up. We knew that wasn't true because Dad was at work. Mom didn't have male friends, or so we thought. I guess she has male drug dealers and boyfriends that we don't know about. She lives a totally different life outside of our house.

I'm starting to wonder if her rapes have something to do with drugs. Maybe she's trading herself for them. That's what Bobbi's brother, Josh, says about her. I always defend her when they talk bad about her because she's my mom, but mostly because I'm embarrassed. I don't want to deal with feeling the shame she casts over our family. The times when she disappears, I often find Dad crying in his room. He pretends like he's not when I walk in, but I know better. I hate her for hurting us all so much.

"Mal," I call out as I watch her going through her clothes and packing things into her book bag. "Don't pack anything. It's too hard to run away when you're carrying stuff. Trust me, I've tried it."

"Then what do you wear when you're gone?" she asks, looking up at me.

"I borrow clothes from my friends. Besides, if Mom and Dad see you packed a bag, they're going to know we're running away," I add.

Just then, the door swings open, and it's Mom. I look at her with disgust. "Get out of here! We don't want to talk to you!" I snap.

"Mal, what's in the bag? What are you doing?" she asks Mal, ignoring my request to leave and sits down on the bed across from me.

Malory looks at her with pure hate. "I'm leaving and never coming back here!"

"You two need to calm down and listen to what I have to say," Mom says calmly.

"There's nothing to talk about, Mom! Heather saw you!" shouts Mal, stomping toward the bedroom door and swinging it open. "Now get out of here! We don't want to talk to you!"

Mom's eyes fill with tears. For a split second, I feel sorry for her, and want to hug her. Then the images of her with that cop appear in my head, and I fill with anger again. "Why do you do this to us Mom? Why can't you just be normal?" I ask, angry.

"Heather, he's just my friend. Nothing happened, I promise!" replies Mom.

Yeah, right!

"Then why was he in your bed?" I ask.

She doesn't respond, and the way she is looking at me, I can tell she is ashamed, but I don't care. "Where is Dad? What's he going to think when he comes home and finds out? How can he be your friend when he's always at our house because of you?" I persist.

Mom stands and starts to walk out of the room.

"Well, Mom? Why aren't you saying anything?" asks Mal.

Mom turns to face us when she gets to the door, and with tears coming down her face, she says, "I'm really sorry, girls," and wipes the tears from her eyes.

Malory, who is still standing by the door, gets in her face and says, "You're always sorry, Mom, but you never do anything to change how it is. Your sorrys mean nothing to us anymore! Now get out!" She screams and uses the door to push Mom out of the room, and closes it shut.

Oh, man, poor Mom. Why do I feel so bad now?

Later that day, Dad still isn't home. I'm not sure where he's at or what's going on. I don't want to talk to Mom, so I can't ask her. I'm still trying to plot out when we're going to leave. We need to do it before Dad gets back. I wonder if they had a fight when they were out last night, and he stayed at Emerson and Norma's.

Emerson and Norma are Mom and Dad's best friends. They've known them since we lived in Ohio. Last year, they moved here, too, so we spend a lot of time at their house. I love going there. They're like an aunt and uncle to us, but whenever they all hang out, they're always drinking.

I stayed with them once for a few weeks when Mom and I were fighting a lot. I really liked being there. They're always so nice to us. Emerson is so much fun to be around. He's always laughing and making jokes. He's really short with blonde hair that goes to his shoulders. He likes to hunt and fish, and he always has his dog, BJ, at his side. He and Dad are very different, but they get along really well. They all fight sometimes when they're drinking together. I don't really know why because we are always outside playing while they're partying.

"Heather, I think Mom is leaving. We can go when she's gone," says Mal, startling me from my thoughts.

"Where the hell is she going, and where is Dad?" I ask, puzzled.

"I don't know, Heth, but we should just go then," she says, paying no mind to my growing concern. I'm starting to really worry about what's going on. *I hope Dad is ok.*

"Maybe we should wait until everyone is sleeping to leave. What if Theo and Johnny are here by themselves if Dad doesn't come home?" I say with concern in my voice.

"Heather, they will be fine! They're always home alone. What are you suddenly so worried about them for, anyway?" she asks, rhetorically.

Curiosity gets the best of me, so I head upstairs from the basement where we've been hanging out all day waiting for the right time to leave. I'm going to find out from Mom what's going on. When I get to the top of the basement stairs, she's standing by the kitchen table, fumbling around in her purse.

"Mom?" I call out.

She turns around and looks at me. She doesn't look very pretty to me right now. Her eyes are all puffy, and she has a cold sore in the corner of her mouth. I try to avoid kissing her goodnight when she has them because if I don't, I get these weird little white spots on my lips.

"Where are you going, and where is Dad?" I ask.

"I don't know where your father is, Heather," she replies.

What the hell? It's very unusual for Dad to disappear, unlike Mom. "Where are you going?"

"Crazy," she says as she pulls her keys from her purse.

What is wrong with her? How could she leave when she doesn't even know where Dad is? We all know what it means when she says she's going "crazy." Mal, Theo, and I have learned how to deal with her, but what about Johnny? He's still so little.

"Mom, you can't just leave us when we don't know where Dad is," I demand.

"Heather, I'm coming back, so cool your jets, ok?"

Ughh...I hate when she says that!

"Yeah right, Mom! You always say that! If you're coming back, then why can't you tell me where you're going?" I ask, but she doesn't respond.

She just stares at me with a blank look as if she has no care in the world except to go on her mission. She starts to walk away, but I stand in front of the kitchen doorway. She's still a little taller than me, but right now, I feel like a giant compared to her.

"I hate you, Mom! You're such a fucking bitch!" I yell with disgust in my voice.

No sooner than the words leave my mouth, she slaps me so hard across the face that my head jerks sideways. I instantly grab my cheek as my eyes fill with tears from the sting.

I'm in shock, not knowing what to say or how to react. She has never hit me before. I look over her shoulder, still holding my cheek, and I see Mal standing at the top of the basement stairs. She's watching in shock with her mouth dropped open.

"Let's go, Mal! We're out of here!" I scream with my eyes locked on Mom's, waiting for her reaction. *Is she going to hit me again?*

"If you girls walk out that door, don't ever come back!" Mom threatens.

"Screw you, Mom! I don't care! It's not like you're going to be here to know that we're home, anyway, so why do you care?" I say to her, walking toward the door where my shoes are. "You leave us here alone all the time by ourselves and don't even care if we're ok or if we eat or go to school, so I don't really care what you think. I don't have to listen to you ever again!" I add.

"Please, don't leave, you guys," cries Johnny from the top of the stairs.

"Who cares if they leave, Johnny? Let them go! It's better here without them anyway," says Theo, who is sitting on the couch nearby, watching TV.

I feel bad about Johnny, but I want to smash Theo's face in. He's too busy protecting Mom to see what she's doing to us.

"Johnny, you're going to be ok," I say, looking up at him. I turn to walk out the front door, following Mal's lead.

"I mean it, damn it! If you walk out, I'm calling the police!" yells Mom, from behind us.

Good! Maybe our leaving will make her stay home with the boys, so they won't be alone. I look over my shoulder and smirk at her as I close the door behind me.

"Mal, we have a long walk, and it's almost dark outside, so we're going to have to take a longer way so we don't get spotted by the cops," I say, following quickly behind her. I turn and see Mom standing on the porch with the cordless phone to her ear. "Shit! She's calling the cops, Mal, run!" I shout, and we both take off.

We run six blocks before we have to stop to catch our breath. Well, Mal could have run further, but I feel like I'm going to die. *Damn cigs!* It's dark now, and the neighborhood we are about to walk through isn't the greatest, so I'm starting to feel scared. "Mal, maybe we should go back?" I suggest.

"Heather, don't be a wimp! I'm here, you will be fine," she replies.

Whenever I'm out at dark now, my mind often wanders to the day I felt like I was almost kidnapped. Maybe he wasn't going to kidnap us after all, but I've never been able to shake the eerie feeling he gave me.

That wasn't my only scare, either. There was another night when I was sleeping over at Carla's. We rode doubles on her bike a block away from her house to go to the pop machine. It was late at night, and on the way back to her house, we were chased by a man in a pickup truck. We were barely able to outrun him. I can't seem to forget about those things. Whenever I'm out at night, I try to stay out of sight as much as I can, and I don't ever talk to anyone I don't know.

We're walking down a dark alley, nearing the end when I see a car pull up with no lights on. It's hard to see what kind of car it is, or who's in it. My heart starts to pound when I hear the squeaking of the brakes as it slows down. Then, suddenly, a spotlight is on us.

"Heather, it's the cops! RUN!" yells Malory as we quickly turn and start running as fast as we can.

"Malory, don't lose me," I yell out as she speeds ahead of me.

"I won't, Heather, just catch up with me!" she yells, barely turning her head to look back at me.

Is she kidding? She breaks records in track, and I smoke like a chimney. There's no way I'm going to catch up to her.

"Girls, stop! Don't make me chase you!" yells out a familiar voice.

Shit! It's Paul. I should just stop running. I can't go back to that hell, so I keep running, faster than I ever have in my life. We dip out of the alley and start running between houses.

"Mal, I think we lost him. Stop running!" I barely gasp out, unable to catch my breath.

"Keep running until I tell you to stop!" she yells back.

We run through three blocks of houses before she suddenly stops and quickly pulls me into an unlocked garage. "We can stay here for a while until we know they're gone," says Mal, bending over, trying to catch her breath.

"Mal, I feel like I'm going to pass out," I gasp.

"Sit down and take deep breaths, and you'll be fine," she replies.

I drop to the floor and lean up against the garage wall. "Malory, maybe we should just turn ourselves in. Paul will be out all night looking for us until he finds us, and you know it. They've probably already been over to Carla's house looking for us."

"No way, Heather! We're not going back! Why are you being such a wimp about it? You do this all the time. I finally came with you, and now you want to go home? No way!" she barks.

We've been in the garage for I don't know how long when Mal says, "Shhhh, Heather do you hear that?" I can hear people talking and it's getting closer. Malory tugs on the handle to the car that's in the garage. "Heather, it's unlocked. Get in! We'll hide in the back seat until they're gone," she whispers, holding the door open, ushering me in.

I jump in the car, and she follows. We're both hunched down on the floor of the backseat covering our heads, hoping not to be seen. I hear the garage door open and my heart leaps into my throat. "Mal, I'm scared," I whisper.

"Heather, shut the hell up!" she snaps back at me in a mean whisper.

I lift my head just a little. I see the familiar beam from the flashlights shining around the room. I put my head back down and stay as still as I can.

Tap! Tap! Tap! It's the sound of the flashlight hitting the window. *Shit! We're busted!*

"Alright, girls. We see you. It's time to come out now." says Paul.

Mal springs up and storms out of the car, "Fuck that! You can't make us go back there!" she shouts.

"Hey, young lady, watch your mouth! You just calm down!" demands a cop I've never seen before.

Paul opens the door on my side where I still sit, feeling defeated. "Come out, Heather, we're taking you girls to the station."

"Taking us to the station? You're not taking us home?" I ask, getting caught up on the seatbelt, and stumbling from the car.

"Not this time, Heather," he replies, not looking me in the eye. *What the hell is he talking about? Where are they going to take us?*

"What do you mean? Where are we going?" I ask quietly.

"I'm not sure yet, Heather. Let's just get to the station, and we'll sit down and figure it out. There's a counselor meeting us there to talk to you girls," he says, meeting my questioning glare. I can tell by his tone and the look he's giving me that something bad is going to happen.

I look over at Malory, who looks worried. "Don't worry, Mal. We're probably just going to the hospital. It's not that bad there. It'll be ok," I assure her.

Chapter Eleven

Once we're at the station, we're taken into the basement, where there is a seating area, a TV, and a small kitchen.

This must be where the cops go to eat their donuts when they aren't out chasing criminals and runaways.

"Girls, have a seat anywhere you like while I go make some phone calls and get the Sister Mary Catherine's counselor over here," says Paul as he disappears back up the stairs.

"Who the hell is Sister Mary Catherine?" I ask, looking at Mal.

"I don't know, and I don't care," she says in a depressive tone of voice as she plops down on the couch in front of the TV.

Mal looks sad. I wonder if she's mad at me because we got caught or if she regrets coming with me. She's never had to go live anywhere else. Well, not since Indiana, but that was a long time ago. I feel like I'm to blame for her being here. Maybe if I could have run as fast as her, she wouldn't have stopped when she did. Maybe if I had kept my mouth shut and hadn't told her what I saw, she would still be at home.

I look around the room and see a few other cops sitting across the way at a table, eating and laughing. I wonder what they have to laugh about working at a job like this where they have to deal with a bunch of low lives and juvenile delinquents like us. One of them catches me staring. "Hello," she says, smiling, and nods her head. *She's been at our house a lot too.*

"Uh...hi," I reply embarrassed and quickly turn back toward the TV.

It's cold in here, and I'm trembling badly. Partially from being cold, but mostly from fear. I wedge my hands under my upper thighs to try to stop the shaking. I've never been brought to the station before. They usually just take me back home. The last time I was taken to the hospital, I was picked up by the cops for running away. Mom had them bring me there to meet her.

I sit, staring at the TV, but I'm not really watching it. For some odd reason, I'm thinking about all the good times we have at home. It seems silly to think about that right now after everything that's happened today. I just want to hate her. I don't want to remember anything good. She doesn't deserve for me to love her as much as I do. I remember the dandelions, birthdays, Christmas, and Thanksgiving. I can almost smell the apple crisp cooking that she makes from the apple trees in the backyard.

I feel the tears start to well up in my eyes and a knot forming in my stomach. My heart aches, wondering why it can't be like that all the time. Maybe if I can gather the courage to tell her how happy those times are and how perfect everything could be, then maybe she would stop.

Sometimes, when things are going ok at home, I lay in bed with Mom at night and watch TV. She'll even rub my back sometimes like Tina used to. I think about telling her how I feel, but I can't; it's too hard. *She should know what she's doing to us right? I shouldn't have to tell her.*

I cherish every good time we have because they don't happen very often. I don't know how she can be two different people at the same time. Sometimes, I know she loves us, and I don't doubt it, but then the other side of her convinces me that the only person she cares about, and loves is herself. Then, there's Dad, stubborn as hell and lost in his own world. I can't tell half of the time if he's on our side or hers.

"Girls!" Paul calls out as he comes walking back down the stairs.

"What's going on? We've been waiting here forever," I ask, startled from my thoughts.

"I know. I'm sorry. It took the counselor a while to call me back because she's working on one of her other cases. She will be here as soon as she's done," he replies, sitting down on the couch opposite us.

"I need to use the bathroom, and we're hungry," says Mal, standing up and stretching her legs.

I'm not really that hungry. The knot in my stomach is taking care of the void in my stomach, but I could go for something to drink after all that running.

"The bathroom is right around that corner if you need to use it. I can get you girls something to eat. How do burgers and fries sound?" he asks, standing up and reaching into his pocket. "There's a pop machine around the corner next to the bathroom. Go get something to drink. I'm sure all that running has you dehydrated," he says with a smirk as he hands us some quarters.

Why is he so nice to us? I wonder if he has kids at home. He looks young, but I bet he'd make a good dad.

"Thanks, Paul," I say as I take the quarters and follow Mal toward the pop machine.

I guess I was hungry after all because I inhaled my burger and fries. I look up at the clock and see it's almost ten. I'm getting sleepy, and my legs feel like Jello from running. I wish I could erase the whole day and be back at home in my bed. I wonder if Dad ever made it home or if Mom left the boys alone so she could go "crazy."

"How much longer is this Sister Mary Catherine's lady going to take?" I ask, looking over at Paul, who is now sitting with the other officers, chatting about sports or something.

"Heather, Sister Mary Catherine's is not a person, it's a place," he chuckles.

"That's dumb! What kind of place is called Sister Mary Catherine's?"

He gives me a look that tells me he's being serious, and I'm afraid of what he's going to say next. "Your mom contacted them. They're a privately funded agency that provides counseling and foster care to families who really need help."

Malory stands up in a huff, and her chair goes flying as she pushes away from the table, "I'm not living in a stupid foster home! I'll run away again!" she shouts.

"I know it's hard, Malory, but you can't keep running away. You girls are going to get hurt out there. Your family really needs to get some help, so we don't have to keep coming to your house and chasing you all over town," he replies with concern.

"This isn't fair, Paul! My mom should be the one who has to live somewhere else. She's the one screwing everything up!" I say with tears starting to fall down my cheeks. He doesn't respond, but the way he looks at me tells me he knows it too.

It's after midnight when the Sister Mary Catherine's counselor finally shows up. Her name is Pamela. She seems ok, I guess. She says they have some grand plan to fix our family, but I see right through it. It's not going to work. *Nothing ever works!* Why does everyone think if Mal and I change, everything else will be fine? They're adults, shouldn't they be smart enough to see what the real problem is?

Pamela says that Mom has been talking to them for some time now, trying to figure out a plan, and they have decided temporary foster care is necessary. They think if we live away from home for six months and get family counseling that we can "reunite." That's the word she used. I ask her if this means Mom and Dad will quit drinking too, and she said we would talk more about that later.

This is a joke! Malory and I secretly agree we aren't going to stay wherever they take us.

I'm surprised when we pull up to the foster home because it's so close to our house. A few of my close friends live right down the street. This makes me feel less scared because I know exactly where

I am and how to get home. I've walked by this house a thousand times but have never noticed who lives here. I hope they're nice to us.

As we walk toward the door, Malory hesitates. "I don't want to be here! I'm not going in that house!" she demands.

"Just be cool, Mal. If we don't like it, we'll just run back home," I whisper, pulling her close to me.

I can tell by the look she is giving me that she's not sure if she should believe me or not, but she continues to walk up the driveway anyway. Pamela is already at the door. The porch light is on, and someone is holding the door open, but I can't see who it is yet.

When we get close enough to see more clearly, I squint my eyes and see an older Black woman wearing her nightgown and slippers. She has rollers that are covered with a hair net in her hair.

"I'm Ms. Peterson. Y'all come in, and I'll show you where you're gonna sleep," she says, visibly irritated with a blank expression.

I can already tell I'm not going to like it here. *Great!*

Pamela says a quick goodbye and that she will be in touch with us soon and leaves.

We walk in the door and linger in the doorway, not sure what to do next. There's an overwhelming odor I don't recognize that almost burns my nose hairs. *Yuck! What the hell is that?* I quickly look at Mal, who has a look on her face that tells me she's thinking the same thing. There's a small lamp shining in the living room, and I can see the antique-style furniture is covered in thick plastic. The vibe I get sends a chill up my spine.

"Well, y'all don't just stand there in my doorway! Get your white asses movin' so I can get back to bed!" she barks.

Oh, yeah, I hate her already.

We follow her through the kitchen toward the hallway, and I can hear her mumbling something about bad ass kids waking her up in the middle of the night. She stops at a door and uses a key to unlock it and instructs us to go in. I wonder if she's going to lock it again once we're inside. I walk into the small room, and there's that smell again, and it's even stronger. It's so strong I can taste it, and I have to fight the urge to gag.

"Now, y'all don't get any ideas about running away now. I have an alarm on every door and every window in this house. If you try to get out, it will go off and the police will be called."

Oh, no!

Malory shoots me a look as if to say "this is all your fault, Heather."

"I'll be back in the morning to get y'all for breakfast. Don't come out of the room until then," she says and then shuts the door.

I don't hear her lock it, and I'm relieved.

"Do you smell that, Heather? It stinks so bad!" says Mal, holding her nose.

"Yeah, I smell it. I can even taste it! What the hell is that?"

"I don't know, but it's gross," she replies, coughing.

"Mal, she seems like a real mean bitch. I don't wanna stay here." I say, scared.

"I know, Heather, me neither," she says, raising the blinds to check the window. "We aren't going anywhere with this on the window," she says, pointing to a little white box sticking on the window frame.

"Mal, it's late. Let's just get some sleep, and we'll figure it out tomorrow. I promise we will find a way out."

There are two beds in the room, but after shutting off the light, we curl up together on the same bed under the window. Malory always acts so tough like nothing bothers her or scares her, but I know she has to be just as scared as me right now.

"Heather, do you remember Mrs. Faulkner?" she asks.

"How could I ever forget her, Malory? She was so mean!"

Mrs. Faulkner was our old babysitter from Ohio. When Mom couldn't get Grams to take us, she would take us to her house. We hated it there. She was old, fat, and mean. My great-grandparents on Mom's side used to own the house across the street from her when they were still alive, and that's how Mom knew her. I think she used to watch Mom and her siblings, too.

I never met my great-grandparents from Mom's side. My great-grandpa died before I was born, and my great-grandma shortly after. My grandma owned their house for a while after they died, and we lived there for a little bit.

I remember Mom cooking in the kitchen and saying she could hear her grandma talking to her sometimes when she would cook. *Weird!* Mom was close to her grandparents. She said she learned a lot about cooking from her grandma and that it connects them.

Sometimes, we would stay at Mrs. Faulkner's for days at a time. In the summertime, she would lock us out in the backyard all day and not let us in even to go to the bathroom. Her yard was fenced-in, and the only thing to play with was a tire swing hanging from a tree. We couldn't play on it because she had a big, mean dog tied to the tree that would bite us if we went near him.

"Hey, Mal, do you remember that one day I got sick of being left out in the dying heat all day while she sat on her old fat ass in the air-conditioned house? I convinced you that we should cuss her out until she let us come into the house?" I ask with a chuckle.

"Yes! That was so funny! Served her right for being so mean," she replies, laughing.

My plan didn't work, though, and I was terrified we would be in big trouble with Dad. I was surprised when he came to pick us up. He just brushed it off like it was no big deal. Maybe he didn't really like her, either. Dad never used to yell at us or spank us for anything when we were really little.

We lay there laughing about it when we hear a bang on the wall and a yell from the other side of it. "Take your asses to sleep before I get the switch out!" she hollers.

I look at Mal with wide eyes.

"Don't worry, Heather. She's not allowed to hit us, and if she does, I'll beat the shit out of her old ass!"

Now I know why Mal was reminded of our old mean babysitter. This woman is a Black version of Mrs. Faulkner. Now that I think about it, her house was a lot like this, even the smell.

The next morning, we are awakened by a bang on the door. "Get out here and eat," she calls out.

We both lie there for a few minutes, stretching and rubbing the sleep out of our eyes when there is another bang on the door.

"I'm not going to keep telling you! Come out here now or I'm tossing your breakfast in the garbage, and you can starve for all I care!"

I quickly look at Mal. "Tonight, we are getting out of here no matter what! There's no way I can stay here," I say, feeling the rage starting to boil inside me.

Mal quickly agrees.

In the kitchen, we find bowls of what looks like slop and toast. We sit down at the small table and we're both hesitant about taking a bite when Ms. Peterson walks in the room. "What's the matter? You've never had grits before?"

Oh, this is what grits are?

My friends at school talk about them, but I've never had them or seen them before.

"It's good for you. Eat it," she says as she walks out of the room.

I look at Mal and shrug my shoulders. "We gotta eat something."

"I guess," says Mal with a funny look on her face as she lets a spoon full plop back down into the bowl.

"It can't be as bad as the powdered milk Mom buys sometimes," I reply, shoveling a spoonful in my mouth. *Here goes nothing.* It's actually pretty good. I think I like it.

After breakfast, we take showers and put the same clothes back on. We spend most of the day in the room, only coming out for meals. Not because she says we have to, but we don't want to be around her. I think Mal is safer in the room. I know if she has to hear much more of Ms. Peterson's racist comments, she's going to explode. I've seen this look in her eyes before, so I'm trying really hard to distract her from being pissed off.

We find a few games in the bedroom closet and keep ourselves busy until it's time to make our move. We also find out what's causing the potent smell while snooping through the things in the bedroom. These little white balls are all over the place: in the closet, under the beds, in the drawers, and in the corners of the room. Mal says they're moth balls. I don't know what they're supposed to be used for, but I'm pretty sure she shouldn't be using them as air fresheners.

We talk her into opening the bedroom window by complaining about the ungodly heat in the bedroom. After all, it is nearing the end of summer, and the only air conditioning in the house is hanging from the living room window. We're hoping she forgets and leaves it open at bedtime so we can crawl out of it later when she's asleep.

Later when it's time for bed, the plan works, and she leaves the window open.

"Don't get any ideas. There's an alarm on the screen, too," she says, and then leaves the room.

Shit! Is that possible?

After hearing Mrs. Bitch shut herself in her room for the night, Malory quickly inspects the window. "Heather, I think she's trying to trick us. There's no sensor on the screen, but just in case we should cut the screen out."

Mal always thinks of everything.

"Where are we going to get the scissors?" I ask.

"I saw a pair on the counter earlier. I'll sneak out there and get them in a little bit once she's asleep," Mal replies.

Twenty minutes later, Mal sneaks out to get the scissors and quickly returns. After cutting the screen we hop out the window.

Yes! Freedom!

Chapter Twelve

We're halfway home, and I know that mean old witch didn't hear us leave, so there's no need to run this time. She thinks we're dumb little white girls, but we showed her. I just hope Mom lets us stay once we get home. I hope Dad is there. Maybe he'll stop her from making us go back this time.

"Mal, what are we going to do once we get there?" I ask.

"I don't know, Heather. Maybe there will be a door or window open. We can sneak in. If not, we'll have to knock on the door and beg them to let us stay."

Once we get to the house, we check the doors, windows, and garage. After not having any luck getting into the house, we sit on the step by the sliding glass door.

"What are we going to do?" I ask Mal. "I don't know, Heather."

"What do you girls think you're doing?" asks Dad, appearing suddenly from the front of the house.

He's home!

"Oh, shit!" I say, startled as I jump to my feet.

"'Oh, shit' is right! You girls just think you can do whatever the hell you want, don't you?" he asks, shaking his head and looking down at the ground. He sounds disappointed, and it makes me feel guilty.

"Dad, please don't make us go back there! They made us go to an old woman's house, and she is so mean. If I have to go back there, I'll just die, I know it!" says Malory, in a desperate cry as she jumps to her feet to face Dad.

He stands there in silence, smoking his cigarette. He's looking at us, but not saying a word. I stand quietly sobbing, not knowing what to say because Mal covered it all.

"Get in the house, and we'll talk about it," he says, tossing his cig to the ground and stomping it out.

Whew!

"Dad?" I ask, following him toward the front door.

"What, Heth?"

"Where were you the other night? Why didn't you come home with Mom?"

"Uhm, 'cause I got pulled over and arrested for drinking and driving. Your grandpa had to come out here and bail me out of jail," he replies under his breath without turning around.

Oh, no!

"Oh my God, Dad, are you ok?" asks Mal.

"I'm fine. Don't worry about it, just get in the house."

When we walk in the door, Mom appears from the kitchen. "We need to call Sister Mary Catherine's and the police to have them picked up," Mom says, her voice firm. It's clear she's pissed, and by the tone of her voice determined to stand her ground.

"Mom, please don't make us go back!" Malory pleads.

I stand in silence, staring at my feet, knowing that Mom's going to do what she wants no matter what I say. I won't waste my time begging her.

Mom stands with her arms crossed, barely looking at us. "No, Malory! You need to go back. You girls can't keep thinking you run the house and come and go as you please. You're eleven and thirteen years old, damn it! You're not adults!" Mom snaps.

I suddenly feel enraged. "Well, maybe if we didn't have to take care of ourselves all the time, we wouldn't act like adults!" I yell back at her.

"Heather, shut up or they won't let us stay," Mal snaps.

Dad is just staring at me but doesn't say anything. He knows I'm right, and so does Mom. They won't admit it; they never do.

"That's what I'm talking about, little girl! You don't have the right to talk to us that way, Mouth!" Mom says with her teeth clenched tight. *There's that stupid nickname her and Dad call me when I'm talking back. Maybe if they didn't give me a reason to run my mouth, I'd shut up.*

I quickly brush past her, and run up the stairs. "I don't have the right to do anything in this house! I don't even have the right to be a kid! I'm not going back there, Mom, and you can't make me!" I shout, running into my room and slamming the door.

"How many times do I have to tell you about slamming the doors Maybe I should come up there and slam your head!" screams Dad.

Uh-oh! I shouldn't have done that. I should have just cried like Malory. But I'm so angry at them, I don't even care.

I sit down on the floor next to the door, trying to listen to what's going on. Malory is still crying when I hear Mom and Dad start to argue. Dad is actually defending us this time.

"I don't know, Lorynn; I think they learned their lesson. We should just let them stay."

"NO!" barks Mom. "If we let them stay, we're just giving them their way, and nothing will change," she adds.

"Well, I don't see why they have to live somewhere else to change. Can't you just take them to counseling with them living at home?" asks Dad.

I'm beginning to feel hopeful because he doesn't stand up to her enough when things like this happen. He just lets her get rid of us. He always wins when he does stand up to her, though. I wish he did it all the time. *I still can't believe he was in jail...must be how Mom ended up with that cop. Wow!* While Dad's sitting in jail, she's sleeping in his bed with the police. *Disgusting!*

"Malory get on up to your room while me and your mom figure this out," says Dad.

"Damn it, Theodore! You always do this to me in front of the kids, and you wonder why they don't listen to me!" cries Mom, with defeat in her voice.

He's going to be in big trouble with her for a while, but at least we won't have to leave.

I back away from the door as Mal walks in. She looks at me with a smile on her tear-streaked face. "See, Heather, Dad cares."

"Well then, why can't he do that all the time, Mal? I know Dad is a better parent than Mom most of the time, but he could do a lot more than he does. Even I know that!" I reply snidely. Mal is closer to him, so she sees past all his flaws. "Mal, you just don't get it because you and Dad are so close. If it were just me, he probably wouldn't have even argued with her," I add.

"Shut up, Heather, that's not true!"

It is true, and I know it. Mal knows it, too. Dad barely ever talks to me anymore. The only time he ever does, he's drunk. I think he's given up on me and sees me as the bad seed. He'll laugh and say I've always been his "little girl from hell." I know he's trying to be funny when he says it, but part of me thinks he means it.

All those games we used to play with Dad when Mom was gone are now collecting dust in the hall closet. It's not fair that Malory gets so much more of his attention than I do. She's getting into trouble now, too, and he still treats her better than me. He probably thinks it's my fault that she's bad. She claims it's not so great getting his attention because he picks out her flaws more than anything. *I'd take that over nothing.*

I love Dad and wish things could be different between us. I wonder if he knows how much more I love him than I do Mom. I know it's wrong to feel that way, but I can't help it. I know he isn't perfect, either, but he doesn't do the same things Mom does. He's different. Even though he doesn't say it, it seems like he cares more about us than she does.

Now that I think about it, though, he does do some pretty messed up things sometimes, too. When he gets really drunk, he blacks out and doesn't know what he's doing. I can't even count how many times he's come into our room in the middle of the night and pees in our closet thinking he's in the bathroom. *Sick!*

He's also really bad at making promises and not keeping them. I hate that part about him the most. He's taken my birthday money from me before and promised to give it back, but he still never has. When I was nine, he got me a piggy bank called "Ernie the Engineer." It was a mouse dressed-up like a train engineer. I loved that thing so much because it reminded me of him. When he kept stealing my money out of it, I cut off its ears and nose. It really hurt his feelings, but that was the point. *How does he think I feel?*

He's not like the other dads of the kids I met in the hospital. He's never hit me for no reason, and he doesn't hit me with a belt like Bobbi's dad hits her. I know it's wrong that he hits Mom, but I would hit her too if I were him. When she comes home in her drunken rage, she hits him for no reason, and she keeps hitting him until he hits her back. When the cops show up, she cries that she didn't do anything wrong. I feel sorrier for Dad than I do Mom, even when they're both wrong. It's her fault our family is so screwed up. I've never seen Dad hit her unless she hits him first. I know I shouldn't make excuses for him. He could just call the cops on her first without hitting her back. I can't deny he has a really bad temper sometimes.

Malory has memories from Ohio that I don't. She remembers hiding with Mom in the closet one night when he came home drunk. She said that Dad reached into the dark closet and pulled her hair by accident. He was trying to pull Mom out of the closet to beat her up, but I don't remember any of that. It's hard to picture Dad being that mean.

I do remember him drinking a lot more in Ohio and sniffing those drugs, too, which I now know was cocaine. Maybe that's why he's different now because I don't think he does that anymore. I think he still smokes pot sometimes. While I was snooping through their room a couple months ago, I found a huge Ziploc bag full of it under their mattress.

Dad used to get in a lot of bar fights when we lived in Ohio. His muscles were a lot bigger then, and he didn't have a beer belly like he does now. Mom says he's calmed down as he's gotten older. There was one night in Ohio I was really scared because he came home from the bar with his shirt off. I found him in the bathroom, cleaning blood off his chest. He had cut marks all over his chest and back. I don't know if someone was cutting him with a knife or scratching him. It was terrifying.

We've gone and lived in a few different battered women's shelters with Mom. I never knew why at the time. After we first moved here, I remember going to one. The one I have the most memories from was in Ohio.

Mom became good friends with a woman named Lisa, who lived there with her two kids. She had a boy and a girl that we became friends with, but I didn't care for the boy. He was older than us. One time, when we were jumping on the bed, he tried to look up to see under our dresses. *Creep!*

They left the shelter before us, and I heard Mom telling her friend a few months later that Lisa went back to her husband. She said he beat her to death in the head with a shotgun in front of her kids. I was so scared and horrified when I heard Mom talking about it. I know my dad could never do anything like that. He doesn't even own guns.

After a while, the arguing downstairs gets quiet, and I hear Mom go into her room and close the door. I can hear the living room TV. I wonder if she's going to make him sleep downstairs. She can't make him do anything. He probably just doesn't want to get yelled at anymore.

I can't turn off my brain, and I'm having a hard time falling asleep. I wonder what's going to happen tomorrow or the day after that. You never know in this house. I've learned to be prepared for anything. And even when things are going good for a few weeks, I know not to expect it to last.

I wonder why Mom had us? She acts like she doesn't want us most of the time anyway. She was married once before. Maybe she should have just stayed with that guy if she didn't really want kids. She says they weren't married very long, and they got divorced because he didn't want kids, and she did. She sure doesn't act like she wants us.

Maybe being a mom is harder than she thought it would be. She tells me all the time that, one day, I'm going to get payback for how bad I am because I'm going to have a daughter that's worse than me. That's not possible because I will never be like her, so I know my kids won't act like me.

"Mal, are you still awake?" I whisper across the room. She doesn't answer.

"Mal!" I whisper louder.

"Ughh! What, Heather? I was just starting to fall asleep!" she answers, irritated.

I know what the answer is going to be, but I ask anyway, "Will you tickle my back?"

"No way! Now shut up so I can go back to sleep!"

"Please? I'll rub yours," I plead.

"No, Heather! You always say that and then you pretend like you're sleeping and don't do it."

She's right. I always con her into doing it and then don't return the favor.

It's been a long time since I've laid in bed with Mom and had her rub my back. I miss it. It relaxes me, and I can't fall asleep right now. I know it would help. There's no way I can get up to go ask Mom if I can lie down with her. She would never let me and says I'm getting too old for that now. Johnny is the only one that still gets to lie down with her. Besides, she's too mad at me tonight anyway.

Over the next several months, things don't get any better. Mom has been making us go to this Sister Mary Catherine's place for counseling. I'm not even trying because she isn't. *Why bother?* I don't know how I'm supposed to turn into this perfect kid she wants me to be when she's still the same drunken lunatic.

I don't like going to Sister Mary Catherine's. Pamela, the counselor, is nice, but I don't like the guy who runs the place. His name is Justin. He looks like he's almost seven feet tall, about 300 pounds, and really gives me the creeps. I feel like he's always looking at Mal and me funny and making comments about how pretty we are in a creepy way. Something is wrong with that man; I know it.

I started the sixth grade, and I hate my teacher! She is so mean to me even when I'm not doing anything wrong. Sometimes, when I'm doing my work and minding my own business, she will call out my name in the middle of class and tell me to go to the hall. I don't know why. I have done some things that were bad in class, so now I think she hates me no matter how hard I try not to act up. I'm doomed as long as I'm in her class, and I know it.

I've already been suspended from school a bunch of times. I'm starting to not give a shit about anything anymore. They keep talking about putting me in the behavioral disorder class down the hall if I keep acting up. Let them take me there, I couldn't give a shit.

My new friends Shaniqua and Sierra have taught me how to master rolling my eyes. That's mostly what I get in trouble for with Mrs. Cintas. It drives her crazy when I do it. Sometimes, she even knows I'm doing it when her back is turned.

There's a class across the hall from us with all the smart kids. It's called the "magnet class." I think I'm smart enough to be in that class, but I'm not well-behaved like the kids in there. I don't really know any of those kids. The girls seem really nice, but I don't have anything in common with them like I do with the girls in my class.

All my friends have a nickname for me. They call me "Heather the Hell-Raiser." Maybe what Dad says about me isn't so untrue after all. I don't mind being called that, and it gets me a lot of respect from the kids in my school. If anyone too tough tries to mess with me, my friends have my back. I rarely have that problem because I'm friends with most of the tough kids. Finally, I feel accepted, and I like it. *Even if we are all a bunch of trouble-makers.*

Bobbi isn't in my class anymore. She's down the hall in a different class, so we don't talk much at school. We are never in the hall at the same time, and she has a different lunch time. After school, I'm either with Shaniqua, Sierra, or Carla.

We started hanging out at Brandy's house more. She doesn't live too far from our house. We have another friend, Beth, who we met through Brandy. Beth's mom is so cool; she buys our cigs. Mal is smoking all the time now, too, so I don't have to worry about her telling on me anymore.

I like the assistant principal at my school a lot. He lets me out of things that I should get kicked out of school for. The principal is mean, and if it were up to her, I would have been expelled already.

Mr. Pierce, the assistant principal, is always asking me how things are at home. I think he knows things aren't that great, but I don't tell him too much because it's embarrassing. He gives me that look of sorrow when I'm in his office. I've seen it many times before, so I know what it means. I don't want people to feel sorry for me or give me the puppy dog look. I can handle being punished!

This year, my teacher knew how I was, so we never even had a chance to get along. I don't mean to take it out on my teacher, but I'm so pissed off all the time and don't know what to do with it. I can't always keep it locked away. Knowing that I'll get my ass beat at home, I save it until I go to school.

In the beginning of the school year, I was in a car accident with Bobbi on the way to school. Her brother Billy's wife, Jamie, brings us to school sometimes. She says she blacked out when it happened, but I'm not sure because I couldn't see her from the back seat. Bobbi was sitting in the passenger seat and not wearing her seatbelt. I wasn't, either. We came to a stoplight, and instead of stopping, Jamie ran right into the car in front of us. We weren't driving very fast, but it was fast enough for Bobbi to crack the windshield with her forehead. She was ok and only needed a few stitches. Jamie hit her mouth really bad on the steering wheel and had to get stitches on the inside of her lip. It looked pretty nasty. I didn't really get hurt. Well, so I thought at the time.

I had my knees up on the seat when we hit. When I flew forward, I hit my throat really hard on my knee. I was fine at first, but over the next three weeks my throat kept getting bigger and bigger. When it was starting to look like I had three chins, Mom finally took me to the emergency room. I'm not sure what was wrong with me. I didn't understand what they were talking about, but I needed surgery to fix it. I was really scared at first, but it wasn't so bad being put to sleep. I got to stay home from school for a week plus eat a lot of ice cream. Mom was extra nice to me. I wouldn't mind having surgery again. Afterward, I was mad at Mom because she kept saying she was going to take Jamie to court over it. She is always embarrassing me, and I hate it. It was just an accident. I begged her to just leave it alone, and eventually, she did.

Mom and the counselors at Sister Mary Catherine's say if Mal and I keep getting in trouble, we're going to have to go back to foster homes. Sometimes, I think I'd be better off living in a foster home, but I'm also afraid. You never know the kind of people you are going to end up with. I wish I could pick who I wanted to live with, then I know I would be happy.

I have been trying not to get in as much trouble lately, but it's been really hard at school. Even when I'm being good, the teacher still finds reasons to send me to the office. I'm going to beg Mom to talk to the principal and see if I can be sent to the class across the hall instead of being in the bad kid class. I'll really miss all my friends, but I can't stand being around Mrs. Cintas. I swear, if she is mean to me for no reason one more time, I'm going to rip her ugly head right off her fat body!

Chapter Thirteen

Dad has taken the car away from Mom again. He does this all the time by pulling some plug out and hiding it so she can't leave. He's tired of her getting arrested for drinking and driving. According to him, she doesn't even have a license anymore. He's no angel, but he's allowed to drive.

Today, she found the plug, and Charlie showed her how to put it back in. In exchange, she gave him a garbage bag full of Dad's dirty magazines. *Gross!* I wonder what started their fight this time.

"Heather, hurry up and get in!" demands Mom as she walks quickly toward the car. "C'mon, Heather! Hurry up before your dad gets out here!" she adds with a huff.

"Ok! Ok!" I respond as I start to jog toward the driveway.

I'm not even sure where we're going, but for some reason, she wanted to take me with her. She's been drinking today and doesn't know that I know, but she's not so smart sneaking it into her orange juice. Mom never drinks orange juice unless it's spiked with something.

We get into the car and close the doors quickly. After strapping on my seatbelt, I look up, and there's Dad, standing right in front of the car. *Uh-oh!*

"Lorynn, get out of the car right now! You're not driving anywhere!" he yells.

"Heather, lock your door now!" says Mom in a panic.

I don't want to be in the middle of this, but I do as Mom says.

Mom starts the car and is ready to pull out of the driveway when Dad jumps behind the car and yells, "If you're going to leave, you're going to have to run me over!"

"Mom, please don't run him over!" I say frantically.

She looks at me as if she's thinking I just made the stupidest remark ever, and says, "Heather, I'm not going to run your father over! Geez...give me some credit, will ya?!"

"Move so I can leave!" she yells, looking at Dad through the back window.

"I'm not moving until you get out of the car!" he yells back. Dad walks around to my side of the car. "Heather, please, unlock the door, dear."

Dear? Since when does he call me dear? It's just because he wants something. What I want more than anything right now is to jump out of the car and run as far away from both of them as I possibly can, but Mom will be mad and think I'm taking Dad's side.

I look at Mom as if to ask "now what?" but I say nothing.

"Heather, please don't listen to him. Don't even look at him. Just keep looking at me," says Mom.

I try to focus on Mom, but he keeps calling my name. The tone in his voice is making me feel bad, so I turn and look him in the eyes. "Heather, listen to me, ok? Just open the door," he says desperately.

I don't know what to do, so I start crying and put my head between my legs. "Why can't you both just leave me out of this? I don't want to be in the middle of your fight!" I yell.

Dad is begging me to open the door, and Mom is begging me not to when I finally can't take it anymore. "I'm sorry, Mom," I say, looking her in the eye. Then, I jump out of the car and run back toward the house. *I hate them both for making me choose!*

A while later, Dad comes to my bedroom door.

"Thanks a lot, Dad! Mom probably hates me now!" I say, still crying.

"Heather, she doesn't hate you. You did the right thing."

"Why couldn't you just let her leave, so I didn't have to be in the middle?" I ask, starting to feel angry.

"Because she doesn't have a license, Heather. She doesn't need to be driving. Especially with you in the car," he adds.

I sit up on my bed and look Dad straight in the eye. Suddenly, I have the courage to ask the question I've been dying to ask for a long time. "Why don't you and Mom just get divorced so we can live with you?"

Dad looks dumbfounded by the question. "Because, Heather. We don't want to separate you kids. You need both of us, and we never want you to have to deal with stepparents or step-brothers and sisters," he replies, looking up at the ceiling. He always avoids eye contact.

Crap, is he trying not to cry?

"Oh! That makes a lot of sense, Dad! Instead, we have to deal with foster parents and not be with either of you! Don't you think we would be better off if you were divorced so we wouldn't have to see you fight all the time?"

"Heather, you don't need to be thinking about things like that, ok?" he says, perplexed, and quickly leaves.

Classic Dad! Avoid talking about anything serious.

He's wrong. I do need to think about those things. And I think about it all the time. He should be thinking about it, too! If I'm smart enough to know our lives would be better with them divorced, why isn't he? *He's the grown-up, not me!* It's their job to figure out what's best for us, and they don't do it. I can't stand this anymore. I have to get out of here. I can't wait until I'm eighteen to leave this house. If all the craziness doesn't kill me first!

It's so typical of Dad to walk away without really explaining his reasons for staying. He never talks about anything. Aside from the occasional drunken lecture, he never talks about anything real. Mom is always complaining that he never talks to her or tells her how he feels.

Join the club, Mom!

Mal walks into the room and catches me trying to climb out of the bedroom window. "Heather! What are you doing?" she asks, quickly closing the bedroom door.

"I'm getting out of this house and never coming back!" I reply, and before I know it, she's got her hands around my waist, trying to pull me back in.

"You can't go out the window, Heather! We're on the second floor. You'll break your neck! Remember what happened to me when I jumped out of the window in Indiana?" she asks, sounding worried.

Oh, yeah. I forgot about that. I don't want to kill myself, so I let her help me back in.

She tried to run away once when we lived in Indiana when Mom wouldn't let her have a sleep over at Laura's. It was stupid. She was only nine. That house was much taller than this one, though, so the drop was a lot farther down. I caught her before she did it, and I begged her not to. I screamed for Mom, who was downstairs, but by the time she made it up to our room, it was too late.

Malory had thrown a pillow out of the window and was convinced she was going to land on it. I told her there was no way she would, especially with snow on the ground. But she wouldn't listen; she was determined. She wasn't even close to landing on that pillow. As soon as I saw her hit the ground, I ran as fast as I could through the house to get to her.

She hit her knee on her throat when she landed, just like I did in the car accident, but she hit hers much harder. Her throat was instantly drooping down. It looked like she had no bones in her neck. All you could see was loose skin hanging below her chin. Mom called 911 and everything turned out ok, but it was one of the scariest things I have ever seen. She had to wear a neck brace for weeks. I'm glad she caught me before I jumped, or I may have ended up worse than she did.

I sit down on the floor below the window. "Great! How am I going to get the screen back on the window now without Dad knowing?" I ask. *He's going to kill me!*

She offers no advice, shrugging her shoulders.

"I mean it, Mal. I want to leave!" I add.

"Heather, what happened?" Mal asks, curious.

She was at her friend's house, and the boys aren't home, so no one saw what happened. She's quiet and not saying much. It's not like it's a big surprise because they fight all the time, but I've never been stuck in the middle like that before. I don't like it at all.

I tell her about what I asked Dad. She is shocked by what I said, but I meant every word of it. I really wish they would get divorced. I know that if we lived with just Dad, it wouldn't be as bad as it is now.

"Mal, I don't care if they put me in another foster home. I'm running away tonight when Dad falls asleep. If I don't like where they take me, then I'll just keep running away until they find me a foster home with real parents who care about me. Then I'll stop running away forever."

"Ok, Heather. I'm going with you. I don't want to be here anymore either."

Dad wrestled the keys away from Mom, but she never came back into the house. I asked Dad later where she went. He said he didn't know, but she took off walking. *Shocker!* Mal and I both know if she comes home tonight, they're just going to fight, and the police are going to get called. What's the point in sticking around for that?

Later, I call Brandy from the bedroom phone that I conned Mom into getting me for Christmas. I tell her what our plan is, and she says if her mom says we can spend the night, she can hide us in her room. Our parents never talk to each other. If she thinks we're just sleeping over, she won't know any better. Brandy's mom, Josie, is kind of mean, so she might say no even though it's not a school night.

Her cousin, Kevin, just moved in with them, but Brandy says he's cool and won't say anything. He lived in foster homes too and just turned eighteen, so the state let him go on his birthday. Kevin's dad is Josie's brother. I guess he molested Kevin, his older brother, and his sisters growing up. When he finally got caught, they were all taken away. It makes me sick to think about how many dads do that to their kids. *It's so disturbing!*

The boys and Dad are sleeping, so it isn't very hard to sneak out. The sliding glass door is so quiet that Dad would never hear it over his loud snoring. On the walk over, Mal and I talk about all the bad things we've done in the last six months. We almost got arrested for breaking into someone's house. I don't even know why we did it. Mal, Brandy, and I, along with some other girls from Brandy's neighborhood, decided it was a good idea. For what, I don't really know, maybe just because we were bored. *Stupid!*

The lady we targeted lives down the street from Brandy. She's really mean to everyone, so Brandy wanted revenge. We didn't steal anything. We just looked for cigarettes and trashed her house pretty good. We dumped her plants out all over her carpet and poured red juice on her furniture. I knew better than to do it. I just wanted to show I could be as tough as the older girls.

We've also slashed people's tires and broken into their cars, looking for loose change and cigs. Brandy lives by the tunnel that we always hide out in. It goes under a factory. The people who work there park their cars in front of the building by the tunnel entrance when the parking lot in the back is full. Those are the cars we targeted. We only did a few cars, and we'll never do it again. It was stupid and mean. I think Mal and I both realize that now, especially after we got chased by the owner of the last car we trashed. He walked out, caught us slashing his tires, and chased us for three blocks. He couldn't catch us, thank God!

Mal still had the knife in her hand while we were running. I told her to throw it somewhere when we got far enough away. It was a really big knife that we found in one of the other cars we broke into. I was so afraid she was going to trip and fall on it. I don't know why I keep doing these things. I know it's wrong when I do it, and I always feel bad for it afterward. *What's wrong with me?*

"Mal, what do you think is going to happen when we get caught?" I ask, trailing behind her as usual.

"I don't know, Heather. They will probably put us in another foster home, but I don't give a shit anymore!"

"Me either," I reply, as we approach Brandy's house.

It occurs to me that it's almost eleven at night, and we can't just pretend we're sleeping over. Her mom is going to wonder why we're coming over so late. "Mal, I don't know if we should knock on the door," I say, hesitant.

"Heather, it's fine. Just c'mon!" she demands as she knocks on the door.

I can hear Brandy's two Dalmatians barking like crazy when Brandy's mom opens the door. "What are you two doing here so late? Do your parents know where you are?" she asks. She seems grumpy.

Uh-oh!

"Yeah," says Mal, adding, "my dad said it's ok if we spend the night if it's ok with you."

Brandy appears behind her mom's large, manly figure. "Mom, can they please stay tonight?"

"I don't know, Brandy. It's getting late, and you girls have no business walking all the way over here at night by yourselves. Get in this house!" she commands as she swings the door open to let us in.

For the next week, we are on the "run." I don't know how we've gotten away with it for this long. This is by far the longest we've ever been away from home without getting caught. During the day when Brandy has to go to school and her mom is at work, we stay at the house with Brandy's stepdad, Tom, and her cousin, Kevin. Tom is cool; he knows what's going on and has helped us cover it up.

We hide out at night so her mom doesn't know we're here. In the evening, she thinks we are just coming over after school. She's questioned a few times why our parents don't mind us being gone so much but has never really figured it out.

"Hey, Heather?" calls Kevin.

"What?" I reply.

"I bet you $5.00 you won't eat this," he says, laughing while holding out a can of wet cat food.

"I am not eating that! That's gross, Kevin," I reply with a look of disgust on my face.

"No one would eat that for $5.00, Kevin. I'll throw some money in on it," laughs Tom.

"No way! I'm not eating that!" I respond.

I listen to them laugh as they banter back and forth about how much each of them are willing to put in on this bet. *I don't care how much it is, I'm not eating it!* The smell alone is enough to make me barf.

"Ok, how 'bout eating it for $20?" asks Kevin.

"No way! I'm not eating it for any amount of money."

"Come on, Heather! Think about the things you could buy with $20. We'll even let you eat it on bread and wash it down with this Mountain Dew," he says. Their chuckles have now turned into belly aching laughter. They are barely containing themselves.

Idiots!

"No!" I reply, unable to hold back my own laughter from the sight of how funny they think this is.

Mal throws a quick jab to my arm with her elbow. "You could buy a carton of cigs."

"Well then *you* eat it!" I say, still laughing. She's right; $20 is enough for a carton. *Hmmmm...*

"No. If you do it, you can't buy cigarettes with it," adds Kevin.

"If I do it, I can spend that $20 on whatever the hell I want!" I respond sarcastically. He hates that we smoke, and so does Tom. "And I'm not eating that whole can!" I add.

"Deal! One bite, on bread, washed down with Mountain Dew, and you can spend your money on whatever you want," he replies with laughter so hard and loud that I can barely understand him. He's leaning over, holding onto his stomach from laughing so hard. When he finally stops and looks up at me, his face is beet red. "Here ya go, kitty. What are you waiting for?" he says, holding out the can.

I can't believe I'm going to do this.

I have a weaker stomach than anyone I know. Mal should be doing this, not me! I couldn't even handle it when Emerson tricked me into eating deer meat. Normally, I refuse to eat fish, anything that's out of the ordinary, or anything that has even a hint of a funny smell. God only knows what they put in cat food. *But hey, it's a carton of cigs.* I don't want to pass that up.

I shove the bite into my mouth so fast I have no idea what's coming. *I just want to get it over with.* Nothing in the world could prepare me for the disgusting taste that I just shoveled into my mouth. I try to chew and feel a crunch, and I can no longer hold it in. As fast as I can, I run to the toilet and throw up more than I ever have my entire life. *What the hell was I thinking?*

All I hear in the other room is the laughter rolling out of Mal, Kevin, and Tom. *Assholes!*

I am starting to have a big crush on Kevin since we've been here this week. Mal says I'm stupid because he's way too old for me and not even cute. I didn't think he was cute at first either, but he is so nice to me that it made me look at him differently. He has a crush on me, too. No one but Malory says anything bad about it. If they think the same thing she does, they aren't saying it. Tom keeps telling us age is nothing but a number. Brandy's mom doesn't know. She would freak out for sure. I know it's wrong for us to like each other, I think. I can't help the way I feel, and I've never gotten this much attention from anyone before. He says he loves me and cares about me. I want to believe him so much. No one else ever treats me the way he does.

"I think I love him, and I don't want to leave. I know I'll lose him forever," I say to Mal, walking toward home.

"Heather, you're so stupid! You don't even know what love is. Think about how weird it is that *he likes you!* You're only an eleven-year-old!" she replies with disgust.

I know she's probably right about him; it is a huge age difference. It's hard not to believe him when he tells me how pretty and perfect I am. I suck the attention right up.

We haven't been caught, but we've decided to turn ourselves in because we are tired of hiding. Every once in a while, we change into Brandy's t-shirts and sweats because we are wearing the same clothes all the time. Brandy tries to sneak us food, but it's been hard to eat at night. I'm starving, exhausted, and just want to go home. Also, Brandy's mom has started to suspect something's up, and it's getting Brandy into trouble.

I wonder why they haven't come looking for us. Not once did Mom or Dad call or come over to see if we were there. Usually, Mom goes pounding on everyone's doors until she or the cops find us. *Where the hell was she this time? Maybe she never came back that day, but why hasn't Dad come looking? It just doesn't make any sense.*

When we approach the house, all the doors and windows are locked but the lights and TV are on, so we know they're home. We knock and knock and even yell out, but Mom doesn't open the door. Dad is already at work for the night, so he can't help us this time.

"What the heck is she doing?" I ask Mal, trying to peek through the front window.

"I don't know, Heather. She's never done this before. It's weird," she says as she grabs the lawn chair from the side of the house. She places it under the kitchen window and stands on it to peek in.

"GO! Get away from the window. I'm not letting you come back this time!" I hear Mom faintly yell from the kitchen.

"MOM!" yells Malory. "You can't just leave us out here all night, what are we supposed to do?" she adds.

"Mal, what is she doing in there?" I ask, standing below her.

"She's on the phone," Mal replies, looking down at me. Just as she says it, I see the lights racing towards the house and the sirens blaring.

"Great, she called the cops," I say, defeated, and sit down on the steps. I'm just going to let them take me. I can't run anymore. I feel the sting from the tears welling up behind my eyes as I watch the cop car stop in front of my house, and an officer quickly jumps out. *Here we go again.*

Chapter Fourteen

ear Diary,
*   I'm on the crazy floor at the hospital again. This time is*
*   different because Malory is with me. We're not on the same*
unit, but sometimes I can see her and wave to her through the door
that separates us. We've been here for almost two weeks now. I don't
think we're going to be here that long, and I already know we're not
going home when we leave. A DCFS caseworker came to see us here and
sat down with our family. We're being taken away by the state and going
to be placed in a foster home once we leave. I don't really understand
what the difference is between us living in a state foster home or Sister
Mary Catherine's foster homes. Mom is really upset. She says now that
the state has us, it will be hard for her to get us back, and she no longer
has any control over where we live. I guess she should have thought
about that when she decided not to open the door for us. She says the
state charged her and Dad with neglect for not letting us back in the
house. Mom said she did it because that's what Sister Mary Catherine's
told her to do when we ran away again. They told her not to let us in and
call the police. Then, Sister Mary Catherine's would pick us up from the

station and place us in their foster homes. It doesn't really make any sense. Can't Sister Mary Catherine's just tell the state that's what happened?

Before we came here to the hospital, Sister Mary Catherine's put us in another one of their homes, and the new lady was worse than the last one but that only lasted two days. The new lady's house was really big, kind of like an apartment. She locked us in the upstairs of the house and wouldn't let us come out. The house was too tall to go out of the window. We tried to pry the door open that she locked us behind, but it was like it was nailed shut or something. We even banged on the door over and over, begging her to let us out, but she wouldn't. She acted like she couldn't even hear us banging on the door. Mom can't do what an agency tells her to do without being charged with neglect, but they can send us to a home with a woman who locks us away like wild animals? I don't get it!

There was another girl locked up there with us. She told us lots of stories about Justin, the guy who runs Sister Mary Catherine's. She said that he's been making her have sex with him for a long time and that he's done it to other girls that go to counseling there too. I knew he was a weirdo! She begged us not to tell, but as soon as the DCFS worker came to see us, I told her everything. I don't know what's going to happen to him, but she said it was going to be investigated. I hope that fat nasty man burns in hell! I don't understand why the other girls haven't told on him.

I had my 12th birthday here last week. It was depressing being away from home for my birthday, but my family got to come here to see me. We had cake and presents in the visiting room. I got the Charlotte Hornets coat I've been begging Mom for, but it wasn't the same as being at home.

I miss Kevin a lot. He sent flowers to me here on my birthday with a big giant card that everyone signed, and a teddy bear. The card was addressed to "Kitty Cat." After I ate the cat food, everyone started calling me that. I can laugh about it now that the taste has left my mouth. Remembering it is enough to make me want to barf again. Mom is really *freaking out about Kevin, big time. She keeps asking me and Mal if he made us do things with him. Linda, the DCFS caseworker, is the same caseworker he had when he got out of the system. She told Mom about him and why he was in foster homes, so now Mom thinks he's a child molester just like his dad. She doesn't believe us when we tell her he didn't touch us. The staff members here keep pressuring me about it, but I'll never tell anyone the truth. They say that even if I think I wanted him to do things with me, I really didn't, and it's considered sexual abuse. He would go to jail for it. I don't understand that. How can I think I want something if I really don't? They say he took advantage of me and confused me into believing I wanted something when I didn't. They're making him out to be a monster so I'll tell them the truth. But I won't! Not ever! I love him, and I don't want him to go to jail.*

Malory has gotten into a lot of trouble since we've been here. She's had to be restrained a few times. One night, I could hear her screaming through the door. So, I ran to the window and saw them dragging her down the hall toward the time-out room. Where the teenagers are, the time-out room is different than it is in my unit. They get strapped down to a bed when they're out of control. I was so scared that I sat on the floor by the door, crying and yelling at her to please stop. I've never seen Malory that angry before, and I was afraid they were hurting her.

I have to go now. Someone is knocking on my door. Numb &
Confused,

Heather, aka: Kitty Cat

"Come in," I yell, tossing my diary in my top drawer. The door opens, and it's Joseph. *He's so cute!* All the girls here have a crush on him, including me. I'll never tell Kevin.

"Heather, pack your stuff. You're leaving tonight," says Joseph.
Leaving? Really?

"What? Where am I going?" This is weird. The other time when I was here, I knew I was leaving a week before I'd gone home. "Are they letting us go home?" I ask excitedly.

"I don't know, Heather. They didn't tell me. They called up from

131

downstairs and told us to have you ready in the next hour. Hurry up, ok?"

"Does Mal get to leave too?" I ask.

"Yes, you're both going," he says, leaving my room.

My heart is beating fast from all the excitement. Soon, I will be home, and me and Kevin can be together again. I don't care what anyone says—I'm going to see him.

An hour later, we say our goodbyes, and Joseph takes us down to the emergency room. I'm surprised when he leads us into an ambulance. *Why are we in an ambulance?*

"Ok, you girls behave yourselves," says Joseph as he starts to close the doors.

"Joseph, WAIT!" I call out in a panic. "Where are we going? I know you must know where they are taking us!" I say once I have his full attention.

"Heather, I really am not supposed to say, but I do know where you're going, and you will be ok. I promise!" he says sympathetically and quickly closes the door.

"Mal, why wouldn't he be allowed to tell us? That doesn't make any sense!" I ask, feeling myself starting to freak out.

"I don't know, Heather. Probably because we won't like where we're going, and they are afraid we were going to try to run away before we got into the ambulance. Now we're trapped in here," Mal replies, testing the handle and seeing that it's locked.

We are riding in the ambulance for an hour before we get to our unknown destination. It looks like another hospital. It reminds me of the orphanage we were in when we were little, only it's a lot bigger. *Damn it! I hate Mom!* This must be the hospital she wanted us to come to.

I've never been downtown before. I've never seen such big buildings. If I were in a different situation, I might be enjoying the view. The hospital is a massive brick building that sits right on the lake. I read the sign as we walk toward the door. "Frontier Children's Hospital." The closer we get to the entrance, the more my heart aches. I don't want to be here. I want to go home. I'm starting to regret running away. If I could go home right now, I would do anything Mom wanted. *I'm so scared!*

I take one last look at the city behind me before walking through the big glass doors. It's so pretty with all the lights from the big buildings shining brightly over the lake. *I wonder why Mom and Dad have never brought us here before?* It's not that far from home, and Dad drives here every day for work. I feel so much smaller in this giant place, and I know already I won't even try to run away here. I'd be too scared of what's out there.

When we get off the elevator on the fifth floor, we're greeted by a nurse who says she's taking us to our unit while the two ambulance drivers leave. I wish so badly that I could follow them back to the ambulance and go back home. Malory keeps shooting me looks that tell me she's pissed, but I don't say anything to her because I'm afraid of what she might say. I know she thinks it's my fault we're here because of the whole Kevin thing. I want to cry, but I don't. I hold it in. *I have to be strong.*

It's late, so we're taken right to our room. This time, we get to be in the same room, which makes me feel better. I can't sleep in this strange place, so I lie awake, worried about what's going to happen to us here. Mom said something about some kind of testing. I wonder what kinds of tests she was talking about.

The next morning, after breakfast, we are taken out into a large day room with the other kids. This hospital is much nicer than the one back home. The spacious room is filled with couches, toys, tables, and a couple TVs. I immediately notice a window that stretches across the whole back wall. From floor to ceiling, it's all window. It almost looks like you could fall out of it. All you can see on the other side of the window is the lake. It's so pretty that it takes my breath away. I'm drawn to the window instantly and find a couch as close to it as I can get. Maybe I can just sit here staring at the water until it's time to leave.

Later that day, one of the nurses tells Malory and me that we have to have exams done by the doctor the next morning. She explains what the exam is about, and it terrifies me. They want to look at our private parts and make sure we weren't abused in any way. I don't want to let anyone look at me down there. *Gross!* The thought of having to let anyone look at me like that makes me sick. Malory refuses and says there is no way she's going to let them.

The next day, when it's time to see the doctor, I am still terrified but less afraid once I learn the doctor is a woman. Malory won't even come out of the room, but they say that we can't leave unless we have it done. I beg her to just let them do it so we can get out of this place. As pretty as the water is, I can't be here another day. I'm so overcome with homesickness that I can hardly stand it. I have never been this far away from home before, and I feel helpless.

"Ok, lay back on the table and relax," says the lady doctor. "I'm just going to take a little look. and it'll be over before you know it."

As I lay there, I try to think of anything else other than what's going on. She has me put my legs up into some sort of contraption and then shows me some shiny metal tool that looks like a duck's beak. When she explains what she's going to do with it, my legs start shaking so bad I don't think I can hold them up any longer.

She knows I'm afraid. She grabs my hand, and I start to cry. "Honey, it's going to be ok, I promise! I'm almost done. It's not going to hurt. You are in a safe place," she assures me.

I don't feel like I'm in a safe place. I have never felt so sick in my life. *Even when I ate the cat food!* I hate Mom for making me go through this. No matter how many times I tried to convince her Kevin didn't have sex with me, she wouldn't listen.

It takes Malory four days to finally let them do it. She knows it's the only way they are going to let us leave, and she hates me for it. "This is all your fault, Heather! If you weren't so stupid and stayed away from him, we wouldn't have to be here!" she says as they take her away.

"Mal, it's not so bad, you'll see. It's going to be ok," I assure her. I get her middle finger in response.

She's probably right. But the truth is, Mom would have freaked out no matter what because we were alone with him. She doesn't trust men at all. Everything she has been through has made her paranoid. She doesn't even trust Dad, and she's married to him. She's always accusing him of sleeping with other women, even with Aunt Phoebe. Maybe she has her reasons for thinking those things, but I think she's just crazy. I have never seen Dad with anyone else. If he has cheated on Mom, he doesn't flaunt it around us the way she does.

I feel guilty for lying to her, but I can't tell her the truth. She will never understand. He really didn't have sex with me, but he did other things. I wonder if they will be able to tell that from the tests. I wrote him letters from the other hospital and told him everything Mom and the caseworker were saying about him. He says we didn't do anything that they would be able to test me for, so he told me not to worry, but he was scared I would tell them. He says they are trying to trick me into telling them by saying bad things about him. He says he loves me, and he would never hurt me, and I believe him.

Linda, our caseworker, picks us up from the hospital a few hours after Malory's tests. She says we are going to live in foster care for a while until our family gets the help that we need. I don't think I like this woman very much. She's tall, skinny, and has really long black hair. She has a couple little hairs growing from her chin and a fine line of hair across her upper lip. I've never seen a woman with hair on her face before. *I wonder why she doesn't just shave it off.* I don't like the way she talks to us, and I can tell by her voice that she doesn't care for us much, either. Kevin says she's a real bitch, and I need to watch what I tell her. He says she can't be trusted. I can tell, he's right.

"Girls," she calls out, looking at us in the rearview mirror. "The Georges are a really nice family. You need to behave while you're there. They will take good care of you."

We nod, but not with excitement. *I hope she's right.* I hope the foster mom is like the one I had in Indiana. So far, she is the only good one I have known.

"You have a court date next week. The judge will help determine

135

what the goals are for your family. When you reach those goals, you can go home," she adds.

Court? I've never been to court before. The thought is terrifying.

"Before you can go home permanently, you'll start with weekend visits, but it won't be right away."

This is too much to grasp. The knot in my stomach tightens a little more. "Are my brothers going to be taken away from home, too?" I ask, breaking my vow for silence.

She looks at me from the rearview mirror and all I can focus on are the hairs hanging from her chin. I don't think I'll ever be able to look this woman straight in her eyes, no matter how hard I try. "No, they will stay home with your parents," she replies.

As she talks, I watch the hairs move up and down. For the first time in almost three weeks, I want to laugh, but I wouldn't dare. This woman intimidates me.

I'm relieved by her response, but it also confuses me. How can my parents be charged with neglecting us but not my brothers? It's probably because we are so bad, and they're not. I'm glad they get to stay at home.

We drive for what seems like hours. It isn't long before we are off the highway and driving down back roads that are surrounded by nothing but corn fields. I have absolutely no concept of where we are right now. Mal is asleep with her head propped up against the window, and drool is coming out of her mouth. I want to giggle, but I remain quiet.

I'm afraid of where we're going, but I'm hopeful at the same time. Maybe where we're going will be better than home, and things can actually be normal for once. I miss my brothers already. I want to be with my parents, but I can't stand Mom anymore. I can't control my need to run away from her, and I want to be a normal kid who doesn't get into so much trouble.

I'm sad because things finally started to get better at school before we ran away the last time. I convinced Mr. Pierce that I was smart enough for the class across the hall. After looking at my grades, he decided to give me a chance. He warned me if I continued to get into trouble, I would have to go to the behavioral disorder class. I liked my new class and teacher a lot. I didn't want to screw things up, so I was on my best behavior at school. Keeping my grades up has never been a problem. The work has always come easy enough for me; it's the staying out of trouble part that's hard.

I also joined the school band after much pleading with the teacher and Dad. *Wow! Me in band?* It's a crazy thought for even me to process. Almost all the kids in my new class play an instrument, and I wanted to be a part of it. The class had already started, so I was going to be behind. The teacher wasn't sure if I would be able to catch up with the rest of the class and was hesitant to let me join. Dad was nervous about renting me the flute because he said it cost a lot of money and wanted to be sure I would stick to it.

After a lot of promises and begging, the teacher agreed to let me join the class, and Dad took me to get the flute. I love that flute. I wonder if Dad already took it back. He told me that if I stuck to it that he would buy it for me, and I could keep it. Now that I'm not at home, I'll probably never see it again. The very first weekend I had it, all I did was sit in my room and practice. When I went to school on Monday, the teacher was shocked when I played "Mary Had a Little Lamb" by heart in front of the class. He told me I did more than catch up; I had passed up everyone in the class. He was proud of me and glad I joined his class. I hope I can play at my new school.

I'm still friends with the girls from my old class, but I started hanging out with a girl named Stacy from my new class a lot after school. She's different from any of my other friends. The girls in my class are good girls, and being around them makes me feel like I'm not such a bad kid after all. I'm envious of the life Stacy has at home and how nice and normal her mom is.

Stacy is shocked by the fact that I cuss and smoke. She doesn't tell on me or want to stop being my friend. She says I should stop, and I know she's right. Being around her makes me want to be a better person. I wish I could be more like her. Someday, when I get away from all the craziness in my world, I will have a life just like hers.

I can't wait to grow up and go to college. I live for the day I have a job and can take care of myself. When I get married and have kids, my life will be so much better than it is now. I hope my kids will grow up to be good kids like Stacy. *I'll make sure of it!*

Chapter Fifteen

ear Diary,
I really like this new foster home I'm in, but Mom hates it and she's trying to get the judge to have us moved. I hate her. She can't stand it that I'm happy. I swear, her number one mission in life is to make me miserable! My foster parents are Bethany and Ronald George. They have two of their own kids: Scott, who is twenty, and Katrina, who is ten. They also have two little girls they are trying to adopt. Ava, who is five, and Candace. Everyone calls her Candie; she's four years old. They're sisters who were taken away from their parents for a lot of the same reasons I was. I guess their mom does drugs really bad, and their dad isn't around.

I wonder if I'll ever be put up for adoption. If I am, I hope I can stay here. Bethany's niece lives here too. She's eighteen, and her name is Kelly. She's cool, I like her. I like my new school, but it started out kind of rough. They put me in the school's bad ass kid class without even giving me a chance in a regular class. I guess I'm automatically a bad kid because I live in a foster home. Whatever! My class only has five kids in it. It's not even in the school! It's in a trailer outside. There are three boys in my class and only one other girl besides me. Her name is Tonya.

She's in seventh grade and all the boys are in eighth, so I'm the youngest only being in sixth grade. I have to go all the way to a school that is around twenty-five minutes away. I guess the school closest to here doesn't have a bad ass kids class. Tonya and I didn't get along at first, but we're good friends now. Not as good of friends as Carla and I, but good friends anyway.

When I first started here, she didn't like me. I'm not sure why because I didn't do anything to her. The boys were always taunting both of us and trying to get us to fight. I didn't wanna fight and have to move again, but I couldn't take the bullying anymore, so I knew what I had to do. I had to show her I wasn't afraid. One day, when the teacher left the trailer, I walked up behind her at her desk and grabbed her by the hair and slammed her head into her desk. The boys cheered and hollered, "Cat fight! Cat fight!" Tonya cried, I smiled and boasted with pride. We've been friends ever since.

Malory is pissed off because I'm doing the same work as her. The teacher says it's easier if we are all doing the same thing. At first, it was really hard, but I've gotten the hang of the fractions we're working on in math. I'm also studying to take the Constitution test. The teacher says if I pass it, I won't have to take it again in eighth grade because my score will go on my permanent record. Mal is also upset that I started my period younger than she did. She started before me, but she's fourteen and I'm only twelve. She says it's not fair. Not fair? I don't get it! It's not like I wanted to start. It's the worst thing in the world to deal with. I wish I could make it go away forever. It's so gross! Mom is sad that I started too because I don't live at home, and she wants to be able to be there for me. I watched her give Malory a crash course on using tampons once before we were taken away, so I kinda know.

We don't get to go home for visits on the weekends yet. I'm not sure when we will. For now, my family comes and sees us here. We're not allowed to leave the house during visits, either, and I can tell Mom and Dad both feel weird about it all. They never want to come inside the house, so we always stay outside for our visits. When it was cold, we sat in the van. We celebrated Malory's 14th birthday in the van a couple months ago. She was really sad about having to do that. I think we all were. I wish my mom would try to talk to Bethany and get along with her. Maybe then, things wouldn't seem so bad. Dad never says much about anything as usual. He just goes along with whatever Mom wants to do. I'm not sure how he feels about Bethany and Ronald, but I know he's sad. I can always tell by his eyes when he's sad.

Bethany is nice, but she's also very strict. She won't take shit from anyone, including Ronald. She runs the show in the house. Everyone knows it and respects her. We have chores we have to do, and I do them without arguing about it. We get an allowance every week for doing our chores. And I know if I don't get my allowance, I won't get my cigs for the week. Bethany lets us smoke; that's why Mom hates her so much. I know I'm not supposed to be smoking this young, so I understand why Mom is so angry about it. But at the same time, I think Bethany is the coolest mom in the world for letting us. She says she only allows it because she knows we are going to be stealing them and sneaking them behind her back if she doesn't let us. She would rather be in control of what we're doing so we don't burn down her house trying to sneak them. We lie to Mom telling her that she's wrong about Bethany and that we aren't smoking, but somehow, she still knows. She can't prove it, so DCFS won't move us. I think they suspect Mom is jealous because we aren't with her. She will find a reason to hate anyone we live with.

Bethany has also let me see Kevin a few times, which is something else Mom knows but can't prove. Bethany tries to tell me I should leave Kevin alone because he's too old. I know she's right, but I'm not ready yet. In my heart, I understand why my mom doesn't like her. But I feel stuck. I love Mom but I also love living here. If I can't be at home, I don't want to be anywhere else.

We live on a cattle farm in a big blue house in the middle of nowhere. They don't own the farm, so we don't have to take care of the cows. I've always lived in a city, so it's weird to see nothing but corn-fields. Sometimes it's even a little creepy, but I like it out here. There's a lot of property for us to play on and a go-kart we ride through a trail Scott made. It's between a big red barn and a few silos that are next to the

141

house. Sometimes at night, we go out into the cow field with Scott and try to tip the cows over. Scott calls it cow tipping. It's a lot of fun, and it makes me laugh so hard I almost pee my pants. Although now, we have to stay out of the field because the farmer brought a bull here. Scott says it's so he can get the cows pregnant. GROSS! Sometimes, we tease the bull from the fence, just to see how mad he gets. When he comes running towards the fence, we take off running.

I hope I get to go home for a visit soon. Even though I like it here, I really miss everyone. I'm glad Mal and I are together, but we aren't getting along very well. They've even talked about moving her a few times. Even though we're always fighting, I really hope they don't. I don't want to live anywhere without her, and I don't know why she doesn't like it here as much as I do. She seems mad all the time. She's really mean to Ava and Candie, but mostly to Ava. I don't know why she gets so mad at her, but sometimes, she even pinches her and pulls her hair when no one is watching. I see her do it, and I feel bad for Ava. I don't want to tell on my sister because I want her to stay here. I don't understand her sometimes and why she has to be so mean to everyone all the time.

I got to go to a concert last weekend. Scott was grounded because of his grades and Malory was in trouble too, so Bethany let me have the ticket. I went with three eighteen-year-old girls. Mom is so pissed about it, but I don't see what the big deal is. She thinks that because the other girls are older, they were going to get me to do bad stuff. She wasn't entirely wrong, but if she only knew, I can do bad stuff all by myself! One of the girls and I got high at the concert with a few boys who were sitting in front of us. I regretted it afterwards, though. I don't know why I do such dumb shit sometimes without thinking about it until it's too late. Mom says she's telling the judge about me going to the concert when she can get our case back into court. I wish she would stop trying to move me out of here. I know she's jealous because I like Bethany so much, and it drives her crazy.

Heather

"What are you doing?" asks Bethany as she walks into my room.

"Nothing. Listening to music and writing in my diary."

"Oh. I don't see you write in that too much," she says.

I only write in it when something is really bothering me. The counselors tell me I should write in it every day no matter what's going on. *What's the point of that?*

"Hey, you have a visitor downstairs," she adds with a weird look on her face.

"Huh? A visitor? Who is it?" I ask eagerly, but she just stands there without answering me. *What the hell?*

I stand up from the spot where I've been sprawled on the floor and start to walk toward the door, but she doesn't move away from the doorway. She's just standing there with a weird look on her face. "Bethany, who's here? What's going on?" I ask, starting to get a little worried.

"It's your mom," she replies.

"What? My mom? What is she doing here? It's not the weekend yet," I ask, confused but also excited. Malory is going to be mad because she's not here. She started going out with Bethany's nephew, and she's over at his house. We didn't know she was coming, and she didn't call. I hope everything is ok.

"Are my dad and brothers here, too?"

"No, it's just her," she says as she moves so I can get through the door. *What's the funny look for?* I wonder as I race down the stairs.

I walk out the back door, and I see Mom pacing back and forth by the car, smoking a cigarette.

"Mom!" I call out, walking toward her. She stops pacing and turns to look at me. The sun is in her eyes, but I can already see it from here, and the excitement I had is gone. *She's drunk!* She always has the same stupid look on her face when she's been drinking. As I approach her, I feel my face turning red with anger. "Mom, what are you doing here?" I ask, annoyed.

"What? I can't come to see my daughters without calling first?" I can tell by her smell and the tone in her voice that I was right. *She is drunk! I can't believe her!* I feel the rage inside of me starting to take over. She is the only one who can make me feel *this* angry.

"NO, Mom! You can't just show up here whenever you want to! We're only supposed to visit on the weekends, remember? What if they find out you came here?" I ask, completely disgusted by her.

She's just standing there staring at me. Her face starts to curl up the way it does when she's drunk and about to get nasty. So I say the only thing I can think of to stop what will come out of her mouth next. "Mom, leave! I don't want you here when you're drunk! Does Dad even know where you are?" *That was a stupid question; of course he doesn't know!* There's no way Dad would have let her come out here drunk. It takes an hour to get here from home.

Her face suddenly turns sad like she can't believe I just told her to leave. *What the hell does she expect!?* "Mom, I said to leave! I don't want you here! Go, now! I can't stand to even look at you when you've been drinking!" I yell, and I turn to walk away, ignoring the tears that have formed in the corner of her eyes. *I don't care if she cries! How does she think I feel?*

"Heather, please don't walk away from me," she pleads with her voice shaking, but I keep walking. "You're *my* daughter!" she cries out.

The sadness in her voice almost makes me turn around. *No! Keep walking, Heather. Don't turn around. How dare she come here like this!*

I turn to look at her one last time before I go inside, and I can see she's crying. *God, I hate how she makes me feel!* How can I be so sad and angry at the same time? I want to hug her and tell her how much I love her, but at the same time, I want to rip her eyes out. *I can't do this with her.* I slam the door shut and go running toward my room. As I quickly make my way through the dining room and living room, I can feel everyone staring at me. I'm crying now. I am pissed off. I just want to be left alone.

"Heather, are you ok?" asks Ronald following behind me as I race toward the stairs. Ronald is always so nice and caring. He's really quiet most of the time, but he has a nice smile and a soft voice. He's short with a thin build. He's always dressed in jeans and cowboy boots.

"Ronald, leave her be," calls out Bethany as I race up the stairs, ignoring him.

Once in my room, I plop down on my bed to bury my face into my pillow. I start crying so hard I can barely breathe. I hate her so much for making me feel bad for walking away from her. *Why am I the one who feels bad? Why can't she ever think about my feelings? If she doesn't quit drinking, I swear to God, I'm never going home.* I lay there crying until there are no tears left. I'm so exhausted that I can hardly keep my eyes open, and I quickly fall asleep.

"Heather! Heather! What happened? Bethany said that Mom came here?" Malory asks as she shakes me awake.

I look at the clock and see I've slept for three hours. "Heather? What happened?"

Still groggy, I tell her what happened, afraid she's going to get mad at me for making Mom leave, but she doesn't. She understands, and for the first time in a long time, Malory and I bond.

We don't talk that much anymore. All we do is fight, so I enjoy every second of sisterly love we share because I never know how long it's going to last. I love my sister so much, and I don't think she realizes how much I need her. She's the only person in the world who can possibly understand how I feel. But most of the time, it seems like we are thinking totally different thoughts. *How can that be when we live the same shitty life?* I know that someday it won't be this way anymore. Someday, she will love me and need me just as much as I need and love her.

Chapter Sixteen

These people are crazy! I gotta get out of here somehow. I'm living with the Brady Bunch from hell! Standing in front of the mirror getting ready for church, I think about how incredibly screwed up everything is. It went from bad to worse overnight.

Penny, Bruce, and their kids: Leah, Lucy, Patrick, Caleb and Lucas. I mean, God! Could they be lamer? I wish Mom would have left things alone so I could have stayed at Bethany's. I'll never forgive her for having me moved. She would rather I be here and miserable than with someone I can actually trust and talk to. God forbid I get close to anyone but her. No matter how hard she fights, I'll never be close to her, and that's her own fault.

"Heather, hurry up, we gotta get going," says Bruce from the other side of the door.

Ugh, I can't stand him, he's so weird. What is this church shit, anyway? How can they try to force me to believe what they believe in? I really don't know what I believe, but I don't believe God is going to damn me to hell for smoking a cigarette or swearing.

They treat me like I'm the devil who needs to be saved. "Ask God for forgiveness and I'll be absolved of my sins if I live the path he has chosen for me."

Blah, blah, blah. Well, the path *He* has chosen for me is shit, and I'm dealing with it the best I can. *Does He really expect anything more from me? Where is God when Mom is out drinking and doing drugs? If God loves me so much, why is He making me live with these crazy-ass people instead of my real parents? I'll start caring about God when God starts caring about me!*

I think I believe in God. Everyone says He's there, but I haven't seen any proof of Him yet. I've never really been a part of a church before. Mom's whole family is Catholic. I was baptized Catholic, but she has never taken us to church. The most church I've seen is when Mom used to force us on the bus on Sundays to go to Grace Baptist. I hated her for that. She is such a hypocrite. We didn't learn anything there. We would sit in a huge room with 100 other kids while someone preached at us for an hour, but no one ever paid attention. We just goofed around the whole time.

They used to come around on Saturdays and try to bribe us with flyers telling us what we would get if we came to church on Sunday. It would always be some sort of toy or treat. No matter how good the prize was, I would fight Mom on going. She was just trying to get rid of us for the day anyway. If she really wanted us to get something out of it, why didn't we all go to a church together?

Penny and Bruce worry that I'm a bad influence on their daughter, Lucy, who is a year older than me. If they only knew how she really was, they would shit their pants. She smokes, cusses, and likes boys more than I do. She was all too excited when I moved in because now there was someone she could share it all with. There's something about her that's different from me. I know I've done bad things, and I'm no angel, but she goes looking for trouble. She's fearless in a way. And most times, no matter how tough I act, most things scare the shit out of me.

A few weeks ago, Lucy convinced me to get into a car with a few guys who I didn't know. I didn't want to at first, but she said she knew them. And even though I didn't trust it, I went along with it anyway. We spent all day and most of the night with these guys who were in fact harmless, but I still knew we needed to get home.

While she was feeling the need to rebel and not having a care in the world, I was worried sick. My caseworker told me when they brought me here that if things didn't work out this time, I would be going to live in a group home. I don't know what that is, but I don't want to find out, either. Everything turned out ok in the end, but when we came home from being missing all day, who got blamed for it? *Yep, I did! The sinning little tramp!* They don't call me that, but I can tell by the way they treat me and talk to me that it's what they think of me.

One thing I don't understand about these Bible-thumping people is that they think because they go to church every Sunday that they are safe and will never see tragedy in their own family. Well, their tragedy lies in the bed across from me. And one day, they're going to see that their little family isn't so perfect after all, and I won't be around to take the blame for it.

After we pile into the station wagon to head to church, Penny turns and says something to me that makes my skin crawl. "Heather, you should really try to find God today. He can set you free of all your sins." *Is she fucking kidding? Will He set me free from living with these judgmental, crazy lunatics? What about Lucy? How can she just sit there all innocent when her parents talk to me like that, and pretend she never sins?* If I knew God would set me free from this crap I would go to the ends of the earth to find Him, but that's not reality, and neither is punching Penny in her hypocritical mouth, which is what I really want to do right now.

As we pull out of the driveway, Bruce starts singing some church song, and they all join in. I know I'm really in hell when he glares at me through the rearview mirror as if to tell me to sing or else. He can glare at me all he wants. It's not going to happen. I'm not going to fake my way through this like Lucy does. I suppose she's used to it since she grew up like this, but I didn't, and they can't expect me to be like them. I like Lucy, but I'm getting sick of how fake she is with her parents. I'm sick of how they think everything is my fault and that she's only acting out because of me. I'm tired of the way they talk about me right in front of my face like I'm not even standing there. I might not be the best kid in the world, and I might come from a messed-up family, but at least I'm not a phony. I don't pretend I'm something that I'm not like their precious Lucy does. I'll make things right with God later. He has to understand that right now, all I'm trying to do is survive, and it's taking everything in me not to explode or run away. After all, if He really exists, He's the one that put me in this mess in the first place.

When we get to church, Bruce tells me to head to my Sunday school class, but I'm already planning to skip it. As soon as the coast is clear, I make a break for it out a side door. I'm not sure where I'm going to hide out until it's over, but there's no way I'm sitting through that again. Everyone else goes to a different class, so hopefully, they will never know I'm gone. Out in front, I spot huge bushes that sit against the church, and I quickly go behind them to find a safe place to sit for the next hour. This will do. No one will see me here, and there's plenty of room to spread out.

I reach into my purse and pull out my pack of cigs. I laugh to myself as I picture the look Penny and Bruce would have on their faces if they knew where I was right now and what I was doing. Everything is a sin in Penny's eyes, and all hell would break loose if she knew I was sinning right here at God's front door. She acts like she has never seen anything bad in the world. Everything shocks her. I'm a tragedy in her eyes. *Well, screw her! I don't care!* Bruce isn't as bad. He told me he used to smoke, too. One time, he caught me smoking behind the shed, but he walked away and acted like it never happened. I guess he can be ok sometimes, but I still don't like him.

The church sits on a rural highway right outside of a small town in Illinois. We live in another small town that is just one town over. A shitty little town, too. I'd never been there before they moved me out here, and I didn't even know it existed. It's so small and boring, and there's nothing to do there. I've been to this small town plenty of times when Mom was working as a waitress. She became friends with a woman named Cindy, who has a daughter named Karen who's close to my age. We used to come out here all the time to see them. I wish she still lived here. I'd walk to her house right now and never look back. I miss her and wonder where they are. Mom and Cindy don't talk anymore. She says they moved away.

School starts in a few weeks. I already know what's going to happen when I start, and I'm dreading it. The girls in town are already spreading rumors about me. I keep hearing that I'm a slut. *A slut? Really?* I'm still a virgin. How can I be a slut? Mom says it's just jealousy because I'm the new girl in a small town, so I should ignore it. She goes right back to the whole "get used to it" talk whenever I complain about it. I wouldn't have to get used to it if I didn't have to move all the time, and it's her fault I had to move here. I'm prepared to have to kick a lot of asses when I start school. I don't want to, but if these small-town bitches want to mess with me, I'll show them what this little "slut" is made of.

As I sit here smoking my cigs and listening to the sound of the trucks buzzing past, I start thinking about Mal. I wonder what it's like where she lives now. They sent her to one of those group homes they threatened me with. So, I know they mean it when they say that's where I'll go next. I haven't seen her in a long time, and I really miss her. She was moved out of Bethany's before me because of how bad we were fighting. At the time, I was happy because I was so mad at her. But once she was gone, I got a sick feeling in my stomach that hasn't gone away. I feel like a part of me is missing when I'm not with her. I wish we could get along so we could have stayed together.

I really don't understand why they sent me here. It doesn't really make any sense because Penny and Bruce know Kevin. Why would they send me here if they want me to stay away from him? Penny and Bruce adopted Kevin's older brother, Andrew. I've never met him because he's away in the Navy. When Kevin found out I lived here, he came out here right away to see me. But Penny told him that he's not allowed to come back as long as I live with them. I still talk to him sometimes, and a few times, I've met him at the park. They can't control everything I do.

There's something different about Kevin. Lately, he's quieter, like there's something he's not telling me. We're just friends, so he doesn't have to hide things from me. I tell him everything. He's the only one I have left in the world to tell my secrets to now that my sister is gone. Maybe that's why I try so hard to keep him in my life. All the grown-ups see is a nineteen-year-old guy with a twelve-year-old girl. What they don't see is that they are taking my best friend away. He's the only person in the world who seems to care about me right now.

I'm not that far away from home. The thought of running away and going home crosses my mind. I wonder what my brothers and parents are doing right now. I know going home isn't an option, but I think about it all the time. Now that I'm a ward of the court, if I go home, my parents can't let me stay or they could get arrested. Mom keeps telling me to stick it out and that we'll be home soon. I don't know if I really believe that, though, and I don't think she does, either.

Mom and Dad hired their own attorney. We go to court once every few months to have our case reviewed, but they always say we have to remain in foster care. The judge tells my caseworker every time we go to court to get us a family counselor, but she still hasn't. If going home depends on that, then we will probably never get to go home. We've already been gone for six months.

On the car ride home, I know Bruce is suspicious of me. He keeps asking questions about how my Sunday school class went like he's waiting for me to slip up. Maybe he just enjoys watching me squirm, but I don't crack, and he leaves it alone. I think he knows that he can't force me to want to learn about God. Maybe he just understands me in a way that Penny doesn't. I'm never going to be like her or her daughters with their long skirts and hair that is so long it takes an hour to brush it. Mom says they wear their hair like that and have to wear skirts all the time because of their religion. *You won't catch me dead in a skirt!*

A few days later, while sneaking a cig behind the shed, two girls come walking down the alley pushing a baby stroller. I think about putting out my cig and sneaking away to avoid them, but I change my mind. If they *are* some of the girls talking about me, I'll stand up to them. Then, they can run back and tell all their little friends not to mess with me. It would be better if I can get this out of the way before school starts. I know if I get kicked out of school, I'll have to go to a group home. One of the girls is short and as skinny as a twig with long dark hair. I'm not worried about her. I can tell by looking at her that I can take her. But the other one is taller and big, so I'm not so sure about that one.

When they approach me, I don't take my eyes off them, and they don't take their eyes off me.

The twiggy one smiles at me. "Hi," she says sweetly. *Oh, maybe I won't need to fight.* Before I have a chance to respond she says, "My name is Selene. Are you Heather?"

"Yes," I say, still unsure if I should let my guard down. "How do you know my name?" I ask curiously.

"I've heard the other girls around town talking about the new girl who lives with the Huffman's. But don't worry, I can't stand any of them either. I never listen to what they have to say. You smoke too, huh? So do we. Don't worry, we won't tell." She's talking so fast I don't have a chance to say anything. I wonder what all these girls are saying about me because I can tell she is nervous.

The other girl just stands there, not saying anything. "Oh, this is Stacy," Selene says when she notices me looking at her awkwardly. We say hi and smile politely.

I look back at Selene, who is fidgeting with the baby in the stroller. "Are you babysitting?" I ask.

"Yeah. Do you wanna come for a walk with us? We were going to walk down to the park," she asks, still smiling. She has really pretty green eyes, and her small lips and smile remind me of Mom. She's so pretty. I bet that's why she has a hard time getting along with other girls, too. I've been tricked before but there's something about this girl that I am instantly drawn to, and I trust her already.

"Let me go ask Penny and Bruce if I can go. I'll be right back," I say, turning to walk back toward the house. I start to feel a sense of relief that I haven't felt in the last three weeks since I've been here. I've been so lonely; it's nice to meet a new friend outside of the house.

Bruce appears from the side of the house. "What are you up to out there, Heather? Who is that you're talking to?" he asks.

"A girl named Selene. She wants to know if I can walk to the park with her them. Can I go? Please?" I ask with excitement in my voice.

"Go ahead, but don't be gone all day. And please, behave yourself," he adds skeptically.

Sensing the hesitation in his voice, I hurry off before he changes his mind.

As I walk away, I hear Penny come outside and scold Bruce for letting me go. She's quietly saying something about Selene and how much trouble her family is. *God! She is such a judgmental bitch! Isn't the Bible supposed to teach you not to judge people? What a hypocrite!*

For the next few weeks, I spend every second I can with Selene, not caring what Penny has to say about it. We've become best friends. *Real* best friends. She's almost exactly a year older than me, but you would never know it. She's so small and fragile; she looks like a nine year old. People who don't know us ask us all the time if we're sisters. They say we have the same eyes, and we have the same raspy voices. I like that people think we're sisters because she's so pretty. Even though people say it, I've never looked at myself as being pretty before.

Her friendship is unlike any other friendship I've ever had. I never thought I could meet anyone so much like me but so different at the same time. She's everything I'm not, and knowing her makes me a better person. She's sweet, loyal, and giving. She would do anything for anyone, and people have taken advantage of her for that. I always tell her that as long as I'm around she won't have to worry because I will stomp anyone who tries to hurt her. *I really will, too!*

Last week, I slapped the shit out of a girl who has been torturing Selene for years. She was so tall I had to jump to do it. She says she looks up to me for being so strong, and she wants me to teach her to be more like me. I don't think she realizes how much I wish I could be like her. There's an innocence and sweetness about her that's untouchable, no matter how hard people try to take it away from her, and that's something I could never have.

Penny says Selene and her family are trouble. *But she's a better person than I am, so what does that say about me?* I've had to sneak to hang out with her, but this town is so small it always gets back to Penny and Bruce. I don't see what the big deal is. The worst thing she does is smoke, but so do I. I'm going to smoke with or without her, so I don't understand why they can't just leave us alone and let us be friends.

Selene's family doesn't seem all that bad to me, either. Her mom likes me a lot. She says that she's going to try to get her foster parent license so I can come live with them. Selene tells me bad things about her family. I know they're not perfect, but I never see that when I'm at her house. Maybe if I lived with her, I could protect her from it.

After weeks of refusing to listen to Penny and Bruce's rules about Selene, they're kicking me out. Tomorrow, I'm being taken to the group home my sister is in, and I don't want to go. It's almost two hours away from here, and I don't know when I'll get to see Selene or my family again. I want to see Mal, but I'm scared because we fight so much. All I know about being in a group home is you're locked in, and you can't just go outside whenever you want to. You can't even make phone calls, and you're watched at all times. I thought about running away so they can't take me there, but Selene's mom convinced me to just do what they say for now. Hopefully, I'll be able to come back to live with them soon. *I hope she means it.*

No matter what happens, Selene and I made a promise that we will never lose touch with each other. I refuse to lose her like I have my other close friends. We're soul sisters now. No number of miles or foster homes could ever take her away from me.

Chapter Seventeen

"I know what you can do," says Cole with a smirk on his ugly face.

"What?" I ask, terrified of what his response will be. *God, please just let this be over.* I've been trying to get away from this sicko for two days. And no matter what excuse I make, he won't let me go. I've thought about running away from him, but somehow, I know if I do, he'll catch me, and I'm afraid of what will happen.

"Suck it," he replies coldly, pointing down at his pants.

"No way! That's disgusting, and I'm never doing that!" I say, surprised by the sudden confidence I have behind my words. I can't be afraid of this guy anymore. I have to find a way to get away from him before this goes any further, but I'm so afraid I can barely move.

"Come on, Heather. Please?" he begs.

"No way!" I say firmly. "Besides, your friend is sitting right there!" I add, thinking he will see what's wrong with this picture and drop the subject.

"So what?" he says, "He's not going to watch. Just do it already!" he demands.

"No, Cole! I don't want to," I plead. Now *I'm* the one begging. I glance around the dark playground and over at the elementary school where I once went. I wonder what Mr. Becker would think if he could see me right now. I wish I could go back to the days when I worried about the girls liking me and getting beat up on my way home from school. Those fears have never seemed as small as they do right now. I feel so sick to my stomach, and I just want to go home. *I did this to myself! I shouldn't have run away again. This is all my fault. If I never left the house when Mom told me not to, I wouldn't be in this situation.*

I've been wearing the same tampon for the last fifteen hours just to stop him from having sex with me. I know my period is over now, and I could have taken it out hours ago. When he insisted we were going to have sex earlier today, it was the only idea I could come up with. My period is not what stopped him from stealing my virginity. Instead, I convinced him that because I didn't have any more tampons, I couldn't take it out or I would be bleeding all over the place the rest of the day. It's really starting to hurt. The end of it started to poke out of me a few hours ago, and every time I walk it feels like sandpaper.

"Heather?" he calls, interrupting my thoughts.

"What, Cole?" I ask, starting to feel defeated.

"Do it!" he demands. Every time he asks, it's less of a question and more of a command. He has now unzipped his pants and is holding it in his hand. Maybe I should just do it. Then, maybe he will let me go, and I will never have to see him again. I've never needed or wanted to be home with Dad so bad in my life. All of the time, we never talked. All of the time, I thought I didn't care that we weren't close. And out of all of the times that I lived away from him, *this* is the first time I've wanted to scream out for my daddy to save me.

"No, Cole! Please stop asking me to do that. I really don't want to," I say with a whimper.

He suddenly grabs me by the back of my head, wrapping his fingers into my hair tightly, and tries to pull my head towards his lap, but I resist.

"You're going to do it, bitch!" he demands, pulling my hair even harder, with evil in his eyes, and a tone in his voice that sends a chill down my spine.

I feel so sick right now that I think I might throw up. I quickly look down toward his friend, who is sitting at the bottom of the slide ten feet away from where we are at the top of the jungle gym. I know he hears everything that we're saying. It's 1:00 a.m., and the only sounds around are my pleas for him to stop. His friend looks up at me, and I look at him with eyes that say to please help me. But all he does is shake his head and gets up to walk away. *Where is he going? Why won't he help me?*

I can't fight him anymore. I can no longer say no. I'm too exhausted. And I'm too afraid that if I scream or fight, he will do something to hurt me. So, I give him what he wants, and pray to God the whole time that he lets me go when it's over. I know I should be fighting. That's what all the women in the movies do, but I'm not because I'm a weak coward that gave in. It's all my fault. Mom was right the other day when she said I was a dirty little slut who would die of AIDS before I turned sixteen. I wonder what she would say if she could see me now. *I hate her!* This is her fault, not mine. If she would just be normal, I wouldn't have left home in the first place.

"Yo, Damian! Do you see this shit, man?" he laughs out in the middle of it, unaware that Damian left.

I can't believe he's laughing! It's funny that someone else may be watching as I do the most shameful thing I've ever done?

Tears are rolling down my face, and I feel anger starting to boil in my belly. I consider biting him as hard as I can, but I'm too scared. I'm only thirteen, and he's seventeen, plus he's a lot bigger than me. I know my 100-pound body is no match for him, so I continue to pray that it will end soon. I try to think of anything other than what I'm doing, but all I can picture are the looks I would get from the people I love if they knew what I was doing. The thought of that makes what's happening more shameful than the act itself.

When it finally ends, he lets me go and says he will see me around.

That's it? After two days of not letting me out of his sight, he finally gets what he wants, so he just lets me go? I'm not going to complain, so I hurry away from him before he changes his mind. It's late, and I'm not sure who's home, or if I can get back into the house. There's nowhere else I would rather be right now than in the comfort of my own bed.

On the walk home, I can't get the horrible things I'd done out of my head. I feel so disgusted with myself for not being strong enough to fight back. I hope no one saw what he was trying to do with me in the dark corner by the door to the school. When he figured out earlier today that he wasn't going to be able to have sex with me, he thought of other ways to get what he wanted. Even though his attempt was unsuccessful, my bottom side still hurts from him trying. I wonder if they have cameras at the school that saw me bent over and crying while he was trying to have his way with me. I wonder if what he did is considered rape, but I know it can't be because he didn't have to physically force me. Like a disgusting coward, I gave in to him, and I will never tell anyone what happened today. The shame I feel right now is overpowering. I know the only person I'll ever be able to tell is Selene.

I wish I was still at the residential home they sent me to, Anchusa, even though I hated it when I was there. Me and Mal were sent there shortly after I was taken to the group home she was in. That didn't last long at all. I was only there for three weeks. Her and I couldn't stop fighting and I couldn't follow the rules. Well, I could, I just didn't care to anymore.

When I was at Anchusa, all I wanted was to come home, but now, I just wish I could go back. Everything was supposed to be different this time when we came home, but somehow, it's worse. I was different when I left there. I even went without smoking a cig for almost a year. Now, who gives a shit anymore? It doesn't even matter when I try. Everything is still the same. *Why bother?*

When I reach the house, Dad's car is gone, I know he's at work. The living room and kitchen lights are on, and the van is in the driveway. Mom must be awake. There's only one reason why she would be awake with all the lights on at this hour, and I know it's not because she's worried about me. *Great, this should be fun!*

I left the other day after one of Mom's drunken rages. Out of nowhere, she called me a little slut and told me I was going to die of

AIDS before I turn sixteen. I don't even know where she comes up with some of the stuff she says. That was by far the worst thing she has ever said to me. I promised myself when I came home from Anchusa that I was never going to run away again, but I was so hurt I just wanted to get away from her. If I would have known what was going to happen, I would have just stayed and taken it. *Now she really has a reason to think I'm a slut.*

I turn the door handle and it's unlocked, so I slowly open the door, afraid of which side of Mom I will find on the other side. The radio is on playing rap music, and it's turned up really loud. *Rap?* I find Mal and her new boyfriend sitting on the couch.

"Heather...you're in so much trouble, where have you been?" asks Mal loudly and giggling. I can tell right away something is wrong with her by the tone of her voice and the look on her face. As I walk further into the living room, I can see they are smoking and drinking! *What the hell is going on?* Mom doesn't even like this guy. *Why is he here, and where the hell is she?*

"Where the hell have you been?" asks Mom from behind me. I turn to see her standing in the kitchen doorway. I can tell by the look on her face and the bottle of Peppermint Schnapps in her hand that she's wasted. The shock of what's going on paralyzes my lips and I don't know what to say to her. *She's letting Mal drink and smoke now? AND have Tony over?* A guy that she has absolutely despised since Mal met him. She has been fighting her to stay away from him for almost a year and now she's partying with them? *What the fuck?!*

I already feel like I'm in an episode of *The Twilight Zone* when she holds the bottle out, "Here have a drink," she says, smiling.

"What? Mom, no! What are you doing?" I ask in shock. All I can think to myself is how incredibly messed up this situation is. I know she can tell what I'm thinking by the look on my face.

"What, you're too good to drink now?" she asks with an ugly, crooked smile on her face.

"Yeah, Mom! I don't drink, and I can't believe you're trying to let me!"

"Well then here, take this," she says, holding out one of her cigarettes.

As tempted as I am to take it because of the last few days I've had, I know I could never smoke in front of my mom, and it's not normal for her to want me to.

"No, Mom. I don't want it! I quit smoking, remember?" I say with disgust.

Mal and Tony get up off the couch and start walking toward the kitchen. As Tony passes us in the doorway, he nudges Mom's arm and says, "Hey, Lorynn, let's go smoke that joint now." *What the fuck! Now she's smoking pot with them too?*

I can't control my anger any longer as I watch Mom walk over to the counter where her purse is and pull out a joint. "MOM!" I yell out. "WHAT THE HELL ARE YOU DOING?" I ask, screaming.

She turns and looks at me with disgust as she walks back toward me. She gets right in my face. We meet eye to eye because I am now as tall as her, and she says, "Don't you dare judge me, little girl! Who the fuck do you think you are?"

"I'm your daughter, and you're supposed to be my mom. You're not supposed to be letting us drink, smoke, and do drugs. It's not normal, Mom!" I say with a quiet desperation in my voice. My tears fall, but she ignores them and turns to walk toward the sliding glass door where Mal and Tony are waiting outside for her.

She turns to face me before going outside. "Screw you, Heather! You think your shit doesn't stink? Well then, just run away again, Miss Goody Two-Shoes!" she says, slamming the door shut on her way out.

I stand there in shock for a few minutes, listening to them laugh on the other side of the door. I know I can't convince Mal that it's wrong because she's having too much fun, and she's enjoying the fact that Mom is letting her see Tony. I wonder what Dad would think if he knew what was going on. I wish I had a phone number to call him at work to tell him, but Mal would probably just beat the crap out of me for it, so I know I can never tell him.

I walk into the living room and turn down the stereo. Feeling completely defeated and exhausted, I sit down on the couch. I can't believe my brothers are sleeping through all of this. When I sit back, I feel something hard poke me in the back. I reach my hand behind me into the couch cushion and pull out a metal spoon. *I knew it! I knew Mom was using drugs again. Why else would she be acting so crazy?* This is not the first time I've found a spoon buried in the couch since we moved back home, and I know it has something to do with her drug habit because of the burn marks that are on them.

I stand up and walk back toward the kitchen doorway, and I'm filled with so much rage and hatred I throw the spoon as hard as I can toward the sliding glass door. It makes a loud pinging noise, and their laughter suddenly stops. "I hate you, Mom! Why can't you just be normal?" I scream out as loud as I can, and then turn to run up the stairs toward my room and slam the door hard enough to hear that old familiar cracking sound.

I throw myself down on the bed and cry long and hard for what seems like forever until there is nothing left. All I wished for was to be able to come home to a normal home and a normal mom. Maybe I would have been able to tell her what happened. I will never be able to do that because what happened was all my fault, and she'll probably just call me a slut again. I know I can't stay here with her anymore, but I don't want to run away, either. I hate living in other homes, but I know what happens here isn't normal, and I can't deal with it anymore. After the incident at Bethany's, Mom finally started to see she needed to change too, and she finally went and got help. She quit drinking for over a year. She did everything she could to get us back, and during that time, I had never seen her act more normal. She was in Alcoholics Anonymous (AA), counseling, and she was even working out at the gym three days a week. She looked amazing, plus she had the confidence and self-esteem to go with it. Things really seemed like they were going to change this time. We've only been home for a month and look what's happening already. Mom fell off the wagon right after we got home. How could she work so hard to get us back just to go right back to it? I worked hard at Anchusa to be different too. *It was all for nothing.*

I miss Selene so much, and I wish I could call her to talk to her about what's going on. I can't because she's on the crazy floor at the hospital now, too. I really hope she's ok. I haven't talked to her in a long time. All I know is that she started dating a boy who lived with the Huffmans after I moved out. Because they were trying to keep him away from her too, she tried to commit suicide. A month later, she somehow got into inhaling things and almost killed herself again and had to go back to the hospital. I can't wait to see her so I can tell her how stupid she was for doing that and make her promise to never try to leave me again. I can't make it through this fucked up life without her. She's the only person I have that I can really trust. *Fuck Mom! I hate her!* I'll never respect her again after tonight.

I go into the hall and see they are all back in the living room again. They all look up at me as I walk over to the picture frame that hangs on the wall holding the poem I wrote at Anchusa that Mom is supposedly so proud of. I look up at it, and then back down at Mom.

"What do you think you're doing now?" Mom asks.

I pull the frame off the wall and walk over to the banister. "You're not my mother anymore, and this doesn't mean shit!" I shout as I begin smashing the frame against the banister. I smash it so many times that my hands start to ache. I don't know what's going on with me right now, but I can't control myself, and smashing this promise of a better life somehow makes me feel better.

"Heather knock it off, you psycho!" screams Malory.

I suddenly stop. Looking down at the mess I just made, I drop the mangled frame on the floor. I grab the poem and go back to my room slamming the door behind me. I sit down on my bed, barely able to catch my breath and look down at my poem.

Sometimes: by Heather Poissant - Grade 7

Teacher: Debbie Thomas

Sometimes I sit and wonder why I'm here, and why I can't go home.
But I guess I'll learn to face my fears. For that's the reason why I'm here.
Sometimes I sit and wonder why my mom drank so much and why she wasn't perfect.
But I guess I'll learn to face my fears. For that's the reason why I'm here.
Sometimes I sit and wonder why my sister beat me up all those times.
But I guess I'll learn to face my fears. For that's the reason why I'm here.
Sometimes I wonder why my brothers bother me so much.
But I guess I'll learn to face my fears. For that's the reason why I'm here.
Sometimes I sit and wonder why my dad yelled and screamed at me so much.
But I guess I'll learn to face my fears. For that's the reason why I'm here.
Sometimes I sit and wonder why I act the way I do.
But I guess I'll learn to face my fears. For that's the reason why I'm here.
Sometimes I sit and wonder why Anchusa wants to help me so much.
But I guess they're teaching me to face my fears.
For that's the reason why I'm here.

I curl up on my bed with the poem clenched in my hands and cry so hard I can barely breathe as I remember my time at Anchusa. I was there for nine months, and I learned so much from them. It's not a normal home for any kid, but being there would be better than being here right now. What happened to the Mom that was changing with me and promising us a new and better life when we came home? She was so proud of this poem and her sobriety. Now, I know it meant nothing.

One day, at the end of class, my seventh-grade teacher told us that we had to write a poem or short story to enter into the young authors contest. Even though we went to school on the residential home campus, the sixty kids who lived there were still a part of the school district, so they wanted us to participate. I dreaded it at the time and had no idea what to even write about. But in the fifteen minutes that I had to do it, I jotted down whatever came from my heart.

I never thought anything more about the poem after I wrote it. I thought the only person who would read it was my teacher. A month later, I was shocked and somewhat embarrassed to learn that I won first place out of all of the seventh graders in the district. I had to go to an awards ceremony and read it in front of a bunch of other kids and their parents who also won. It was really hard to do because I knew none of them could understand what I was talking about. They were all normal kids with normal parents, and reading it to them made me feel more shame than pride.

Now, looking at my poem, I know that the tears of pride Mom cried weren't real. She told me I was special, and I had a gift that she was proud of that she never wanted me to give up on. *Look at us now. I'm a dirty little slut who's too good to party with her.* I shove the poem under my mattress and promise myself that I'm going to get out of here someday soon. I'm never going to be like her, and even if I have to go back to being locked away in a home until I'm eighteen, I'll do it. I can't stay here with her anymore.

Chapter Eighteen

Dear Diary,

Are you ready for this massive update, Diary? I know it's been a long time since I've written, and I should be sorry, but I'm really not. Life has been extra crazy. This past summer was the worst summer of my life. Mom was more out of control than I had ever seen her, and if I'm being honest, so was I. I stopped caring about everyone and everything. I lost my virginity to a boy named Bryant, who I thought I loved more than anything in the world. He came along right after the incident with Cole and promised to protect me from him and everything else bad in my life, and he did...for a while. I wanted so badly to trust someone and have someone that would save me from all the hell I have been living. So, when I met him, I was willing to do anything to keep him. That only lasted so long with how chaotic my life is. We tried to stay together through all of it, but it was too hard.

On top of my life being crazy, his mom doesn't like me because of our four-year age difference and the family I come from. I can't blame her. I don't like them most of the time, either. She sent him off to military school in the fall and that was the end of us. But not before I made the mistake of having a little heart and his initials tattooed on my ankle like *an idiot. Selene tried to warn me that I would regret it, but I was so convinced we would be together forever. We still talk and write letters whenever we get the chance, but I know there is no hope for us to ever be together again as long as I'm locked away in this hell.*

There were a few other boys this summer, too. Like I said, I was pretty out of control after me and Bryant broke up and shortly before I was taken away again. I don't know why I keep doing it. It's like I can't stop myself or something. I knew at the time I should have said no, but for some reason, the words just wouldn't come out of my mouth. I get so wrapped up into someone wanting me and feeling loved that it doesn't feel wrong until it's too late. I didn't realize until after the last boy that I was being used. I didn't feel that way with the others, but the last one let me know afterward I was only good for one thing, so I think I learned my lesson. I'm going to wait until I meet someone who really loves me before I ever do it again. At least now, I finally live up to what my mom thinks I am anyway. Maybe that's why I did it, who knows.

I'm in another stupid residential home. It's not as big as the last one; there are only ten girls living here. It's a private residential home, so some of the girls who live here are here because their parents paid to put them here, and the rest of us are state kids. There are a few girls who only come here for school. It's more like a boarding school than anything. It's called Woodland Academy for Young Women, and it lives up to its name. It's set back in a forest preserve where the house can't be seen from the road. It would almost be a fairytale-like setting if we were all princesses instead of a bunch of wayward girls. I guess the guy who owns the place owns other homes like this in other states. I always heard about how mean he is, but in the time I've been here, I've never met him. I suppose he probably started out with good intentions, but dealing with a bunch of lost causes probably wore him down like I have many of my caseworkers and counselors.

I've gone through so many of them, I've lost count. Before I was brought here, they sent me to another group home that was three hours away from home. I only lasted a few weeks there. Another girl and I came up with a scheme to run away and somehow managed to make it all the way back home. We found a payphone where she called some older guys she knew, and they came to get us. Now that I think about it, I realize how stupid that was. One of the guys gave me the total creeps, and I'm lucky and thankful nothing bad happened.

I didn't even have a reason to hate that place. They actually let us smoke there. Once an hour, we were allowed to go outside for a smoke break. There were basically no real rules at all other than "don't leave unless we tell you that you can." We made our own meals and took care of ourselves for the most part. The staff members were basically glorified babysitters. It was a very strange place. It was almost too easy to run away from. Something about being there was unsettling, so I had to go. I think I just hated knowing that I was that far away from home.

. *A lot of good running did. I'm just as far away from home where I am now, and I've only seen my family a few times. I don't think they plan on making the trip to see me here very often. They say as soon as I earn my way up their level system I can go home for weekend visits. They're actually going to put me on the train to go, and Dad will pick me up in the city since it'll save him hours of driving. I'm nervous about that but also excited. I thought about running away from here a few times when I first got here, but I'm tired. I know it's only going to make things worse if I do. This place isn't so bad. There's a payphone in the day room that we can use during our free time, and I can call whoever I want. I've met so many different types of kids since I've been in the system that come from different types of situations. Most of them make me feel lucky to have the parents I do, as crazy as they can be. A lot of the kids I've met (most of whom have been girls, since I'm usually in all-girls homes) have been sexually abused. I used to think I was lucky to have never gone through that until I came here. Months back, I opened up about the situation with Cole during group. They've made me realize that what he did is considered sexual assault. I really thought that because I didn't fight him back, I was the one who did something wrong. When I first told my counselor, she made a phone call to DCFS. They tried to go after him legally, but because so much time has gone by since it happened, they said there was nothing that they could do. I hope he burns in hell for what he did to me. I hate him even more for the way he made me feel afterward and for how much I've blamed myself.*

As much as they try to tell me over and over it wasn't my fault, I still feel dirty. It's hard to make those feelings go away, but I'm working on it. As much as I've learned about it over the last few years, I'm still shocked at how many sick people there are in the world hurting kids like that...sometimes even their own kids. I don't understand it or what makes them that way. How many other kids are there in the world blaming themselves for what happened, never telling anyone, and just silently suffering and beating themselves up over something they had no control over? It makes me sick to think about it. I'm thankful I've had the staff members here make me talk about it and help me understand it wasn't my fault. I hope all the kids out there that are suffering in silence have someone walk into their life to make them brave enough to talk about it too, so they don't have to suffer forever.

I feel bad for my mom. I know the abuse she went through isn't her fault. That's why it's so hard to stay mad at her. I'm not sure if she ever told anyone when she was young. I get confused by that part because when she talks about it after drinking; she makes it seem like my grandma knew about it when it was happening and didn't stop it or believe her. She hasn't said that exactly. It's just the impression she gives and hints she drops, but maybe she's just referring to the physical part of the abuse. That definitely wasn't a secret. It's hard to tell what she means when she's drunk enough to talk about it. If my grandma did know, and even if she only knew about the physical abuse, how could she love a man so much that she chose not to protect her daughters? Maybe some-day, when me and Mom are in a better place and she's not drinking, I can ask her about it. I hope she can tell me the whole story so I can understand her more. I know now for sure it's why she's so messed up. Like she's always trying to run and hide from it. No matter how much she hurts us in the process, she just can't seem to stop herself. I under-stand the running part. I'm the queen of running. But I'll try for the rest of my life to keep the promises I made to myself to be different, no matter how hard it gets. And I swear to God, when or if I have kids of my own, I will NEVER let anyone hurt them. And if they do, God help them!

I have a good friend and roommate here named Ashley. She's from Wisconsin, but where I am in the state isn't far from the border. She makes living in this hell more bearable. I can talk to her about anything and don't have to worry about her judging me. No one can ever replace my friendship with Selene, but she's been a good stand-in. I'm going to miss her when one of us gets to leave. Her dad put her here because she's been out of control since her mother's suicide. She found her mother dead one day when she came home from school and hasn't recovered from it. She also found a suicide letter that her mom wrote to her. It makes me sad because sometimes she reads it over and over in our room. She has to be on seizure medication, and when she gets in depressive moods, she refuses to take it. Those days are by far my worst days here. It scares me to death knowing that at any time she could have a seizure. When it happens, I feel helpless because all I want to do is take her pain away. All I can do is scream for help and watch as the paramedics come and take her away. I cry and beg her to stop because I love her so much. It hurts to watch her suffer, but I can tell she has more problems than I could ever understand. I try to be here for her and be her friend, but all she wants is to die. She talks about dying and killing herself all the time, and it terrifies me.

I have never thought about killing myself, and I don't understand how anyone could be so sad that they would want to end it all. I don't have to deal with the things she does, though. My mom is still here. As angry as I get at her sometimes, I know I would be lost without her and don't want her to die. This life sucks, there is no doubt about that, but I still hang on to the hope that, someday, it will be better. So, I will continue to live this train wreck of a life anyway. There HAS to be something good at the end of it all, right? The daydreams I have about how good my life could be someday are the only things that keep me going. Without those dreams, I would be just as sad as Ashley. I wish I could save her, and I hope that someday, daydreams of a better life are enough to keep her going, too.

I'm not sure how much longer I'll be stuck here. But when I leave, I have to go back to another group home. They're going to send me to the same one my sister is at again so at least I'll have her. It'll make adjusting to a new place easier. It's not the same one we were at together before. It's in a different town somewhat closer to home. Group homes are a step down from residential homes, so I'll have more freedom there, but not as much as I would in a foster home. The only real difference between residential homes and group homes is that you get to go to a normal public school when you're in a group home. The doors are still always locked. There are alarms and staff members who are always watching you, so running away is hard, except for the last place, of course. I really am tired of running, though, so I just hope I can survive it long enough to make it to whatever will come after that.

Heather

Chapter Nineteen

"Who are you talking to?" I ask as I walk into the bathroom.

"Can't you knock?" Mal snaps, giving me the look of death through the reflection in the mirror.

Ughh! Whatever!

She looks back at her own reflection and smiles at herself as she continues to scrunch her hair, and I roll my eyes. "You were talking to yourself again, weren't you?" I ask annoyed.

"Shut up, Heather, you're just jealous because you're not as fine as me!" she replies in her normal overconfident tone, still smiling at her reflection.

Yeah, sure. That's what it is! "Mal, that's so weird! Normal people don't talk to themselves in the mirror," I say, rolling my eyes, this time making sure she sees I'm annoyed.

"Shut up, bitch, before I punch you in your ugly face!" she growls, turning to get in my face. I feel her breath on me, and I know I better shut up before World War III begins.

"Wanna sneak a cig?" I ask, quickly changing the subject. "The staff are in the office sitting on their asses. They won't catch us," I add, pulling the hair dryer from the vanity drawer.

"Ok," she replies.

I hate fighting with her. Sometimes, it's hard to keep my mouth shut when she's really pissing me off, but I'm learning my limits with her. I'm usually good at judging just how far I can take it without getting slugged. *Really though, who talks to themselves like that?* I catch her doing it all the time. She'll stand in front of the mirror saying things like, "Girl you're so fine; you're so hot; no one in the world is prettier than you." And she'll even kiss herself in the mirror! *Weirdo!* Sometimes, I get so sick of her. She's so full of herself, thinking she's the hottest, toughest girl in the world. *God, she's pathetic!* There are times I wish I was tougher so I could pound her face in. Then we'd see whose face is ugly!

"Why do you always have to be so mean?" I ask, hunched over the toilet by the window, trying to light my cig with the hot coils in the blow dryer.

"Because I can and it don't cost me nothin'," she replies with the same cockiness as before, taking the cig from me as soon as it's lit.

"Hey! That's mine! I should get the first couple of drags," I demand.

"You gonna take it from me?" she asks with a grin and her eyebrow raised.

Of course, I'm not going to take it from you, bitch!

I sit down on the edge of the tub with a huff and wait patiently for my turn. I watch her as she stands on the toilet, trying to get as much of the smoke out of the window as possible. As I watch her, I realize how much I really hate her. I'm tired of being intimidated by her. I don't understand why it makes her feel good to make other people feel bad.

"It's all yours," she says, interrupting my thoughts as she hands me the cigarette.

"Damn, Mal! Thanks for saving me some!" I snap, noticing she smoked almost all of it.

"Ha, ha!" she teases as she walks out of the bathroom, but not before turning to look at herself one more time in the mirror...winking and blowing a kiss at herself.

Psycho!

I quickly finish what's left of the cig and head back out to my bedroom. I'm glad I got the big room with the bathroom in it. Without it, I wouldn't be able to get away with smoking here. Knowing I don't want to be downstairs around the head case right now, I pull my journal out from under my mattress and stretch out on my bed.

Dear Diary,

I hate my life! I hate my sister! I hate school, and I hate living in this stupid group home! Why is Malory such a bitch all the time? She thinks she's so tough and so beautiful. Little does she know, her nasty-ass attitude makes her the ugliest girl on the face of the planet! I wish someone would just kick the crap out of her and bring her down a couple notches for once.

It doesn't make any sense. When I come home from school crying because the girls at school are so mean to me, she pretends like she gives a crap. She gets so angry that she can't be there to defend me, but then she's just as mean to me! Whenever I ask her about it, she laughs and says it's because she's the only one who's allowed to be mean to me. Really, I think it's because she's crazy! If she had a heart, she wouldn't want to be mean...would she?

Anyway, school has been awful! I try so hard to keep my mouth shut with these girls, but it's getting harder and harder every day. They think I'm a coward because I don't defend myself, but they don't understand my life. If I get in trouble at school, I don't get to go home to my parents and get grounded for a week. If I get in trouble, I don't get to see my parents at all! I don't have any friends at school, and I don't think I've ever felt this lonely. I go to school, and everyone hates me and misunderstands me.

I come home, and I walk on broken glass around Miss Tough hot-ass. I hate it. What's the point of all this? Yesterday, school was the worst. I went to the bathroom during the passing period. As I walked in, a few girls were walking out and laughing at me. When I got all the way in, I saw that they had written "Heather Poissant is a dirty nasty slut" in red nail polish all over the walls. They've done it before, but the last time it was inside the stalls. This time...it was everywhere! I ran to the principal's office crying again, but he does what he always does: NOTHING! I hate him!

Sometimes, I wonder if he thinks I deserve it because I live in a group home and because I don't come from perfection like the rest of those snobs. There's got to be more he can do, right? I don't even understand how this happened. My first few days of school they made me feel like a movie star. Everyone wanted to be my friend. A few days later, I was hearing rumors that I am a slut, and it's been a nightmare ever since.

How can I be a slut? I can't even leave my house without an adult! The only window we can even open without the alarm going off is in my bathroom, and that's just because it's too small for anyone to fit through. If they knew the truth, they'd really have a reason to call me a slut. Maybe I do deserve this, and they don't even realize it. I'm trying so hard to stay strong, knowing that I won't have to be around these bitches forever, but I can feel myself starting to break. It's been going on for almost four months now. Every day, I come home crying from all the bullying. I feel like such a wimp. What can I do???

The counselor here keeps telling me I'm doing great, and there's only one month left until eighth-grade graduation. Then, I'll be away from them forever. I sure hope when I move to Aunt Phoebe's in Ohio that high school is not as bad as junior high has been. I can't wait to go live with her and Uncle Roger. It's going to be weird living so far away from home, but I'm excited anyway. I'm ready for a fresh start.

Mal is not happy about it at all. God forbid she get away from Tony. She's going to live with Uncle Derek and Aunt Claire. She's already plotting out how she's going to run away from there so she and Tony can be together. She's so stupid; she's going to get caught! She's on probation, too, so she'll end up in juvie until she turns eighteen if she doesn't quit getting in trouble.

I think I have finally had enough of this shit. I just want to have a normal life for once. I'm tired of running, and I'm tired of living in new places all the time. I've lived in so many foster homes now that I can't even remember some of the people's names. I'm tired of leaving my friends and having to make new ones. I don't even want to get close to anyone anymore because I know I'm just going to have to leave them anyway. Selene is the only friend I've always kept in touch with. I don't care how hard it is, I will never stop being friends with her. She is more of a sister to me than Mal can ever be. It would kill me if I lost her.

I'm too damn scared to run away anymore since learning that two friends from my hometown, Lisa and Ophelia, were killed. To think they got picked up and murdered from the same dark streets I've run a million times makes me feel sick. It could have been me so many times, and it makes me realize that I'm not invincible. Now, I get what Paul was trying to stress to me all those times he picked me up. They released a sketch of a man who was last seen with Ophelia, and I swear to God, he looks just like the man that stopped me and Bobbi that day. I told Mom right away, and she was so mad that I didn't tell her when it happened. What the hell does she expect? I don't tell her most things! She took me to the police station so I could tell them what I remembered about him, but they couldn't do anything because I didn't get a plate number or anything for them to look for. I'll never forget his creepy face and the way he made me feel that day. What if it was him that killed my friend?

I think about death and God a lot more now. I wonder if He really does exist. I want to believe that my friends are in heaven and not just buried in a box in the ground. But who really knows what happens until they actually die? I know I don't ever want to end up like that, so I have to try to stay put no matter how bad things are. I gotta go. I hear someone coming down the hall. It's probably Miss Full of Herself!

Lonely and defeated,

Heather -Aka- The dirty nasty SLUT!

"Heather, what are you doing? You've been up here a long time," Mal says as she walks into my room. "Are you crying? What's wrong?" she asks.

I quickly wipe my eyes. "Nothing, I'm fine," I say as I roll over to hide my face and change the station on the radio.

"Heather, are you thinking about those girls at school again?"

Please! As if YOU really care!

"Heather, forget them! You need to stop letting it bother you and just kick one of their asses! You know you can! They are just jealous of you because you're pretty, and they know you can steal their boyfriends if you wanted to!" she says with fury.

"Says the girl who just said they were going to beat my ugly face in!" I reply, annoyed, not making eye contact.

"Heather, you know I don't mean it when I say those things!"

"Then why do you say them? You know my life at school sucks, and instead of being my friend and sister, you are just as mean to me as they are!" I say, fighting the urge to cry.

"Whatever, Heather! Carol wants you downstairs in ten minutes, it's time for your counseling session," she says, and closes the door.

Yeah. Whatever! That's all she's got to say about it. *Hypocrite!*

While I still have a few minutes, I pop in an old cassette tape that I've played so many times over the last few years, it's about worn-out. Whenever I get in moods like this, I play it, and no matter how many times I listen to it, it never gets old. It makes me sad but hopeful at the same time. It came out a few years ago when things were really crazy at home and I was running away a lot. It's called "Runaway Train." *How ironic!*

I've never related to anything as much as I do to this song. I feel like the singer knows me somehow and every single lyric was meant for me. As sad and tragic as the song is, it gives me hope. It inspires me to be different, so I don't end up like one of the missing kids they post in their music video. Or worse, like Ophelia and Lisa. I wonder if the kids in the video were ever found and if they are alive. When the song ends, I shudder at the thought, wipe my tears, and head downstairs to my session.

"Hi, Heather. How has your week been?" asks Carol as I sit down in front of her.

Carol is nice. I like her, and she's pretty. Not in a glamorous kind of way, but in a more natural way. Her bouncy, short red curls make her green eyes stand out, and her subtle freckles line her high cheekbones. She always wears these swaying skirts that remind me of a hippie. She's always so happy. How can she be so happy being around a bunch of troubled girls like us?

"It was ok, I guess. Was the same as all the rest of the weeks since I moved here," I reply, biting my fingernails, a habit that's become quite bad lately. I bite my nails so low my fingers ache.

"What's going on, Heather? You seem extra distracted today. Is it school again?"

"It's always school! What else is new?" I reply, dropping my head a little.

"You don't have that much longer to go, and you've done so well ignoring them. You can't give up," she says in an "'atta girl" tone of voice. *She doesn't get it.*

"Just because I don't stick up for myself doesn't mean I'm ignoring them. I hold onto everything they say. I can't help it." *I'd like to see how she'd deal with it, or anyone else in this house for that matter!*

"Heather, what's wrong? Did something else happen?"

"I was just thinking that maybe I deserve this," I reply, knowing what she will say next.

"Heather! No one deserves what you are going through, so you can't ever blame yourself."

"I know, but..." My voice trails off, and I pause. "But I believe in karma, and I was just thinking that this is my karma for the way I've acted in the past."

"Karma for what exactly?" she asks.

"Well, I know it was a long time ago, but there was this girl I made fun of in the third grade, and..."

"Heather, you are not being punished for something you did in the third grade."

"I know, but let me finish, it gets worse," I interrupt. "I was making fun of her because I wanted to be friends with this group of mean girls that always picked on me. I knew it was wrong, and I hated doing that to her, but I wanted them to like me so bad. I thought if I could be cool like them, I wouldn't have to be the one they bullied anymore. I know now how stupid that was, but..." I take a deep breath.

"Heather, what happened?" she asks anxiously.

"Well, the girl, her name was Shenille. She was overweight. We used to call her hippo and stinky whale, cruel things like that." I lower my head in shame as I picture the look of hurt on her face. I remember it like it was yesterday.

"Heather, kids say and do mean things like that sometimes, and although it's wrong, I can tell you learned from it, right?"

"Yes, and I quit doing it almost as soon as I started. I didn't care what the other girls thought anymore, and I told Shenille how sorry I was; and I never did it again, but..."

"But what, Heather?"

"I found out she died last year from heart failure. No matter how sorry I told her I was, I know now I can never forgive myself for being a part of that, especially now," I blurt out quickly with my head still lowered, and I feel the familiar sting behind my eyes. I look up at Carol, and for a moment, she's speechless. I can't tell if the look on her face is sorrow or shock. Maybe it's both.

She reaches over and puts her hand on my knee and lowers her voice. "Heather, I am so sorry you had to learn such a valuable lesson in such a tragic way, but you have to forgive yourself. You had no control over what happened to her. You learned from it, right?"

"Yeah, but that doesn't change it. So, I feel like I deserve this for what I did to her. It's karma, isn't it?" I don't give her a chance to respond as I ramble on. "Plus, if these girls at school knew my past, they would have a *real* reason to call me a slut. I feel like that's my karma for actually acting like one."

"Oh, Heather, you are not a slut. Why would you think that about yourself?"

"Uh, because I've slept with more than one guy already, and I'm only in the eighth grade! You already know this about me," I say in a "duh" tone of voice.

"I know, Heather, but that doesn't make you a slut. Sometimes, we do things for the wrong reasons, but that doesn't make us bad people, right?"

"Why couldn't I say no then?"

"You were searching for something you weren't getting at home. We're going to work on that so you don't repeat past behaviors in the future, ok?"

"Ok," I reply, but I'm doubtful. It was easy not to say no. Now that I look back on it, I don't think I even wanted to say no. It's been almost a year since I've had sex, and I know I should be proud of that, but it doesn't change that I did it in the first place.

"How have your weekend visits home been going?" she asks, interrupting my thoughts.

"Ok, I guess. We're all just pretending our way through this whole thing, anyway."

"What do you mean?" she asks.

"Well, I know my parents are still drinking. They just pretend like they're not when we're there. They're never going to change," I say, and my attention wanders toward the window.

I can't wait to be able to go outside whenever I want to without a staff member holding my hand every step of the way. It's spring and before I know it, it will be summer and I'll be at Aunt Phoebe's. Pictures of the beach when I was little flash through my mind and my heart aches momentarily at the memories. *Life should have been better than this! This is so unfair!*

"Heather, what are you thinking about?" Carol asks, snapping me back to reality.

"I don't know. Starting fresh and hoping things will be different once I move."

"Things will only be as good as you make them. Our time is up for now, but if you need anything, you know where to find me, ok?"

"Ok," I reply and quickly scurry off to my room where I can be alone.

Chapter Twenty

"Hey, Heather! Where are you going in such a hurry? Do you have a dick to suck somewhere?" yells Mindy, one of my biggest bullies, as I walk down the hall, trying to make it to my next class without an incident.

I should have known I couldn't. Mindy and her twin sister are so little and scrawny. If only I didn't have so much to lose, I'd squash them both like bugs.

"Heather, just ignore them," says Alex, who is walking next to me and carrying my books. I wonder why he even likes me. He's one of the popular guys in school, and I know everyone gives him hell for talking to me, but he couldn't care less. He's my only friend, and I love him for it.

"Dick-sucker! Dick-sucker!" yell out a bunch of the girls in unison as everyone else laughs.

I feel myself fill with rage and want so badly to scream at the top of my lungs. I suddenly have flashbacks of the night at the park with Cole. The thought of ever doing *that* again after what he did to me makes me sick to my stomach. As they continue to taunt me, the rage boiling beneath my surface is one I'm not quite familiar with. The devil inside me says to turn around and show those bitches what I'm really made of. "Heather, are you ok?" asks Alex when I suddenly stop walking and squeeze my eyes shut.

Fuck, what do I do? Run, Heather! Get the hell outta here before you do something you will regret.

Without even taking my books from Alex, I run as fast as I can to the principal's office, knowing that if I don't get there now, the bad in me will take over. As I push my way through the office door, I bend over to catch my breath and lose all my bearings, falling to the floor crying harder than I ever have. I hear the secretary call out to the principal, and seconds later, he's standing above me.

"Heather, what happened this time?"

"Please, make it stop! Make it stop, or I'm going to lose it on one of them. I can't take it anymore!" I cry in the most desperate, pathetic voice I've ever heard come out of my mouth.

Without saying a word to me, he grabs my arm and helps me off the floor. "Take her to the nurse's office," he instructs the secretary.

Asshole! Why won't he stop them? I wonder as the secretary leads me to a cot. I've been going through this for months, and he never does anything. He never writes them up, calls their parents, or even considers kicking them out of school.

I dry up my tears, and as I sit here stewing, I get more and more enraged. I can't calm down no matter how hard I try. My breathing is so heavy that it feels like my chest is going to explode.

When the bell rings, the secretary tells me to get to my next class. I grab my books that Alex brought me and storm out of the office, rolling my eyes at the asshole principal as I pass him. The way I'm feeling right now, I don't trust myself. I know that the next person to say anything nasty to me is going to get it, so I avoid going to my locker and head straight to the gym for P.E. *Hold your head up, Heather! Only one more week until graduation, and then you will never see these fucked-up people again!*

We're playing dodgeball today. This brings some relief to my rage as each ball I throw makes me feel better every time it hits someone.

My gym class is huge, consisting of about thirty girls. They keep us separated from the boys with a thick, heavy curtain that splits the gym in half. This junior high is big. There are only seventh and eighth graders in the school and around five hundred kids, maybe more. I've never been to a school this big before.

Everything is new because the town was devastated by a tornado that ripped through here a few years ago. From what I hear, this town used to be nothing but corn fields, but now, there are subdivisions and businesses popping up all over. Everyone who lives here has money.

The house I live in sits all by itself on a road heading out of town where we aren't really a part of the community. Everyone in town has lots of things to say about us girls who come from that house. I think that's why the asshole principal hasn't done more to stop the bullying. *He's one of them. I'm a bad kid, so I must deserve it.*

The next ball I throw is at Sarah, one of the biggest snobs in the school. She doesn't threaten me the way the bullies do, but she's one of the ones who will whisper things and laugh when I pass her in the hall. She walks around with her nose stuck in the air like she's better than everyone. I throw the ball as hard as I can and nail her right in her snotty back. I feel a smile spread across my face as she grabs her back and makes a grunting noise. *Ha! That felt great.* She turns around and looks at me with her face all scrunched up. *God she's so ugly, I want to hit her so bad.* My feet stay planted firm as I stand there, staring at her smiling, secretly daring her to say something to me.

A few seconds later, I'm tagged with a ball, and it's my turn to walk off the floor. Just as I get to the side line, I hear her laughing loudly with her equally as snobby friend. I know she's talking crap about me. The rage starts to come back as I stand there with my arms crossed and my fists squeezed tight trying to calm myself. *One more week, Heather. One more week.*

"I swear to God, if that bitch says one more thing, I'm going to beat the living shit out of her!" I say to the girl standing next to me as I watch them across the gym, continuing to laugh and whisper to each other while staring right at me.

"Yeah, right! You aren't going to do anything!" she laughs back at me.

That's what these girls think of me. They see me as a coward because I never fight back. I never even say anything. I walk around with my mouth shut and my head down all the time. Instead of giving them back what they dish out, I run to the useless principal, crying every day.

I'm not a coward, and it's time I show them!

As the laughter continues, I storm across the gym with nothing but Sarah in my sights and the thought of how bad I'm going to pound her in racing through my head. I make it halfway to her when she turns and sees me coming toward her. Her laughter suddenly stops and an "oh, shit" look appears on her face.

That's right, bitch! I'm coming for you, and you better be scared.

"If you got something to say, bitch, say it to my face," I shout as I approach her, pushing her so hard she flies backwards and lands on her ass.

"HEY!" she yells. "You can't push me!" she says in her snotty tone of voice as she picks herself up off the floor.

"Oh, I can do a whole lot more than push you! Say another word about me, Sarah. I dare you!" I antagonize.

The entire gym gets quiet and stops staring in shock, probably wondering what the *coward* is going to do next.

"Hey, what's going on over there?" I hear the gym teacher yell out from across the gym.

"What are you going to do? You BITCH!" says Sarah with her ugly snotty face scrunched.

Everything in my world suddenly turns black as I lunge toward her with my fists swinging, punching her everywhere I can. I punch her in the face, chest, and head. Anywhere my fists will land, I punch swinging harder than I ever have. As we fall to the floor, I grab her by the hair and start banging her head off the gym floor in between punches to her head and face. I can hear everyone screaming out in the background. All the boys in front of me are watching with their heads tucked under the curtain as I attack her like a caged-up lion. I continue to pound on her as our heavy-set female gym teacher tries to pry me off, but she's no match for my 110 pounds of pent-up rage.

Both gym teachers are on me now, pulling me off as Sarah screams out for help while they try to cover her head and face.

"You stupid bitches wanna keep messing with me? I'll fucking show you! I'm no coward!" I scream.

I'm completely out of control with spit flying out of my mouth as I yell. I feel like Ralphie from *The Christmas Story* when he finally had enough from his bully. I don't care how stupid I look, either. The only care I have is how good this feels. *Finally! No more, it's finally going to be over. God, why didn't I do this a long time ago?!*

When they finally pry me off, I look down at my still balled up fists and see a huge clump of her hair in my left hand. I heard it rip out when they pulled me off her. *Who am I right now?* I drop it on the ground. *Gross!* I look up and see Sarah crying; her hair is everywhere, and her face is beet red. The boy's P.E. teacher is holding onto her, and our teacher has a hold of me by my left arm.

"You bitch!" Sarah cries out, and without even thinking about it, I punch her in the face as hard as I can.

"HEY!" yells the boy's teacher as he pulls Sarah further away from me. "That was a cheap shot!"

"That's what the bitch gets for fucking with me!" I gasp out, looking at him with an evil grin. Even though I can hardly breathe, and my chest is burning so bad that it feels like it's on fire, I have never felt so good in my life.

"Let's go, little girl. You're in some major trouble!" says the teacher as she pulls me by the arm, leading me down to the principal's office.

Mr. Clueless is at a loss for words as usual and doesn't have much to say to me. *Shocker!* He tells me that I have to serve two days of "in school" suspension. And since the day is almost over, he has me sit in the nurse's office on a cot for the rest of the day. *That's it? Just two days of ISS and it's over?* I've gotten in way more trouble for way less in other schools. Maybe the asshole knows he shouldn't do much more to me since he let them torture me all this time. I tried to warn him that I couldn't take it anymore, but he didn't listen.

As my big ego diminishes and my feelings of pride start to subside, I realize what will be waiting for me after school, and I'm suddenly filled with panic. I'm supposed to be leaving to go live with Aunt Phoebe in a little over a week.

Oh, no! What did I do? What if they don't let me go now? It's Friday, and Dad will be there to pick me up after school for my weekend visit. I'm sure I won't be able to go now. He's going to be so disappointed in me.

I lie there on the cot the rest of the day, worried sick about what will happen to me when I get home. For the first time since I've been coming to this dreadful school, I find myself wishing I could just stay here.

When I return to the house, Tabitha, the head staff member in charge at the group home, is waiting for me at the dining room table. She's a heavyset Black woman who stands about six feet tall. We all know better than to piss her off. She's one of the nicest, funniest women I've ever met, but she's also very strict. If you're smart, you respect her and stay on her good side.

"Oh my God, Heather, what happened?" Mal asks, running down the stairs toward me with a big smile on her face. *She already knows.*

"Not now, Malory! All you girls get up to your rooms while Heather and I have a talk," demands Tabitha before I have a chance to respond.

Oh, shit! I stand there frozen, unable to look Tabitha in the eye for fear that I will start crying and begging her not to make me stay here any longer. I have to stay strong and defend why I did it. *No more crying!*

"Have a seat, young lady," she says in a calm tone pointing at the chair across from her.

I hesitate before sitting, still afraid to make eye contact. Minutes that feel like hours of silence pass while I sit there with my head down, worrying about what's coming next. *Get on with it already, I can't take this anymore.*

Finally, the silence is broken when she reaches out and grabs my hand. "Heather, look at me," she says in a low, sympathetic voice. I look up at her, determined to stand my ground if I have to. "I know it's not appropriate for me to say this to you, but you're leaving in a week, so I'm going to say it anyway." She pauses. "It's about damn time, girl!" she says with a smile.

Wait, what?

I look at her, shocked and speechless. I'm pretty sure my mouth has dropped open.

When she smiles at me, she continues on to say, "You have been so strong for so long now. You have taken some of the worst bullying I have ever witnessed in my life from those girls, and I've seen a lot. You've kept your head high, and you did what you knew you had to do." She pauses again. "But honey...look at me please."

I look up, trying hard to fight back the tears.

"There is only so much one person can take before they break. We all have our limits, and you finally reached yours. There are no words to explain how incredibly proud of you I am for trying so hard. You are one of the strongest girls that has ever walked through that front door, and I will not punish you for that." She pauses again, and I feel a tear fall down my cheek. "So, the only punishment you are getting is what-ever they have given you at school. Nothing changes in this house for you. Now, get on up to your room and pack your bags. Your dad will be here soon."

Wow! I think as I stand up and hug her as tight as I can. "Thank you so much, Tabitha," I mutter. I can't help but cry tears of relief as I thank her repeatedly before racing off to my room.

I'm in shock when I return to school on Monday and everyone in the school is dying to be friends with me. *Really? That's all it took...for me to kick one of their asses?* Now, I wish I would have done it in the beginning, but I don't care because I'm never going to see these fake bitches again after graduation in a few days.

Everywhere I turn in school, I have someone in my face, laughing, wanting to talk about the fight and how bad I kicked her ass. They're all kissing my ass now and telling me how cool and tough I am. *Blah! Blah! Blah! Fake asses.* Sarah's face is filled with bruises. I actually feel bad about it now. I know the rage that I had inside came from a million different places, and it wasn't all meant for her.

For the rest of the week, I keep to myself. Even when the girls try talking to me, I just smile and nod my head. There is no point in making friends now. And besides, I don't want to be friends with people like them—people who only treat me well because they are afraid of me. They may all live with their parents and not live the crazy life that I do, but in my heart, I know I'm a better person than any of them. I can leave this place with my head held high, knowing that no matter how bad it got at times, they never changed who I am.

I've been taught by a lot of counselors that everything happens for a reason and that God doesn't put anything on your shoulders that you aren't strong enough to carry. At the time, when bad things are happening, I can never understand the reason behind them. What good, loving God would ever put me through the things that I've been through? Why would He put Sheneille, Ophelia, and Lisa through what they went through?

There are still so many things I can't make sense of, but this time, I finally get it. I've seen the kind of person I know I will never become. Even though I've made mistakes in the past, I will never treat someone as bad as those girls treated me. I feel stronger than I ever have, and I will never forget the words that Tabitha spoke to me. I will be forever grateful to her for understanding.

The day comes when it's time to go to Ohio. Our caseworker drives Mal and me to the airport with our parents following behind. Ohio isn't a far enough drive to need to get there by plane, but the caseworker says they can't be held liable in case of a car accident. They have no choice but to fly us. I've never been on a plane before, so I don't mind.

After we say our goodbyes to Mom, Dad, and the boys outside the airport, I tilt my head back and take one last look up at the hot June sun and take in a big breath of fresh summer air.

Bring it on, God! There's nothing I can't handle. I'm ready for this next chapter of my life and whatever it has in store for me. Nothing will ever break me down, and if it does, I will get right back up again!

Runaway Train

Light at the End of the Tunnel

Part Two

"And just as the phoenix rose from the ashes, she too will rise.
Returning from the flames, clothed in nothing but her strength,
more beautiful than ever before."
-Shannen Heartzs

Chapter One

"Hi, Heather. My name is Kyleen, and I'll be your counselor here at Personal Support Group. We're going to assign you a mentor as well. Do you know what a mentor is?"

I shake my head no without looking her in the eye.

"A mentor is someone who will spend extra time with you after school and on the weekends. She's a social worker that will always be there if you need something. Can you tell me more about yourself?"

I look up at the smiley-faced heavy-set women sitting on the other side of the desk. *Here we go again.* Another person who will pretend to understand me and how I'm feeling, but she won't—she couldn't possibly. She'll try, and I'm sure she will have the best intentions, but she will fail. Everyone who has tried to help me fails.

I look back down in my lap and start picking at my fingernails. "What do you wanna know?" I ask.

She smiles politely. "Whatever you want me to know. Tell me about the foster family you're living with now. Is Ellen nice to you? Are you happy there?"

I shake my head yes. *I actually am.* For the first time in a long time, I feel like I belong somewhere. I'm afraid of those feelings, though, because I've felt this way in the past, and I was wrong. So now, I know better than to expect too much, and I know it probably won't last.

"Well, why don't you tell me about your family? Where did you live before you moved in with Ellen?" she continues.

"All over the place," I reply, starting to feel annoyed by all of her questions already.

"Well, can you be more specific? Where were you last that made you happiest?"

The answer to the question is easy so I answer quickly, "My aunt's in Ohio."

"What made you happy about living there? Why did you move back here?"

Jesus! This lady is not going to let up on the questions, so I drop the act and give her what she wants.

I tell her about how horrible the group home was, and how I had such high hopes of a brighter future when I got on the plane that day. I tell her how happy I was at my aunt's, but no matter how hard I tried, I still couldn't be good enough. I couldn't stop smoking, and my aunt and I fought about it constantly. In the end, I just quit trying altogether.

I tell her all about school there and how much different it was. I had so many friends and a boyfriend who was on the varsity football team. I tell her how my heart was ripped right out of my chest the day I had to leave to come back to this dumpy city that's filled with nothing but bad memories. I tell her how unfair it feels that I had to leave, and how hard it is to be perfect so someone will want me to stay. And how angry I am at my aunt for giving up on me and taking away the happiest days of my life.

Mom told me when I started high school that they would be the happiest days of my life, and at first, living with my aunt, I saw exactly what she was talking about. They really were the happiest days of my life, but it didn't last four years like it was supposed to. It only lasted six months. Ever since I came back to Illinois, I've given up on trying to hold on to anything good. I know it will eventually be ripped away from me, anyway. I just want to get through this time of my life and still be breathing at the end of it. All I cared about when I moved back here was surviving; I didn't want to feel anything real for anyone anymore. I was pissed off and not afraid to let people know. *Fuck 'em all!*

Now, after months of being bounced around to numerous foster homes, four different high schools, and even back with my parents for a couple weeks, who now live an hour away in Indiana, I find myself ready to stop being so angry because I've met someone who I really want to believe cares. She doesn't just say she cares like everyone else does; she actually shows it and I'm scared to death to get too close to her. I don't want to lose her and what I have at her house. It feels like home with her. I've never felt that before. Not even at my own house. For the first time in a long time, I don't want to run anymore.

I wonder why it took them so long to send me to her house. My caseworker says it's because Ellen never has openings because she's one of the best foster homes they have, and I believe it. I've gone through almost all the foster families in this area, and I've passed her street so many times and never knew she was there. I wish I could have met her in the beginning.

I feel broken now. My innocence that was once there has been gone for a long time, and I don't know if I can be what she needs me to be. I don't know if I can ever be fixed or be someone that any mother could love, but I at least want to try now. I want to try harder now than I ever have. I'm done running; I want this to be it for me. I know that if I don't stop, I will never make it to where I want to be, and she's the perfect person to help me. She makes me want to be a better person. If I can only manage to not be my own worst enemy like I always have been, I know I can make it this time.

After my hour-long session with Kyleen, she takes me out to the waiting room and introduces me to Robin, my mentor. Robin drives me home from counseling, and in the brief time that we talk, I already know I like her. She seems different from the other social workers who have tried to relate to me before. She doesn't have that fakeness about her like a lot of them, and I'm instantly drawn to her.

"Would you mind if I pick you up after school tomorrow? Maybe we can go see a movie?" suggests Robin as I'm getting out of the car. *I knew I liked her.*

"Ok," I agree anxiously with a smile and then head into the house. "How did it go?" asks Ellen as I sit down at the kitchen table in front of her.

"It was good. Robin seems nice. I like her a lot already," I say, lighting a cigarette.

Ellen lets me smoke. She says she knows I shouldn't be, and she wishes I would quit, but she has the same take on it as Bethany did. She knows I will do it anyway and doesn't want to fight with me over it all the time. I have to find a way to pay for my own cigarettes, so I buy them with the allowance she gives me for doing chores around the house and babysitting. I'm fifteen now, and looking back at my time at Bethany's, I know why Mom was so angry about us being allowed to smoke there.

What the hell was she thinking? I was only twelve. Mom knows that I smoke here, but she isn't going crazy over it like before. She knows she can't stop it.

"That's good that you like her. She seems nice, and you need someone you can trust and talk to about things," says Ellen.

Doesn't she know that I trust her too? I know I'm bad at telling people how I feel because I'm afraid to be rejected, but I trust Ellen more than I've ever trusted anyone.

I was brought here in the middle of the night after being caught on the run from another foster home. Ellen sat me down at the table as soon as I got here and said, "I don't care what you've done in your past or where you've been. I will never judge you for anything, and I will trust you until you give me a reason not to. I will love you and accept you as one of my own as long as you let me. If you're always honest and follow the rules, you will do just fine here. I can be your best friend or your worst enemy; it's entirely up to you."

Ellen is strict, strong-willed, and in many ways, very intimidating. She's a large woman who gets a fierce look in her eyes and a growl in her voice like a bear when you cross her that lets you know she will not be messed with. At the same time, she's funny, loving, forgiving, and will open her home, arms, and heart to anyone—no matter how battered and broken they are. I respect her more than I've ever respected anyone. The last thing I want to do is hurt her or disappoint her.

The house looks very small from the outside, and it amazes me that ten people fit in this tiny home, including Ellen, her husband, Jerry, and their daughter, Brook, who they adopted when she was a toddler. There are two other teenage foster kids. April is the one I share a room with, and Riley is a senior in high school. David, Priscilla, and Katrina are siblings that Ellen and Jerry are in the process of adopting, and Liam is the baby of the family, whom everyone adores. Ellen has three of her own kids from her first marriage who are all grown and on their own. Jerry has a son from his first marriage who is also grown and on his own.

Liam's story is tragic. Ellen has had him since he was only a few months old. He was brought here with numerous broken bones throughout his tiny body and even a concussion. I'll never understand how anyone could ever hurt their newborn baby. Ellen nursed him back to good health like she does for everyone, and she hopes to adopt him too.

The house is never quiet or empty. It's completely chaotic, but I love every bit of the togetherness I feel amid all the chaos. There are always more people here than who live here. The front door opens and closes probably 100 times a day from people coming and going. People who are really family and people who have been accepted as family, and there are lots of them. That's the thing with Ellen—once she lets you in her heart, she never lets you out of it, and you'll always be welcome and a part of the family.

Everyone calls her "Mom," and I have even started calling her mom, too. I thought it would feel weird or like I was being disloyal to my own mother because she's still a big part of my life, but nothing has ever felt more natural. I imagine myself coming back here someday to visit like the others do.

A few weeks after my first counseling session, I had the winter formal dance at school. A boy I was talking to from school asked me to go, and I was so excited I could barely stand it. I love school dances. I went to my first one in the beginning of the school year when I lived with Aunt Phoebe. Mom drove all the way to Ohio just to see me off. She couldn't stand the idea of missing my first real dance, and I was so happy she was there. I love dressing up and feeling like a princess for a day. For a little while, I can pretend I'm someone else—someone special, beautiful, and worthy.

Ellen took me shopping for my dress, and I found a white one that I fell in love with. Robin took me to have my hair and nails done, and everything was perfect. Mom wasn't there to see me off, but that was ok. I had Ellen and Robin, and everything felt right in the world. Robin and I are getting close and spend a lot of time together. It feels like I have an older sister again. *One I never fight with.*

The time came that my date was supposed to pick me up, and before I knew it, he was an hour late. I tried to call him but didn't get an answer. I recognized the looks of pity Ellen and Robin were giving me, but I still had hope until another thirty minutes passed. I had never felt so stupid as I did in that moment. *How could he do that? Jerk!*

All was not lost, though; Robin took me downtown to a nice steak house and made me forget all about him. I don't know what I would do without Ellen and Robin. They have been such positive influences in my life. Without them both, who knows where I'd be. I've never been more thankful and feel so blessed to have real love in my life.

I never talked to that boy again. Well, after I hunted him down at school and gave him a piece of my mind. And, of course, I slapped him after hearing his pathetic excuse for why he stood me up. I changed schools shortly after, but not because of him. I was so far behind in school, and it was impossible to catch up. I am almost to the end of my freshman year and haven't earned one credit all school year.

The only school I stayed at long enough to get a report card was in Ohio, but I was so busy socializing when I was there that I wasn't paying attention to my grades. I thought I could skate through it like I have everywhere else. I've learned real fast how different high school is and that I need to be stable somewhere to focus if I ever want to graduate.

My new school is an alternative school for students who are behind and need to be able to work fast. It's a very small school. There's only a handful of classrooms with around fifteen students in each class.

The school day is very short. I'm only here three hours a day, and that's definitely my favorite part. Everyone works at their own pace and on different subjects depending on our individual needs. The teacher is here to help us if we need it, but there is no instruction in front of the class like a normal school. April goes here too, so that made it a little easier to change schools again.

Selene and I have finally been able to spend time together now that I live here. I go visit her all the time. In the spring, she introduced me to one of her friends named Ben, and we were inseparable for a few months. He took me to his junior prom, to the top of the Sears Tower, and promised to love me forever, but he turned out to be a jerk like everyone else. To make matters worse, he dumped me for the town slut. I heard he cheated on me with her, and I was devastated over it. I don't understand what she has that I don't and why I wasn't enough for him.

Ellen says I need to stop worrying about boys so much. She says I'm boy crazy, and she's probably right. I always have a boyfriend, but it's not like I go looking for them. There's always someone there, waiting, and even though I know it will probably be short-lived, I suck up every bit of attention I get from relationships. I know I should be strong enough to say no, but I can't seem to help myself.

"Heather, you need to get over Ben and stop crying over him. He's a jerk and doesn't deserve you!" says April, standing over me at the table I'm sitting at in school. She sees me trying to scribble out "I love Ben" that's plastered all over the outside of my notebook. *God, I'm pathetic.*

"I know, April. I'm fine, I swear! I hate him!"

April taps me on the shoulder. "Hey, you see that guy standing out in the hall?"

I turn to look and see two Black boys standing outside the door laughing and messing around. "Which one?" I ask.

"The hot one with the light skin," she replies.

"Yeah, I see him. What about him?" I ask uninterested and turn back to my notebook.

"His name is Shane. He's in my class, and he asks me about you all the time. He thinks you're hot and wants to talk to you."

"April, he's Black! I can't date him!" *Shit! Why did I say that?*

"So what, Heather? Are you a racist?" she asks me shocked.

"No, of course I'm not," I reply quickly, trying to redeem myself from sounding like a total bitch. "You know me better than that, but my mom and dad would kill me!"

The boy who stood me up was Black, and Mom gave me the, "I told you so! I told you they were no good and to stay away from them," speech. I know Mom is wrong. Not all Black people are the same. They are people just like us. We all make mistakes and screw up sometimes. How does the color of our skin have anything to do with it? Bad people come in all colors. Besides, look how Mom acts. She's not perfect just because she's white! I've never been racist. I've always given people a chance no matter who they are, where they came from, or what color their skin is. Mom's family is mixed race, so what's the big deal, anyway?

I look over my shoulder toward Shane again. *He is really cute, and screw Mom! What does she know?* His skin is light and reminds me of silky caramel. For a split second, he looks up and we make eye contact. I can see all the way from over here that he has the prettiest light brown eyes I have ever seen. They almost glow in a way. He has high cheekbones and perfect lips. The way he looks at me sends a chill down my spine, and I feel the butterflies in my stomach start to flutter. *Oh, no!*

I quickly turn my head back to my notebook. "I don't know, April, is he a gangbanger? I don't want anything to do with guys like that!"

She laughs. "No, Heather, he's not. I swear. Do you want me to say something to him?"

"No, don't do that right now. I don't even know him, April." I hesitate and then quickly add, "I'll think about it, ok?"

"Ok," she replies with a quick smirk.

"April! I mean it. Don't say anything to him!"

The bell rings and she heads to her class, smiling at me over her shoulder.

Damn her!

After school, Shane approaches me outside and says hi. *I'm going to kill her!* We make small talk, but I'm hesitant, trying to keep my responses short and not making too much eye contact. The attraction I have to him scares me, and I'm not ready to trust anyone yet. *Hell, I can't even trust myself!*

In the weeks that follow, he is very persistent and tries to sweet talk me every day until I finally give into his charm. April was right. He is different, and him being trouble is the least of my worries. Mom is going to flip out when I tell her about him, but not just because of his race, but he's also nineteen. I don't care. Maybe I won't even tell her. I don't see my parents that much, anyway. They live an hour away. *They would never have to know.*

Chapter Two

"Tell me more about your family," says Kyleen. "In all the months we've been seeing each other, you don't talk about them very much."

"I don't talk about them because I don't know what to say. I don't see them very often anymore. I guess now that I'm happy where I am, I try really hard not to let what goes on at home bother me so much. I really do miss them," I reply, and my words sadden me. I feel as if I'm being disloyal to my family for feeling happy.

"Well, what's going on with them? Tell me about them," she prods.

"Well, Mom is a mess." *What else is new?*

"How so?"

"I'm not sure what's going on with her lately because, like I said, I barely see them, but I know things aren't right at home."

"Heather, I'm going to need you to be more specific," she says teasingly with a smile on her face.

"Well, in the beginning of the school year when I lived with Aunt Phoebe, Dad was arrested in a drug bust that was all Mom's fault." As I say this, I feel my sadness quickly start to turn to anger at the thought of the memory.

"How did that happen?" she asks, looking up quickly from her notepad with one eyebrow raised.

"He bought her a junky car to drive because he was tired of the van getting towed every time she gets arrested for drinking and driving. When they moved to Indiana, she said it was because she wanted to get my brothers out of the town before they were old enough to get involved in gangs. But I think it had more to do with Dad getting her away from all of her drug dealers."

"I see; keep going."

"When they first moved there, she drove the car out here on a drug binge and traded it for drugs. Dad eventually came out here to try to find the car and found it on the side of the road with the drug dealers standing next to it. He told them if they didn't let him take it, he would call the police." I pause for a second to think about what they could have done to him. *Thank God nothing bad happened!* "He still bowls in a league here. And a week after he got the car back, he drove out here to go bowling and was pulled over for not stopping at a stop sign or something. The cops arrested him and told him they had been watching his car. They knew it was used to deal drugs, but I know they were watching the drug dealers and not my dad!" I add with anger. "I don't know why he stays with her sometimes. She always ruins everything for everyone!"

"Heather, try to stay on track. Keep telling me the story. Then you can tell me how you feel about it, ok?"

I let out a sigh and continue. "They stripped the car down and found a bunch of cocaine hidden inside the back seat. He tried to explain what my mom had done, but they wouldn't listen to him. Grandpa bailed him out of jail, so he wasn't there long, but the railroad told him they couldn't let him work for them until his name was cleared."

"Were they able to clear his name?"

What are you writing, a book?!

"I don't know what Mom had to do to fix everything, but eventually, Dad's name was cleared, and he could go back to work. I was so ashamed of her when that happened. I was glad I was far away and didn't have to deal with what all my old friends were saying about it. The whole thing made it to the front page of the newspaper. I'm sure they didn't make it front-page news that Dad was innocent when it was all over, either."

"I can tell you're angry, but what else do you feel?"

"I feel sorry for Dad sometimes, but I'm also angry that he doesn't do more to stop her. I miss my brothers, and I feel sorry for them, too. But I'm glad; right now, I'm happy, and I'm free from all of Mom's craziness. I still love her more than anything, but I've learned to accept that we will never have the relationship I've always wished for."

Kyleen looks at me with sad eyes and says, "You know, you shouldn't have to accept that, and none of this is your fault. You're allowed to be angry at her, Heather."

"I know, but I'm sick of being angry all the time. I just want to be happy for once. I can't change what she does, so what's the point in being angry about it all the time?"

She smiles and gets an "ah-ha" look on her face. "You know, that's very true, Heather. Do you think that's why you've run away so much? Because you're so angry all the time?"

Duh, lady! I think to myself, but I'm wise enough not to be a smartass about it toward her.

"Yeah, that's the only reason I've ever run away, and maybe sometimes because I was scared, too."

"What were you scared of?"

"I don't know...new places, starting over, and living with strangers, I guess. Some of the people I lived with weren't nice, so I would just leave."

"Does your dad use drugs too, or just your mom?" she asks, changing the subject.

"My dad didn't do that, if that's what you're getting at! It was all Mom's fault. He didn't do anything wrong!" I snap back at her, starting to feel defensive.

"I know, Heather, I believe you. I was just wondering if he has ever done drugs too, or if he just drinks."

Oh.

I relax a little in my seat and tell her the few memories I have of Dad doing drugs when I was little, but I have no memory of him doing it after we moved away from Ohio. If he does do drugs, he's good at hiding it.

"Tell me about your sister. When's the last time you talked to her?"

"I haven't talked to Malory in a long time, and I really miss her. She only lasted a week in Ohio at Uncle Derek's. He didn't do anything wrong. She just couldn't take being away from her stupid boyfriend, Tony. I swear, he is ruining her life. I wish she could just leave him alone; she will do anything for him."

"How did she get all the way back here?" she asks.

"He sent her a bus ticket, and she ran away in the middle of the night. I knew she was planning to do it. I didn't want her to go, but she's my sister, so I couldn't tell on her. She was caught about two weeks later."

"Wow! That's a long time to be gone. Where did she stay?"

"She was staying in a tent in some woods by his house. My mom knew she was there and didn't want to turn her in, so she was taking her food and stuff. She got caught because she got a bad kidney infection, and my mom had to take her to the ER.

"After that, she moved around for a while before they sent her back to Anchusa. She got into legal trouble there for beating a girl up on the school bus, so the judge sent her to detention. Now, she has to stay there until she turns eighteen." *I wonder what she's doing right now. I wish she could come live at Ellen's with me. She would love it there, too.*

"When was the last time you saw her?" she asks, looking down at her pad of paper where she's been scribbling notes.

"When I first came back from Ohio, Mal and I lived together in a foster home for a little bit. We got along well there."

"Why do you think you got along better there?"

"I don't know, probably because we equally hated the place and the people we were with. We got to go home together for a few weeks after we left there, but it didn't last because Mom was just as much a mess as both of us."

"Why do you think you were a mess?"

"I was still pissed off about having to leave Ohio, and Malory didn't care about anything as long as she couldn't be with Tony. We went to school there for one day and didn't even make it through the whole day before leaving the school. Later that night, we stole Mom's junky car to run back here. We stayed with older friends of ours at their apartment for the weekend before we turned ourselves in. We've been separated ever since."

"Tell me again why you were so happy in Ohio. What was so different there?"

I've told her about this before. She is always asking me to repeat things, and it's really annoying.

"I don't know. It was just different."

"In what way?" she prods.

"I didn't get bullied there like I did before. I had a lot of friends, a boyfriend, and I got to be with family."

"What happened, exactly? Why did you have to come back? You said before you got in trouble for smoking a lot, but I know there must be more to it than that. So, I'm just wondering what else could have happened?"

"Like I told you before, me and my aunt got along really well at first. But then, she started spazzing out all the time on me for smoking, so I was always grounded for that. Toward the end, I know there were other reasons."

"What do you mean by that?"

"I don't know. I was really close to my uncle when I first moved there. We got along better than me and my aunt did. And in the end, he wouldn't even talk to me anymore."

"Why?"

"I don't know...maybe because I was always fighting with my aunt. Or maybe because she was always yelling at him and accusing him of treating me better than my cousin, Christopher. My mom said she was jealous."

"Do you think he treated you better than your cousin?"

"I guess maybe in a way, but I think it was only because I was a girl. He was the same way with his seven-year-old daughter, Gracey. Plus, I think he felt sorry for me in a way."

"Oh, yeah? How so?"

"I can just tell by the way he looked at me sometimes that he felt bad. I've seen that look enough times."

"Ok, back to my original question: was there something specific that happened to make your aunt think he was treating you better?"

"I don't think so," I say, trying to remember.

Oh, wait!

"There was one time when Christopher and I were going to the Friday night football game. My uncle gave me $10.00 and only gave Christopher $5.00. I know that wasn't fair. I felt bad about it at the time because Christopher and I were close. I know it must have hurt his feelings. That was the only thing he ever did that I can remember. We talked more than he and Christopher did, but they never got along, even before I lived there. I guess it was after that when I would hear my aunt fighting with him about it all the time. She couldn't let it go. And one day, he just quit talking to me altogether."

"How did that make you feel?"

"Really sad because I finally felt like I had a real dad in a way. One that really talked to me, instead of criticizing me all the time. When I look back at it now, I know he was the one who really pushed for me to come live there."

"How do you know that?"

"Because whenever we would go there to visit them during Christmas or Thanksgiving, he would always pay a lot of attention to me and tell me how much he wished I could come live with them. When I found out we were going there, I was so happy and I knew it was him who really wanted it. Not that my aunt didn't, but do you know what I mean?"

"Yeah, I know what you mean. Have you talked to your aunt or uncle since you left?"

"Just my aunt once or twice on the computer, but we don't say much. Things are different now."

"What's different?"

"I'm mad at her."

"Tell me more about that," she says as she continues to write.

Holy hell how many times do I have to explain myself?

"I feel like she took everything away from me. I mean, I know I wasn't perfect when I was there, but I don't think I was that bad, either. She definitely didn't see me at my worst, and I just wish she would have given me more of a chance. One day, I even heard her say that the state still wasn't paying her for me to be there like they were supposed to, and that upset me. Because what am I...her niece or a paycheck?" I say, wiping the tears that have suddenly started falling down my cheeks.

After moments of silence, she changes the subject. "Tell me about Ellen. What makes her so different from anyone else you've had in your life?"

"It's hard to explain. I can talk to her, for one. I've never been able to talk to my mom, my aunt, or anyone like I can talk to her. I trust her more than I have anyone, and it scares the crap out of me."

"Why does it scare you?"

"Because I don't want to lose what I have there. And every time I ever feel like things are finally going to be ok, I'm wrong."

"Sometimes, when people have abandonment issues, they find ways of protecting themselves from being hurt. With the first signs of trouble, they will shut down in order to shield themselves, or they act out so they can be the ones to leave instead of being left. Do you think you've done that at all with your aunt or your mom or anyone else you've lived with?"

I never really thought about it that way before.

"Yeah, I guess I probably have."

"Well, I'm going to work with you so that doesn't happen at Ellen's and try to teach you new ways to deal with things because it sounds like Ellen really cares about you. It's a good place for you to live. How has your mom dealt with your happiness at Ellen's? From what you've told me before, it sounds like she's gotten a little jealous in the past when you've gotten close to other mother figures."

"Surprisingly, she's not jealous of her. I think she has accepted the same things I have about our relationship. She used to be so uptight about everything all the time, and now she's so quiet about everything. She almost seems defeated in a way and sad. Or maybe she's just tired of fighting, just like I am. I feel bad about it sometimes."

"Why do you think you feel bad?"

"Because I talk to Ellen about everything: boys, sex, Mom, Mal, and my childhood...all of it. I've never been able to open up to my mom the way I can with her. She doesn't judge me for anything. She just gives the best advice she can. Of course, she lets me know when she thinks I'm wrong and what I can do better, but I don't get mad at her for it. I love her for it. Plus, I've been calling her 'Mom,' but everyone calls her 'Mom,' so it feels normal to call her that. I kinda feel like I'm not being loyal to my mom by getting so close to her."

I wish I could be that close to my mom. I let out a chuckle. "I've learned I can't tell Ellen a lie, either. Not that I was ever big on lying, anyway, but I can't even try with her."

"Why do you think that is?" she asks. "Because I respect her too much, I guess."

"Well, that's good, Heather. That's how a mother and daughter relationship should be. Trust, respect, and good communication are the biggest keys, and I'm really happy you've found that with her. Ok, our hour is up, but I'll see you next week. Until then, I want you to continue writing in your journal and talking to Robin and Ellen whenever something is bothering you, ok?"

"Ok," I say as I get up to leave the room.

It's summer now, and things with me and Shane have gotten pretty hot and heavy. My instincts tell me he's trouble and I should leave him alone, but I can't seem to break away from him. He tells me everything that I want to hear. Even though I know in my heart it's all lies, I pretend to believe him anyway.

I found out he has a one-year-old son. He swears he's not with the mother anymore, but when I page him, he doesn't answer for two days. I know he's lying. He seemed so different at first. But as soon as he knew he had me hooked, he started showing me the real Shane. He's everything bad that April swore he wasn't, and I know I need to find a way to break free before I get stuck forever.

I've gotten close to Shane's friend, Darius, and sometimes, he hints at things about Shane. He won't come right out and tell me what's going on because he's afraid to piss Shane off. I've heard from Darius' girlfriend that Shane and all his friends run trains on girls at Darius' house. She tells me to watch out because they might try to do it with me, too, but I don't know if I believe her because she tells me these things when she and Darius are fighting.

At first, I didn't know what a train was, and I felt stupid for not knowing, so I didn't ask her. Later, I talked to Darius about it and he explained to me that a train is when multiple guys sleep with a girl at the same time in a sort of tag team fashion. I was so disgusted. The thought of Shane doing that makes me sick to my stomach. Darius tells me not to worry and that Shane hasn't done that since we've been together. The thought of him *ever* doing that is just gross, and I know Darius isn't telling me everything.

Shane and his friends have a nickname for me. They call me "Bay Watch." Darius says it's because I'm different from the other girls they have around. He says I look like a Barbie doll with my long blonde hair, tan skin, and thin frame. I think Darius has a crush on me, but I know he would never tell me or disrespect the friendship we have.

He says I don't need to worry about Shane ever trying to share me because I'm his little trophy, and he gets pissed off when other guys even look at me. I'm not sure if I take that as a compliment or not. It seems so degrading. If all I am is his little "trophy" to show off to all his friends, what's he doing behind my back when he's not answering my calls for days at a time? I wonder all the time if he's still with the mother of his child. I've never met his family or his son, and sometimes, I feel like he's trying to keep me hidden from his real life. *Hidden from what, though?*

Ellen doesn't like Shane, but she says I need to learn from my mistakes. She knows if she tells me I can't see him, I will do it anyway, and I need to figure it out on my own. He never comes over here and hangs out. Ellen doesn't like that. She says it's disrespectful. She can tell when I haven't heard from him because I walk around upset, and she can't stand it. She's right. I probably would be with him, anyway, even if she told me I couldn't. For now, I'm glad that's a fight I don't have to have with her.

Chapter Three

One hot summer night a few weeks later, Ellen, Robin, and I are sitting at the table playing Scrabble when my world starts to spin. If I knew just how out of control things were going to get, maybe I would have changed everything, but then again, maybe not.

"Whoa!" I say, grabbing the table to stop myself from falling when I suddenly feel dizzy. *I must have stood up too fast.*

Ellen looks up from the board, gives me a funny look, and pauses for a minute before she asks, "Heather, are you pregnant?"

"What?" I ask in shock, almost spitting out a mouth full of pop. "No, Mom, I'm not pregnant!"

The look on her face tells me that she isn't buying it. I look over at Robin and she's staring at me in shock.

I look back at Ellen's questioning glare. "What, Mom? Why are you looking at me like that? I'm not pregnant, I swear!"

"Are you sure, Heather? When's the last time you got your period?" asks Ellen.

"I don't know, but I know there's no way I'm pregnant!" I insist.

"Well, getting lightheaded like that is a pregnancy symptom, and I've noticed it's been happening to you a lot lately," she replies.

I stare down at my tiles and think about what she's saying, but I know there's just no way. "I just stood up too fast, that's all."

"I don't know, Robin, what do you think?" asks Ellen, looking at Robin.

"Maybe we should get her a test," Robin replies. "Ughh...you guys, stop! I'm not pregnant!" I laugh.

Ellen isn't going to let the subject die. And after the game is over, Robin goes to the store and comes back with a test. *They're crazy.* I know I'm not pregnant, so I'm not worried about taking the stupid test. *Should I be?*

After Robin shows me how to use the test, she leaves the bathroom and I find myself wondering if it's possible. I don't really keep track of my periods, so I don't remember when the last one was, but I don't think it's been that long. I pee on the stick, leave it on the sink, and go back to the kitchen.

"Ok, done. Are you happy now?" I ask, smiling at Ellen.

"It's nothing to smile about, Heather, and I'll be happy when I know you're not pregnant!" says Ellen sternly.

Robin looks up at me, and I can tell she's worried. "Robin, don't worry I'm not pregnant," I reassure her.

"Heather, are you on birth control?" she asks. "No," I say quietly, lowering my head.

"Has he been using condoms?" she quickly asks.

I continue to look down at the table without answering, and she knows.

"Oh, Heather! What were you thinking? Don't you know you can catch things from guys, too? Honey, you don't just have to worry about getting pregnant!" says Robin in a panicked voice.

My mind goes back to the first time Shane and I had sex and all the times since. I never even considered I could get pregnant, or catch anything from him. It seems stupid when I think about it now. I guess I wasn't thinking. I thought I was invincible to these things. *I'm so dumb!*

My heart starts to race when Robin goes to check the test. She's only gone for a moment, but it's the longest moment of my life. *Shit! What did I do?* When she walks back into the room with the test in her hand she has a huge grin on her face, and the overwhelming fear I am feeling is instantly turned to relief.

"See! I told you I wasn't pregnant!" I say with excited relief, looking at Ellen, but the look on her face scares me. *Shit...she's not happy.*

"I'm still not convinced. Maybe you're not that far along. We need to get you into the doctor to have you checked out for everything. I should have been talking to you more. I didn't realize you were having unprotected sex. I thought you were smarter than that, Heather!" she snaps with a frown on her face.

But who have I ever really had to talk to about these things until now? My mom is so overbearingly protective that she won't even have a conversation with me about any of it.

"I'm sorry, Mom. I wasn't thinking," I reply, feeling my world once again crashing down around me. I hate making her angry.

"Yeah, I guess you weren't. From now on, use that smart brain I know you have in your head, little girl," she says with a sigh, and her angry look turns to sadness.

Shit, that's even worse!

A week later, Robin takes me to the doctor, and I am shocked when they tell me I am in fact pregnant. As if it couldn't get any worse, they tell me I also have a yeast infection and a sexually transmitted disease. I've never felt so many different emotions at once. I'm angry, sad, and confused. I feel completely disgusted with myself, and I'm scared as hell. *How am I supposed to tell my mom and dad about this?* They don't even know that Shane exists. Now, I have to tell them I'm pregnant, my boyfriend is Black, *and* I caught an STD from him? They are going to kill me. *Dad is really going to think I'm his daughter from hell now.*

"Heather, what are you going to do?" asks Robin, breaking the silence that filled the car. Robin has been crying ever since the doctor told me, but I can't cry right now. I just feel numb. *This can't really be happening.*

"What do you mean? I guess I'm going to have a baby," I reply with a hint of sarcasm. I know about abortion, adoption, and all of that, but those things haven't crossed my mind as options. I don't feel like I have any other options. No matter how much I know that I can't possibly have a baby at fifteen but killing it or giving it away just doesn't seem right either. *I'm trapped!*

"Heather, I'm going to tell you something I don't ever tell the kids I work with, but we're close enough, and right now, it's appropriate," says Robin, pausing. "I gave a baby up for adoption when I was seventeen," she continues, crying even harder.

"Really?" I ask shocked.

She tells me the whole story about her and her high school boyfriend and how hard it was to give up her son. She tells me how she had an open adoption, so the parents still send her pictures of him. Someday, she will be able to meet him. The whole story makes me sad because I can see how much it hurts her. I know she's telling me to let me know that I have that as an option, but I just don't think I can do that. *Look how sad it makes her.*

Dear Diary,

The last four weeks have been some of the hardest weeks I've ever been through. Just when I think life can't get any worse...BOOM! A bomb blows up in my face. I can't blame anyone else but myself this time though. I can't believe I was so damn stupid. From how far along I am, I know I must have gotten pregnant the very first time I slept with Shane. How could I have not considered getting pregnant or catching a disease from him? I hate myself for being so dumb.

I'm due February 28th, which is only four days after my 16th birthday! How ironic! Instead of getting a car for my sweet 16, I'll be getting a baby. Happy freaking birthday to me! Ellen has been great, but Mom is a total mess over it. Shane hasn't been the greatest, either. I keep getting pressure from everyone to do different things, and I just don't know what to do. My heart tells me that abortion is wrong, and I know I will never be able to do that.

Ellen doesn't believe in abortion, so I don't need to ask her opinion on that. She says she will support whatever decision I make. She says if I decide to keep the baby, I can still live with her, and she will do anything she can to help me. Ellen's sister wants to adopt the baby, and Ellen thinks I should consider that. How could I have a baby that I've given up, but still see it all the time and watch it call someone else "Mom"? I know that would hurt too much, and I won't even consider doing it.

It took Mom a while, but she finally told Dad. When I asked her what he said about it, all he said was, "I ain't raising it!" I couldn't believe that's all he had to say about it! Where's my dad? Why don't I have a dad who will tear down walls to protect me? Why doesn't he want to kill Shane for getting me pregnant? Why isn't he mad? He should be screaming at me, but instead, he just avoids looking at me or talking to me. I know it seems stupid for me to wish for that because I don't want any more pressure. But for once, it would be nice to have a dad that tries to protect me.

I don't know why I'm so surprised by his reaction. He has never protected me from anything. Maybe he doesn't protect me because my mom tries to do enough of that for the both of them with her craziness, but I know that's just me making excuses for him. Mom wants me to have an abortion. I keep telling her there's no way I can, but she keeps insisting it's my only choice. "Heather, you're living in a foster home. How are you supposed to have a baby? They may tell you that they won't take it away from you, but you can't trust the state. They WILL take it away from you!" I swear, she beats those words into my head on a daily basis. She is also convinced it's going to be harder on me because the baby will be mixed. She says I'm being naïve, and that people aren't as accepting as I want to believe they are. She thinks the kid will have it hard in school, and everything will be harder for me because I will always be judged for it, and blah, blah, blah. I think she's the one who isn't as accepting of it, though. She's the one who will judge me more than anyone. How dare I shame our family. Puke!

I know Ellen will be here for me. When she says she's going to do something, unlike Mom, she actually does it. Shane has been acting extra crazy since I found out. He wants me to have an abortion, too, and we *fight about it all the time. A few weeks ago when I paged him, the mother of his child called me back, asking who I was. At first, I was scared to death because all I ever hear about her is how crazy and mean she is. I thought about pretending I paged the wrong number, but then decided to tell her the truth. She was pissed when I told her everything, and she threatened to beat my ass. I kept asking her why she was so mad at me. I didn't know about her, either. Shane is the one that's doing something wrong, not me or her. She wouldn't listen to me. She hung up on me and hasn't called back. Shane was really mad at me for telling her, but how does he expect to keep a baby hidden from her or anyone else? He denies that he's with her, even though she told me enough for me to know he's lying. I still can't leave him alone, though. How the hell can I now?*

I'm so scared, and I don't want to be alone, so I keep putting up with him, hoping that somehow everything will magically be ok. I hate him for what he's putting me through. I think I hate myself even more for being such a dumbass for him. You would think after giving me a disease, I would never want to talk to him again, but I'm such a sucker! The medicine they put me on for it made me throw up every day for a week. They were huge pills that were hard to even get down. Every day like clockwork an hour after taking it, I'd be in the bathroom at school, throwing it right back up. I don't know if it was the pills or the pregnancy making me so sick, but I was terrified that the disgusting STD wasn't going to go away since I couldn't keep the meds down. Somehow, it still did its job because they rechecked me and it was gone. I'll never forgive him for it. And to make matters worse, he accused me of giving it to him! I haven't been with anyone but him since I met him, and I can't even believe he would think that. I sit at home crying over him all the time. How could I be with anyone else?

Ellen's daughter, Darcey, just had a miscarriage and was so depressed over it she laid in Ellen's bed for two weeks. I can tell by the way that she looks at me now that she hates my guts. I don't think she's ever liked me that much to begin with, and I guess I don't blame her. It's gotta be hard to see your mom loving so many other kids. Now, here I am, carrying around a baby that I don't know what to do with when she wants nothing more but to be a mom. I feel really bad for her. I'm trying to understand why she's mad at me. It's not like I wanted any of this to happen. I wish I could make it be her and not me. I would give anything to turn back the clock on the mistakes I've made.

Robin is the only one who doesn't give me an opinion of what she thinks I should do. Everyone else thinks they know, and they don't hesitate to tell me, but not Robin. Even though Ellen says she will support whatever I do, I know how strong her opinion about abortion is, so I can't talk to her about that being an option. I really don't want that as an option, anyway. Robin just listens when I need to talk about it. She lets me know how much she loves me, and I know she means it. We've gotten so close since I've lived here. Ellen keeps saying it's not appropriate how close we have gotten. She thinks we are more like friends and says it isn't healthy. I look up to her like an older sister, not a friend. She feels like family now, and I don't know what I'll do if they take her away from me. Even Kyleen and my caseworker both think we're too close. I don't understand it. They wanted me to be close to someone. They wanted me to open up. I finally found someone I can do that with, and now we're too close so they want to take her away??? Make up your fucking minds, people!

The lady who owns PSG, where I go to counseling, has offered to pay for the abortion if that's what I decide to do. I can't tell anyone she's offered because there could be huge consequences for her. She doesn't want me to feel like I don't have that as an option because it's expensive, and I can't come up with the money. But I don't want that, even though I know I'm too young to have a baby. I don't want to be a teenage mom, but having an abortion seems so wrong. I don't want to go to hell, so what now, God? Where are you when I need You the most? If You're really up there...why can't You find a way to tell me what I'm supposed to do? I swear to You, if You could make this go away like it never happened, I will find a way to make it up to You. I would do anything to be able to start over and make this whole nightmare end.

Ellen says I can't see Shane anymore because of how he's acting and treating me. How can she expect me to break away from him now when

I'm carrying his baby? I can't leave him now, and I think it's crazy that she expects me to. I hate everything he's put me through and all the lies that he tells, but I feel stuck and so confused. I love Ellen, and I respect her, but I just can't follow that rule. I've been sneaking around to see him. I've gotten caught, and I keep getting in trouble, but I just can't stop. I know she's right. I know he's trouble. I know he's going to keep hurting me, but I'm carrying his baby, so what am I supposed to do?

I have to go now. It's almost midnight, and everyone's asleep. He'll be waiting for me out in the alley soon, so I need to get ready. I'll write again soon, Diary.

Lost & trapped, Heather

Chapter Four

Weeks later, I'm sitting on the couch next to Ellen when I finally gather the courage to ask her, "Mom, do you care if I go for a walk?"

Without looking up from the blanket she's been crocheting for Liam, she looks at me with suspicious eyes. "A walk where?"

"Down by the river to read my book," I reply quickly, lying through my teeth.

"Are you sure that's all you're going to do?" she asks, looking over at me with that "I know what you're up to" stare.

Fuck! I hate lying to her.

"Heather, I asked you a question. Are you SURE that's what you're doing?"

I know she can tell when I'm lying to her, but I can't tell her the truth—not about this. I look toward the TV to try to avoid eye contact. "Yeah, I'm sure, Mom," I reply as I feel her gaze burning a hole right through me. *Crap! My ears are on fire. I wonder if she notices.*

"You know, Heather, I try to guide you in the right direction and teach you how to make the best decisions. But if you're going to insist on seeing him anyway, I know I can't stop you. I just wish you would realize how much better you deserve."

"I know, Mom. I swear I'm just going to read my book." *Liar, liar, pants on fire!* I can't stand letting her down, and I'm ashamed for still wanting to see him because I know I shouldn't. He's become like a drug that I'm hooked on. I know he's poisonous, but for some reason, I just can't stop. *What the hell is wrong with me?*

I got caught sneaking out of my bedroom window in the middle of the night a few weeks ago. I can't do that anymore because she's watching for it. Instead, I started going out the back door, but I got caught doing that the first time I tried. When I came home, I snuck in real quiet. *Or so I thought.* The house was pitch-black. And just when I thought I got away with it, I heard her call out from across the dark living room, "Have fun, did ya?" Startled, my only reaction was, "Oh, shit!"

We laugh about it now, but I was grounded after that. I hate hurting and disappointing her. She knows it, so she doesn't yell at me. She just tells me how much she's worried about me. I feel bad for being so sneaky and lying all the time. *Is this what Kyleen was talking about? Am I inadvertently setting myself up to fail?*

After I poorly convince her that I'm just going to read my book, I start walking toward our usual meeting spot. There's an abandoned baseball field behind the YMCA a few blocks away. It's far away from the road where no one ever goes. It's the perfect spot for us to meet and hang out. Behind the field, there are some woods with a bike trail that leads down to the river. Sometimes, I go there by myself just to think. There's a bench right by the water where I sit when I need time to myself.

Something about being by the water always relaxes me and helps me clear my head. Maybe it goes back to my childhood at the beach and all the good memories I have of my family spending time there. Most of the time, I take a book with me and spend hours reading, but not today. Today's book is just a decoy for what I really have planned. I love that spot, though; it's my favorite place in the whole world when nothing else seems to be going right.

Shane has been so demanding about me having an abortion that I've actually been considering it. I made an appointment last week, but I couldn't bring myself to go through with it. He doesn't know it yet. How am I supposed to tell him I couldn't do it? I'm so scared of what his reaction will be. I feel so ripped apart by what everyone else thinks I should do that I can barely think straight.

Maybe Mom is right and an abortion is the best choice. I know there's no way I can go through my whole pregnancy, get attached to my baby, and then just give it away. I know I would end up keeping the baby. But I also know that having a baby at fifteen is crazy. On top of all of that, I'm a ward of the court, so my baby will be, too, which makes everything harder. *What if I can't be what this baby needs? Will they take the baby away from me? Then, will the baby end up having a life just like mine?* I can't stand the thought of that.

As I approach the parking lot by the baseball field where his car is parked, I start to get nervous. He has his radio turned up loud, and his friend, Jeremy, is with him. I can see from where I am that he has a forty-ounce bottle of beer wrapped in a paper bag in his hand. And from his demeanor, he seems drunk. He's stumbling around, singing the rap song that's playing while waving his free hand in the air. Seeing him from this angle makes me wonder what I'm so attracted to. I give Mal such a hard time about Tony, and now look at me. The level I've sunk to makes me no better or different than her.

He turns. and sees me approaching. "Hey! What took your ass so long? You think I got all day to wait on you?"

Oh, goody! He's in a great mood.

"What the hell, Shane? You know I have to lie to her to get out of the house, and sometimes it takes time. You don't have to talk to me like that!" I respond as I approach him.

He smiles, leans in, and plants a hard kiss on me that jams my lips into my teeth. *Ow!* I can smell the beer on him, and for a moment I cringe. The smell takes me back to my childhood, and I suddenly want to jump out of my skin.

"You know I'm just playin' wit you, girl. Get your fine ass in the car so we can go," Shane says, laughing as he slaps me on the ass.

Wow. What am I doing here with him? Ellen is right. He has no respect for me. My gut is screaming at me not to get into the car. *Just go home, stupid girl!* I ignore my instinct and climb into the back seat.

"Where are we going?" I call out over the blaring radio as he heads down Route 45.

"We're going to a party, girl. We need to celebrate," he replies, turning down the radio.

"Celebrate what?" I ask.

He turns the rear view mirror to make eye contact with me. "You know what girl, stop playin'!" he says, giggling.

Is he freaking kidding me? He wants to celebrate killing our baby? Man, is he going to be pissed when he finds out there's nothing to celebrate. Who has parties in the middle of the day, anyway? It's barely noon!

We pull into the trailer park that's close to the highway by the mall. I've never driven through here before. It's a nicer trailer park compared to some I've seen. The trailers are newer and well taken care of. It reminds me of the campground Grams used to spend her summers at. I loved staying there with her. I would fish the pond every day and make my own poles out of sticks. I'd find old line and hooks that were tossed out along the shore line, and I'd use cigarette butts as bait when Grams wouldn't let me use up all her bologna. The memory makes me smile. *Grams must be disappointed in me right now.* I don't know if it's the pregnancy or the shame, but I suddenly feel nauseous.

I don't recognize most of the people here, and I'm starting to feel really uncomfortable. Shane keeps leaving me alone to sneak off to the back bedroom with some other people. *I wonder what he's doing back there.* Everyone's drunk, and I keep dodging all the offers to have a drink or take a hit of pot. My gut is telling me not to trust anyone right now.

I spot Wendy, who has a really bad reputation among all of Shane's friends. I latch onto her even though I have a nagging suspicion she's slept with my boyfriend. I've heard that she let all of them run a train on her once. Even though the thought disgusts me, she's the only familiar face in the room. *She'll have to do...for now.* I find a spot on the couch next to her in the tiny living room and watch all the partying going on around me.

I try to distract myself from the uneasy feeling by talking to Wendy when Shane comes back from the bedroom for the third time. He plops down on the couch next to me. "Here, drink this," he says, holding out a bottle of beer and looking at me with a look in his eye I've never seen before. Something is different about him, and I wonder if he's on something besides pot and alcohol.

"No, I don't want it," I reply, pushing the bottle out of my face. "Why don't you want it, Heather?"

"Because I don't feel like drinking," I say quickly.

The tone in his voice turns angry. "Why not? You're allowed to now, aren't you?" he asks suspiciously.

Shit!

I tell the first lie that pops into my head, "Yeah, Shane, I'm allowed to but I can't. I have to go back home soon, and I can't go home smelling like alcohol." This is not the time or place to tell him the truth.

I try to avoid his questioning glare by turning back toward Wendy. He elbows me in the arm. "Hey! Don't look away from me when I'm trying to talk to you!" he demands.

"OW! What the fuck, Shane? What the hell is wrong with you?" I ask, grabbing my arm. "Let's go," I say, standing up. "Take me home!" I demand.

"We're not going anywhere until I fucking say so," he says as he pulls me back down on the couch by the back pocket of my shorts.

"Shane, knock it off! What's wrong with you?" I feel all eyes on us as the room grows quiet.

Shane reaches out and grabs me by my cheeks. He squeezes hard as

229

he forces me to look at him. "You didn't have the fucking abortion, did you?"

Oh, no! I don't want to answer him, so I just stare at him with tears starting to fill my eyes from the pain on my cheeks, and the embarrassment from everyone watching. I start thinking about the conversation I just had with Ellen before I left the house. *Why didn't I listen to her?*

"Shane, let me go—now!" I cry, pushing his hand away from my face. He cups his whole hand over my face and pushes me backward on the couch, making me fall into Wendy. He lets out an evil, twisted laugh.

What the fuck? I quickly regain my composure and stand up, heading quickly toward the bathroom.

"Heather, are you ok?" Wendy asks, following me.

"Guess what, you dumb bitch?" Shane yells out, still laughing. "I'm still fucking my baby momma! And guess what else? We're still together, and I live with her, you dumb cunt!"

Oh my God! How stupid have I been?

My embarrassment quickly turns to rage as he laughs. *He thinks this is funny? I'll show him!* I turn to look at him right before I reach the bathroom door. "Well, guess what, you stupid asshole? I'm still fucking pregnant!" I know saying it is a mistake as soon as it leaves my lips, but I don't care right now because I'm so angry that I could scream at the top of my lungs. The look of shock on his face is priceless, and it makes whatever is coming next worth it. I knew all along something wasn't right about him. And instead of trusting my gut, I kept listening to all of his lies.

"What the fuck did you just say?" he asks, jumping off the couch and walking quickly toward me.

Crap! He's not laughing anymore. I turn and hurry into the bathroom before he gets to me.

"Shane, leave her alone!" screams Wendy as I try to quickly shut the door to lock it, but he jams his foot in the door before I have the chance to close it.

"Shut the fuck up, Wendy, and mind your own fucking business!" he yells, shoving her out of the way.

I'm holding myself against the door as hard as I can so he can't get in, but he's too strong for me. I get knocked into the wall as he pushes the door open and slams it shut behind him. "Why did you lie to me, you stupid bitch?" he yells as he grabs me by the hair and pulls me real close to his face, clenching his teeth and spitting on me as he talks.

I don't know what to do to get away from him, so I say the first thing that pops into my head. "I was just saying that because you pissed me off. I really did have the abortion, I swear," I cry out.

"You fucking liar! I know you didn't do it!"

Shit! I bet Darius told him. I tell Darius everything. I trusted him when he said he wouldn't tell Shane. I should have known better. Ellen tried to warn me not to trust him. As usual, I didn't listen.

He lets go of my hair and slams me against the wall, pinning me by my shoulders with both of his hands. "Shane, I'll do it. I swear to God, I just got scared. Please, just let me go," I beg as I start to cry harder.

Wendy is banging on the door. "Shane, let her out before I call the police!"

"If you call the police, I'll kill you, bitch!" he screams out. The banging stops. After staring at me like he's going to rip my head off for what feels like an eternity, he lets me go and steps out of my way. The look on his face scares me. He's breathing heavily. I quickly walk out of the bathroom, grab my purse off the couch, and head out of the trailer as fast as I can.

Wendy follows as I walk down the road toward the entrance to the trailer park. "Heather, are you ok?" she asks from behind me. I'm walking so fast she can barely catch up.

"Yeah, I'll be fine. Thanks, Wendy," I say, wiping the angry tears from my face. I turn to look over my shoulder, and I see him coming out of the trailer and jogging toward me. *Fuck!* "Wendy, he's coming! Go call the police!" I say, starting to panic.

"Heather, STOP!" he yells out from behind me.

Without turning to look back, I yell out in a pleading tone, "No,

231

Shane! Please, just leave me alone! I'll have the abortion, and you'll never have to talk to me again!"

When he reaches me, he grabs me by the arm to pull me back toward him. "Heather, stop so I can talk to you!"

"There's nothing to talk about, Shane. I just wanna go home," I cry, looking up at him. He's squeezing my arm so tight that it's starting to ache.

"Shane, just leave her alone!" shouts Wendy.

"I told you to mind your own business, you dumb bitch!" With his free arm, he reaches out and shoves Wendy so hard she stumbles backward.

I love her for trying to help me, but I don't want her to get hurt too. "Wendy, I'll be fine. Just go, ok?" I say to her with a stare that screams, "Help me. Go call the police. Do something useful besides stand here and piss him off more." She turns and walks back toward the trailer. *God, I hope she read the look in my eyes.*

"Shane, let me go!" I yell, trying to pull away from his grip, but it's too strong. He's giving me that "I wanna rip your head off" look again. I stop struggling to get away and look up at him and ask in the most desperate, tear-filled voice, "Shane, what do you want from me? Why can't you just let me go?"

"Because I want you to have the goddamn abortion!" he yells as he begins punching me in the stomach. "Why couldn't you just have the fucking abortion and I wouldn't have to do this?" He punches me hard three times before letting me go and turning to run back toward the trailer.

Trying to catch my breath from the blows to the gut, I can see Jeremy off in the distance watching us. As Shane approaches him, he yells at him to get in the car.

Oh my God, what is he going to do? Run me over?

Snap out of it, Heather! He's going to come back, and God only knows what he might do. I turn and start running as fast as I can. As I run, I notice all the people standing outside their trailers, watching. *One of them will call the police, I know it.* I don't have that far to go. I can see the traffic on Route 50 just ahead of me. If I can make it that far, there's no way he will hurt me in front of all those people in the middle of a busy street.

Just as I'm rounding the curve close to the entrance, his car races past me and screeches to a stop. I quit running and stand still, trying to figure out what he's going to do next.

He jumps out of the car, opens the back door, and calmly says, "Heather, get in, and I'll take you home." *Yeah, right!*

I start to walk toward him like I'm going to obey his orders. As I approach the car, I continue to walk past him. "That's ok, Shane. I'll walk to Denny's and call Ellen. She'll come get me." I can see the restaurant in the distance. I know if I make it there that I can use the pay phone to call Ellen. *No way am I getting in his car now.*

"Heather!" he yells out from behind me. "Get your ass back here and get in the fucking car!"

I start to walk faster, and from the corner of my eye, I see another onlooker. Just as I turn to look at the older man standing on his porch, Shane grabs me by the back of my hair and starts to pull me backward.

"Help me!" I scream out, looking at the man, but he just stands there and watches. *Why isn't anyone stopping him? Why is that man just standing there?* I wonder as Shane drags me toward the car.

"Shane, please," I beg as we approach the car. I grab at his hands to try to get him to let go of my hair. I can feel it starting to rip out. He's pulling it so hard my neck is starting to ache from being pulled backwards, so I turn my body to gain more control. I see Jeremy sitting in the front seat, watching with a look of shock on his face, but he's not doing anything either. *Coward!*

For a split second, my mind goes back to my childhood and all the ass beatings Mal used to give me. I try to remember how I would get myself out of these situations, but my mind can't think fast enough. I wish Mal were here right now. She wouldn't just stand there and watch like all these other people. She would kick his ass!

"Ellen will come get me. Just let me go, damn it!" My desperate cries turn to anger as he pulls me toward the open back door. *Don't let him put you in that car or he's going to kill you!* cries my inner voice.

"Get in the fucking car, you dumb bitch!" he yells as he struggles to push me into the car, but I'm not going in without a fight. With both hands, I grab the top and side of the door frame and push my back toward him as hard as I can to stop him from shoving me in. But it's no use; he's too strong. My back gives way as he shoves me inside and slams the door shut.

Chapter Five

I sit in the back seat, terrified and crying, contemplating my next move. "Where are you taking me, Shane? I wanna go home!"

"Shut up, bitch! I'm gonna take you somewhere to make sure you don't have that baby!"

He speeds out of the trailer park so fast that there's no way I can jump out of the car. As soon as he gets to the stoplight at the corner of Route 50 and another road, I can jump out of this car and run as fast as I can.

"I'm gonna take your dumb ass over to Rita's house and let her beat that baby right out of your ass," he adds.

I can't believe the things that are coming out of his mouth or the way he's acting. I've never seen him this out of control before, and I believe every word. I know I need to do whatever I can to get away from him. I say nothing, and I sit in silence in the back seat, waiting to make my move. My whole body is shaking with fear. As soon as the car stops, I jump out as fast as I can, ignoring all the beeping horns as I try to run across the street, careful not to get hit as I run between oncoming cars. *I just need to make it to Denny's. It's so close!*

I almost make it across the street when I feel him grab the back of my hair again. "Shane, please let me go!" I scream, fighting him as he drags me back toward the car. It's the middle of the day, and we're at one of the busiest intersections in town, and no one is doing anything. *Why are they just staring?*

"What the hell is wrong with you, lady?" I scream at a woman staring out her car window. "Don't just stare at me! Help me! Call 911! He's going to kill me!"

"Shut your fucking mouth!" he yells as he tosses me back in the car like a sack of potatoes.

We're on Route 50 now, and it's just my luck that the next three stoplights are green as he speeds right through them. I find myself wondering if jumping out at this speed will kill me. I know it probably will, so I don't even try.

"Let me out of this fucking car, Shane!" I scream as loud as I can. "Or what? What the fuck is your little ass going to do about it?"

I gather all of the anger and fear inside of me and scream, "Or I'll kill you! You disgusting piece of shit!" From behind him, I throw the hardest punch I can and hit him right in the side of his head. The car swerves, and he throws the car in park right in the middle of traffic. He turns around and starts slapping at me from the front seat.

"I'll fucking kill you, bitch, if you ever touch me again!" he yells as he continues to slap at me. I'm reminded of the days when I was a kid when Dad would pull the car over and slap us from the front seat.

As soon as he turns back to start driving again, I jump out of the car and start running down the cement divider that separates the four lanes of traffic. People are yelling and beeping, but they're still not helping me. Again, he chases me down and drags me back to the car. Once we get back inside, he tells me he's taking me to where his brothers live outside of town. He's going to have them kill me and dump my body where no one will ever find it.

Now I know I'm fighting for my life. I don't know his brothers. All I've ever heard about them is how mean they are, and for all I know, he's telling the truth. Dead bodies get found near where they live all the time. It's the dumping grounds out here for garbage, dead bodies, and whatever else you don't want found. All that's out there is a bunch of double-wide trailers, dirt roads, and cockroaches.

That's where Lisa's body was found, and there is no way in hell I'm going to end up like her. So, at the next stoplight, I jump from the car again. I start screaming bloody murder for someone to help me. Just like my attempts before, I fail, and he gets me back into the car.

This time when he puts me back in the car, he clicks on the child safety locks so I can't open the door from the inside. *What is he, stupid?* The windows are down. So, at the next light, I open the door from the outside and run for my life, screaming louder. Once he gets me back to the car, he pulls off the main road and heads toward the back roads east of town. I see cornfields to my left and houses to my right. *This is it.* Once he makes it to Route 17, we'll be completely out of town. There will be no more stop signs or lights, and I'll never be able to get out of the car again. *This will be the end of my life.*

There's a stop sign coming up, and I know this will probably be my last chance. As soon as he stops, I'm going to run to the nearest house screaming because my life really does depend on it. The car stops, and I jump out and start running. I hear him behind me, yelling and cussing, but I keep running as fast as I can. He catches me and starts dragging me back.

"Shane, please just let me go. I swear to God, I'll have the abortion, and you'll never hear from me again. Just let me go, please!" I plead as I fall to the ground and roll over onto my back, kicking my feet at him.

Jeremy gets halfway out of the car. "Shane, why don't you just let her go, man?" he asks in a pleading voice.

"Stay the fuck out of it, J, and get back in the car," he yells as he pulls me off the ground by my hair. He tosses me back into the car, holding me only by my hair and the back of my shorts. *He's going to break my neck!*

Jeremy listens and gets back in the car. *I don't get it, why isn't he helping me?* "Jeremy, please, stop him!" I beg, crying.

"Sorry, Heather, I don't wanna get in the middle of it," he says quietly, continuing to look forward.

"Why? Are you scared of him?" I ask sarcastically. "Why do all you guys do whatever Shane says? Can't you fucking think for yourself? He's not tough! Look at him, beating up on a pregnant girl! He's a pussy!" I scream, and then I spit on Shane from the back seat.

"Oh, now I'm a pussy?" he asks, wiping the spit off the back of his head. "First, I'm a piece of shit and you hit me. Now I'm a pussy and you spit on me? I don't know what the hell has gotten into you, bitch, but you got some nerve talking to me that way!" he yells as he slams on the brakes and turns around, slapping me on the side of the head so hard my ear starts ringing.

"Fuck you, Shane! Fuck you! I will die trying to get away from you! I'll keep jumping out of this fucking car until I get away!" I scream, holding the side of my head.

Shane rolls up the window in the back on the driver's side with the power button in the front seat, "You're not jumping out of this car anymore you dumb, WHITE BITCH!"

Oh, shit! What to do next occurs to me so fast that I don't even know where it comes from. I jump to the passenger side and hold my finger down on the button so he can't roll up the window. When it works, I start laughing. (Half because I defeated him and half because I'm becoming numb and exhausted to what's going on.) I look down at myself and half of my shirt is ripped off. I can feel that he ripped the back of my shorts too.

"Jeremy, move her fucking hand so I can get the window up!"

No, Jeremy! Don't do it. This little black button is all I have left in the world right now.

"I'm not getting in it, Shane," replies Jeremy.

Oh, thank You, God! He's a coward for not helping me, but at least he's not helping Shane, either.

Just then Shane turns right and starts to drive back toward town. My racing heart regains some hope. *Maybe he is going to take me home.* I can't trust anything right now, though. As soon as he gets to the stop sign to turn back on to Route 50, I jump back out of the car, this time losing my shoes and my purse. I know I look like a crazy lunatic, racing away from the car, but I don't care about anything except getting away from him.

I see a pay phone on the side of the Shell gas station and make it my only mission in life to get to that phone and dial 911. I hear him running after me again. *God, where are You? Please help me! I swear to You, I will do whatever it takes to turn my life around and never talk to him again if You help me just this once.*

"Stop running away from me, BITCH!" he yells as he grabs me by the back of my hair again. "If you would just keep your fucking mouth shut. I am gonna take you home, but you keep running that pretty little mouth of yours and pissing me off!!"

Oh, God, is this my fault? Maybe I would be home if I had just stayed silent and got in the car in the first place. I could have pretended to Ellen that none of this happened. I start thinking about what Dad always says to me about running my mouth and how I need to learn how to keep it shut sometimes. They call me "Mouth" more than my own name.

As he's pulling me away from the gas station toward the car, I see two big, burly white men standing at the closest gas pump. They look like big strong farmers. *Yes! They can help me!* I start screaming, "Please, help me! He's going to kill me!"

They don't do anything. They just keep standing there, staring at me as if thinking, *Dumb little white girl. That's what she gets for messing with those Black boys.*

My parents' voices start ringing over and over in my head, "You should have kept your mouth shut, dummy!" I know I shouldn't have called him names, spit on him, or hit him, but all I can think about is fighting him back and getting away. Part of my brain is working logically. The other part is in fight-or-flight mode.

Shane has me halfway into the back seat, and just as I start to lose faith in all things good, I hear a siren. Shane stops dead in his tracks and lets me go before shutting the door. I jump out as fast as I can and start to run back toward the pay phone. When I make it to the phone, I dial 911 as fast as I can.

"911, what's your emergency?"

I'm crying so hard I start to lose my breath and hyperventilate. "Please, help me. My boyfriend is trying to kill me, and I'm pregnant."

"Where are you?" asks the female voice on the other end of the line. I tell her where I am, who I am, and a brief description of what's going on. "Oh my gosh, sweetie, we have gotten about twenty phone calls about you. You stay right where you are and an officer will be right there."

I hang up the phone and turn around to see the same two big farmer men and about five other people standing across the parking lot staring at me. *Fucking hillbilly assholes!* I sit down on the ground, prop myself against the building, and wait there for the police. I wonder if I should call Ellen, but I'm too afraid of what she will say so I decide to wait.

I can hear sirens off in the distance. I know they're chasing Shane. Thirty seconds later, I see two more police cars race past the gas station in the direction he took off. Another police car pulls into the parking lot next to where I'm sitting.

An officer gets out and helps me off the ground. "Are you ok?" he asks.

"No," I say as I start to bawl my eyes out.

"It's going to be ok. We got you now. Why don't you sit in the back of my car and catch your breath. There's an ambulance on the way for you."

The ambulance arrives a few minutes later, and the officer tells me they're going to take me to the hospital to make sure everything is ok with the baby, but that I'll have to come back to the station afterward and give a formal statement. He tells me he's also going to call Ellen and let her know what happened. *This is going to be it for me living at her house, I know it.* I find myself wishing I could turn back the clock. I wish I would have just listened to her.

"This is your baby," says the doctor as she turns the monitor toward me and points at the screen.

"Wow," I say, but I don't smile. I'm too numb. *I can't believe I really have a person inside of me.*

"Looks like you have a thumb-sucker," she laughs. I know she's just trying to make light of a bad situation. "Everything is fine. He didn't hurt the baby at all, and it looks like you're just about 11 weeks along. Those little guys are tough in there and protected by everything growing around them, but if you have any bleeding or cramping, you need to come back right away, ok?"

"Ok," I reply and sit up as she turns off the monitor. She hands me a picture to take home with me. *I'll be damned; it is sucking its thumb.*

"You look pretty scared. Are you going to be ok?" she asks. "I don't know."

"Do you have a plan for this baby?"

"How can I have a baby with someone that would try to hurt us like that?" I reply bluntly.

I am expecting to find Ellen waiting for me in the waiting room, but I'm surprised to find Robin and Mom instead. "What are you doing here? Where's Ellen?" I ask, looking at Mom. She looks at me with sad eyes. *Oh, shit. I hurt her feelings.* I didn't mean for it to come out that way and I try to recover. "I'm glad you're here Mom. I'm just surprised," I say, giving her a long hug.

"Ellen's going to wait at the house while we take you to the police station," she replies, brushing the hair away from my face and looking at me with tears in her eyes.

"Are you ok, baby girl?" asks Robin.

"Yeah, I'll be fine. Let's just go so I can get this over with." Mom remains quiet, but she has that look on her face, and I know she's in attack mode. "Where's Dad? Does he know what's going on?" I ask worried.

"Yeah, he knows. He's at home with your brothers."

When I get to the station, I tell them everything that happened from beginning to end. When they ask me if I want to press charges, I say of course. *The bastard should fry, and I never want to see his disgusting face again.* The police tell me that they had to chase him for a few miles around town before he finally gave up.

"Good! Jail is where he belongs," I say to the officer.

"You know the 911 dispatch center was swamped with phone calls about you. We were driving up and down Route 50 looking for his car," says the officer.

I'm glad people had the good sense to call it in, but still feel sickened that no one tried to stop him. He could have killed me before the police found us, for all they know. I don't know what would have happened to me if he wouldn't have turned off that desolate back road.

Afterward, Mom and I have a brief talk about abortion again. "Do you think you're ready to do it now, Heather?" she asks.

"Yeah, Mom, I think I am," I reply. I'm surprised at how sure I feel about it now.

She hugs me and tells me she loves me. She says that she's going to make another appointment for me as soon as possible and call me later. I still feel sickened by the idea of abortion, but now I feel like I have no other choice. I don't want to see him ever again. *How can I ever get away from him if I have his baby?*

Robin and I get in her car after Mom leaves. She turns and looks at me before putting the car in drive, and with tears in her eyes says, "I'm going to take you to stay at my house tonight, ok?"

"Why?" I ask quickly. *I already know the answer.*

"Because Ellen needs some time to think about things and what you guys should do next."

"I knew it! I knew she was going to kick me out over this," I say, beginning to cry. "Robin, I don't want to live anywhere else!"

She looks at me, and tears start falling down her cheeks. She reaches out and hugs me hard. "I know, honey. I know." We hug and cry for what feels like forever. I needed a big hug. It really helps to know someone really cares about me.

I call Darius from Robin's house later that night. I know I shouldn't talk to him, but I want to tell him what happened and ask him why he told Shane about me not having the abortion. I thought he was my friend, and the betrayal stings. He denies telling Shane. I don't really expect him to be honest and admit to it, but I know better. He already knows what happened because Rita bailed him out of jail and he's already running the streets again. *I can't believe that he didn't even have to spend the night there!*

I'm so sickened by the fact that she would bail him out. She must be real stupid to bail him out after what he did. I don't care how tough she supposedly is, she's dumber than I am. Darius tells me I should call her and tell her everything because maybe she doesn't know the truth. *How could she not know, though?* I decide I'll call her and he gives me her number.

I talk to Rita for about thirty minutes and tell her everything that happened that day and all the days since I met Shane. She was different this time. There was no yelling or accusing. She knows that he's the one that's wrong. She says she would never hit a pregnant girl, so nothing would have happened if Shane had brought me to her house. The conversation ends with me telling her that I'm having an abortion and never speaking to him again. I also tell her she should be stronger and get away from him too. From what she says, he's hit her before too. I will never give him the chance to do it to me again. I never want to be that scared again as long as I live.

Chapter Six

"Mom, I don't think I can do this," I say, shaking so bad I can barely bring my cigarette to my lips. Today, she decided to let me smoke. She says not to get used to it, and that it's only because of what I'm going through. We're standing outside the abortion clinic, waiting for them to call me in. We've been waiting a long time. The longer this takes, the more I want to change my mind.

They have already made me take a bunch of pills and stuck some metal rod looking things inside of me to make me dilate...*whatever that means*. They had us leave for a few hours and go eat lunch. Mom's counselor, Deb, the one that she's gotten really close to, drove us here today. After eating lunch, I threw up all over her back seat, and even accidentally got it on her purse. *Gross!* They said I might feel nauseous, but that was an understatement.

"Heather, you *have* to do it! You can't change your mind now. It's too late. What do you think those things inside you are doing to the baby right now?" Mom replies with desperation and a hint of irritation in her voice. "Look at me, Heather Rae," she says calmly. I look over at

Mom and start to feel the stinging in the back of my eyes. "He will kill you if you don't do this. He will hunt you down and kill you. Do you understand that? You're doing the right thing. You need to get whatever anyone else has told you about abortion out of your head. God will forgive you. I promise, everything is going to be alright."

I know she's right, so I shake my head in agreement and wipe the tears from my eyes, but it doesn't make what I'm about to do any easier. I have so many doubts about what's right and wrong.

Back in the waiting room, I start flipping through a magazine. I can't read it because my mind won't quit racing about everything that's happened in the last week. A few days after the incident, I had to go to court to ask a judge for a restraining order. Mom took me to court that day, and she has been at my side constantly since. She insisted on talking to the prosecutor while we were trying to find out what's going to happen to him. Mom wanted him to be charged for attempted murder for trying to kill the baby, but they said I wasn't far enough along in my pregnancy. Also, she wanted him to be charged with statutory rape, but they said something about us needing to be exactly five years apart in age or more.

I wasn't really paying attention to everything that was being said. I've been so numb, going through the motions. Everything has been happening so fast that it feels like a blur. All I know is that he's being charged with a felony that will follow him around the rest of his life. He's not in jail, but he will be on intensive probation for four years. If he breaks the law again, he will go to prison for the rest of his probation period. It seems unfair that he hasn't had to spend one night in jail. But if I know Shane, he'll screw up and end up right where he belongs.

Mom wants him to be charged with everything possible. She won't stop until he's locked away, and I couldn't possibly love her more for it. For the first time in a long time, I feel like I have my mom again. She actually made the comment that he'll be lucky if she doesn't run into him. If she sees him, she is likely to run his ass down with her car. And the way she has been acting so protective lately, I wouldn't be surprised if she actually did it. She's been the only one who has acted like she really understands me since this whole thing happened. This past week, things have been different between us, and I can't quite figure out why or what's changed. But for now, she's everything I need from a mother.

"Heather, it's time for you to come back now," says a woman's voice from the doorway a few feet away. I suddenly start shaking, again doubting why I'm here. The only thing that gets me out of the chair is that voice in my head, *He'll kill you, Heather. You have to do it or you'll die.* I never want to feel that fear again, so I get out of my chair. Mom follows behind as I walk through the door.

"Ok, just lie back on the table and relax. I'm going to give you a shot so you won't feel any pain," says a nurse.

Relax? Is she crazy? Who could relax lying on this table? Maybe Darius' girlfriend, who has had five abortions already, according to him. *She's disgusting.* The nurse has me roll on my side and sticks me with a needle. I immediately start to feel dizzy. Mom is to my right, holding my hand. When they tell me they're going to start, she begins to cry.

I suddenly hear a buzzing sound coming from a scary-looking machine I notice in the corner. It looks like a giant vacuum cleaner with hoses coming off of it. Before I can think about what they're using it for, the intense pain I begin to feel makes me cry out. Mom squeezes my hand even harder. "Heather, look at me. Just keep looking at me. It won't take long," Mom tries to assure me with tears falling down her face.

I try to focus on Mom but I can't. I just want it to stop so I yell, "Please stop! I don't wanna do this! I changed my mind!" I start to sit up, and for a split second before two nurses come running to hold me down, I see what the clear hoses are being used for. It's an image I know will never leave my mind.

Oh my God, what am I doing? I have never hated myself more than I do right now. *I'm a murderer!* All the shameful things I've ever done could never compare to what I'm doing right now. I'll never forgive myself for it. I'll never forgive Shane. I hate him now more than ever.

I'd rather he beat my ass and threaten to kill me a thousand times than ever have to go through this.

Dear Diary,

I know it's been a long time since I've written, and I'm sorry. I've just been so busy with my crazy life and trying to start over again. I did it, Diary. I had the abortion three months ago, and I feel horrible about it. The more time that goes by, I realize I did the right thing. But I can't stop wishing that I would have never been stupid enough to get pregnant in the first place. I can't stop dreaming about it. I am waking up in the middle of the night, sweating from nightmares of being on that table, feeling that awful pain again, and seeing my unborn baby being sucked through a tube. I was having nightmares almost every night at first, but now, it doesn't happen as much. I know it's probably God's way of punishing me for it. Or maybe it's just me punishing myself. I can't stop looking at the ultrasound picture, either. Mom says I shouldn't have it. She offered to take it for me and put it away. She promised she wouldn't throw it out, but I can't let her take it. I don't know why I can't stop staring at it. Maybe I need the constant reminder so I never put myself in that situation again.

I'm living at Bethany's again and at high school number five. It's hard to believe I've already been to five high schools and I just started my sophomore year. I know I really need to slow down and be stable somewhere. I really am trying. After everything that happened with Shane and after I made another appointment for the abortion, Ellen said I couldn't live there anymore. She says it was her way of protecting me from him and that I needed to get as far away from him as possible. Part of me can't help but think it's because of the abortion. She would never tell me that, but I know how she feels about it. I could tell Darcey wanted to rip my head off more than ever when she found out what I was going to do. I can't blame her. I can't blame Ellen either because I went against her rules way too many times for Shane. I'm sad that I had to move because it really felt like home there. But I'm glad that I got to come back here, where it's familiar, and not go somewhere new.

Now that I'm older, Mom has lightened up, so she doesn't hate Bethany like she used to. There's a lot less tension this time, and I can tell I'll be happy here. I hope! Mom has lightened up about a lot of things lately. We talk on the phone all the time, and I feel closer to her than I ever have. She opened up to me more about her past, too. I found out that she has had three abortions. I'm not really sure how I feel about that either. I don't understand how she could go through that hell more than one time, but the other part of me is glad she really understands how I feel. I've been able to talk to her about everything since then, and instead of yelling at me, she actually listens and talks to me. I'm really starting to gain a trust in her that I've never had before. I wish that it didn't take something so horrible for us to become close, but I'm so thankful we are.

I know Mom is still a mess with alcohol, but I don't see her that much to be affected by it. She's been staying in Iowa with some guy she met because she and Dad have been fighting a lot. I know it probably won't last because she always goes back home, but something feels different about it this time. I hate that she's so far away, and I hate that my brothers are in the middle of all of it. Part of me wishes I were there to protect them, but the other part of me is thankful that I don't have to see any of it.

Johnny is still the same sweetheart he's always been, but he's becoming quieter every time I see him. Theo seems angry all the time, and he blames me and Mal for not being at home. I don't know how he could think this is all our fault. But I know he's just trying to find his own way of dealing with everything. I can't imagine how different it must be at home without Mom there. Dad is just as quiet and distant as always. He's never said anything to me about Shane, the pregnancy, or the abortion. Sometimes, I wish he would just yell at me or something. At least then I would know he cared or felt some kind of emotion. He seems so empty and sad most of the time, almost cold in a way. People who don't know him take his silence and lack of expressions as him being mean. I think after going through so much, he must have just built himself up that way to stop things from hurting. I pray that whatever is going through his head about me that it's not shame. Not knowing whether or not he hates me now because of all of this is killing me.

I haven't seen Robin since the day I moved away from Ellen's. They didn't even let me say goodbye. I had to find out over the phone that they were going to be sending someone new to see me. I'm still pissed off and hurt that they could take her from me like that. How can they expect me to keep opening up to people if they are going to take them away from me once we get too close? I like my new mentor. She's nice, I guess, but she's not Robin. She doesn't understand me the way Robin did, and I don't see the point in getting close to her. The few things I have told her leave her speechless because she comes from a background where she can't even begin to relate to me. She doesn't know what to say to me half the time, so how do I get close to someone like her?

I met a boy that I am so insanely head over heels in love with. I know what you're thinking, diary. Am I ever going to learn? But this one is different; I know I've thought this a thousand times before. But this time, he really is. As I go back and read things I've written in my old stack of diaries (I have in a box in the closet), all I talk about is this boy or that boy and how in love I am. When I look back at it now, I see how wrong I was. I wish I would have waited for this boy. THIS is my first real love. Right now, Ryan, is just my friend...my best friend. I tell him everything, and he never judges me for any of it. When I first met him, I would have never thought that I would have the feelings I have for him today. He's not my normal type, but that's probably a good thing given my track record. After months of being just friends and getting close, I have never seen anyone more beautiful than him. I'm finding myself more attracted to him than I have ever been to anyone. Mom says that's what real love is. When you can start off just as friends, and it grow into something amazing that didn't start off as lust. I don't know if I will ever tell him how I really feel about him. He knows more about me than anyone, even more than Selene. I'm too scared that if I show him, he'll reject me because of all of the mistakes I've made. I don't know if he feels the same way. Sometimes, I think he must, or he wouldn't spend so much time with me. He respects me too much to try anything. But I wish he would!

I've never known a guy like him before. Most guys only care about getting in my pants right away. And like a dummy, I have thought for them to really want and love me that I had to give into them. Now I know better thanks to him. Maybe someday, I'll gather the courage to tell him how much I love him for all the things he's teaching me.

    Hopeful Again, Heather

Chapter Seven

"Mom, you were right about Bethany a long time ago. She's weird, and she keeps doing strange things. I don't trust her anymore."

"What do you mean by that?" Mom asks, sounding worried.

"I don't know. I keep catching her listening to my phone conversations. She's probably listening right now! At first, I would catch her standing around the corner listening, so now I come out to the garage to call people, and I can hear her picking up the other line to listen in."

"Well, why the hell would she do that?"

"I don't know, Mom. It's not like I've done anything to make her suspicious of me. She's just a weirdo! AND I'm pretty sure she killed the frog Ryan got me for Christmas, too!"

Mom laughs. "Come on, Heather, don't be ridiculous. I'm sure she didn't kill your frog!"

"Mom, don't laugh. I'm serious! I turned on his heat lamp before I went to school that day. And when I came home, he was dead, and his heat lamp was off. I asked her if she found him like that and turned the light off. She said she hadn't been in my room all day. The heat lamp wasn't burned out, so obviously someone turned it off. Why would she lie about it? Unless she didn't want me to know she was in my room snooping around? Why would she be in there snooping, anyway? I don't have anything to hide!"

I hear a sigh on the other end of the phone. "Well, Heather, you're just going to have to suck it up for a while. There's nothing you can do about it. You're the one who wanted to go back there so bad, remember?"

"I know, Mom, but I didn't see this side of her before. It was different back then."

"The grass is never greener on the other side, is it?" she says with a sigh.

Sure isn't!

"How are things going with Ryan? Have things gotten any better with his mom?" she asks, changing the subject.

"No!...it's gotten worse! She hates me, and that's never going to change. She *still* calls me by his ex-girlfriends name! We've been dating for three months and have been friends for six months. You'd think she'd have my name right by now. As if I can't tell she's doing it on purpose! Now, she's decided she doesn't want us talking at all anymore, so I'm not supposed to be calling there or seeing him," I reply dramatically and begin to cry. "I don't understand, Mom. I finally found something good, something *really* good, and people still want to take it away from me. What did I do that was so bad that she hates me so much? I can't live without him, Mom. I love him so much," I say, sniffling.

"Listen to me, Heather Rae, you didn't do anything wrong! There's something wrong with that woman, and it's not your fault. Do you hear me? Don't you ever let her make you feel like you're not good enough or that she's better than you—because she's not!" Mom says in a protective tone.

I get quiet and think about what she's saying, but I still don't understand it. She didn't like me from the second Ryan told her that I live in a foster home. She keeps telling him I'm trouble and that he needs to stay away from me. It's not fair to be judged by my circumstances. She won't even try to get to know me.

"Heather, do you hear me?" asks Mom, breaking the silence. "Yeah, Ma, I hear you. What about you?" I ask.

"What about me?"

"Are you going to go home soon? How long are you planning on staying in Iowa?"

"I don't know, Heather, we'll see. I don't want you to worry about me, though, ok? I'm going to be fine."

"I know, Mom, but what about the boys?"

"The boys are fine, Heather. Your dad is taking care of them."

"Have you talked to Mal?" I ask.

"Yeah, I've talked to her a few times on the phone, and we've written some letters. I'm making plans to go see her soon."

"I wanna go with you! Do you think they'll let me come, too?" I ask anxiously. *I miss her so much.*

"I don't know, Heather. I'll talk to your caseworker and see what they say."

"Mom?"

"Yes, Heather?"

"Are you and Dad going to get divorced?"

"I don't know, Heather. We're not talking about divorce right now, so stop worrying about everything, ok?"

I say ok, but I secretly say a prayer that this time will be like every other time and she'll go home soon. How can she expect me not to worry about her? She's living eight hours away. She's never been this far away from us before or for this long, and she's staying with some guy none of us have met.

All the times that I wished that her and Dad would get divorced, I never thought it would feel like this. I barely get to see her. Now that we've gotten closer, I find myself wishing I could be home again. I know things would be different this time. Not because she quit drinking or because she and Dad quit fighting. Things would be different because I've finally forgiven her. Even though everything is still fucked up, I'm not angry at her anymore. She's shown me in the last six months that I can really trust her. When everything in my world is crumbling down around me, she's been the only person still standing there to help me clean up the mess. When everyone has lost hope and given up on me, there she is, my mom, still loving me and wanting me unconditionally. I love her more now than I ever have before. The guilt I feel for how shitty I've treated her at times in the past is overwhelming. We've both said our own versions of "I'm sorry" since we've gotten close, but I don't know if mine could ever be enough.

"Heather, are you still there?"

"Yeah, Mom, I'm here."

"I'm gonna go for now, but I'll call you soon, ok? If anything happens and you need someone to talk to, I'm only a phone call away, ok?"

"Ok, Mom."

"Heather?"

"Yeah, Ma?"

"Keep your head up and your nose clean, ok? Everything is going to be alright. I promise!"

"I know, Mom. I love you."

"I love you too, Heather Feather."

She hangs up the phone, but I stand there for a second. With the phone still to my ear, I am wishing she was still on the phone; wishing I could reach out and hug her; wishing I could erase my whole childhood and start over; and wishing everything between us would be just like this, forever.

"Heather, what are you doing in my car? Everyone is looking for you! When they couldn't find you, they came to my lunch and asked me if I knew where you were. I knew you would be out here," says Ryan, opening the door.

"I was gonna stay out here the rest of the day and wait for you," I reply.

"How many classes have you skipped?"

"Who cares?" I reply.

"You should care!" he snaps.

Crap, he's mad at me now.

"You say you will do anything to make sure we stay together, but skipping class is just going to get you kicked out of Bethany's, and then what are we going to do?"

"Screw Bethany!" I reply without looking him in the eye. "You know she's crazy, Ryan. I don't know how much longer I can take living with her. She's fake! You're the only reason I've stayed with her this long," I add, starting to feel scared that he may be right. When she finds out I skipped class, she's probably going to kick me out. She threatens me with it constantly, and I know it's just a matter of time. She hangs it over my head in her sick twisted way. *I hate her!*

"Heather, look at me," Ryan says, grabbing me gently by the face and kissing me softly on the forehead. "Babe, you have to stay out of trouble or we won't be able to stay together," he says desperately. "What happened? What made you angry that made you come out here?"

I start to feel angry again thinking about it. "Mr. Asshole driver's ed teacher picking on me again for no reason!"

"What did he do this time?" he asks.

"He's such an ass! I was driving, and he wouldn't shut up. He said, 'You're driving too fast, you're driving too slow, you're off-center, you're not at ten and two'...bitch, bitch, bitch. I swear, everything I do is wrong! I finally told him to stop yelling at me or he was going to make me wreck, and you know what he said to me?"

"What?"

"He actually said I'm the worst driver he's ever had and that I'll never have my license because I'm going to get in accidents all the time! Can you believe him? Where does he get off?" I say in a huff. "So then, I looked at him and told him to kiss my ass. I wasn't taking his crap anymore, so I pulled the car over and walked back to the school. I've been sitting out here ever since."

"Heather, why do you let what other people think of you bother you so much? You know he's just a jerk, and he doesn't know what he's talking about. You should have just laughed at him instead of getting mad."

Too late now!

After a while of silence, Ryan looks at me and says, "Let's go, Heather. You have to go back into the school and face it."

"I know, but I don't want to. I woke up in a bad mood today as it is. That asshole just made it worse."

"Why did you wake up in a bad mood?"

"I'm not telling you. You'll just laugh at me."

"What? Why would I laugh at you? Just tell me. You can tell me anything," he assures me. He is going to laugh because it seems so silly, but he's right, I can tell him anything.

"You swear you won't make fun of me?" I ask. "I swear. Now, just tell me!"

"I had a really bad dream last night." A smile spreads across his face. "See! I told you that you were going to laugh at me!" I say, punching him in the arm.

"Heather, I'm not laughing, but whatever it was about, it was *just* a dream!"

"I know, Ryan, but it felt so real. I've never had a dream feel so real before."

"Heather, come on! I'm sure it wasn't that bad. What was it about?" I hesitate to answer him. "Come on, woman. Spit it out!" he says.

"Ok, but don't laugh. Let me tell you the whole thing before you say anything, ok?"

"Ok," he replies.

I know he's going to think I'm crazy.

"Everything was perfect between us like it has been in real life. And one day, for no reason at all, without any explanation, you just disappeared. I was running around everywhere in my dream looking for you, but I couldn't find you. I had the worst feeling in the dream that something was wrong. I finally found one of your friends and asked him where you were and if everything was ok. All he kept saying to me was, 'It's over, Heather—he doesn't want you anymore, so stop chasing him.' I know it sounds crazy, but I actually woke up with my eyes wet like I had been crying in my sleep. That's how real the dream was. I haven't been able to shake it all day." The smile on his face gets bigger, and he bursts into uncontrollable laughter. "I told you not to make fun of me, you jerk!" I say, smiling and slugging him on the arm again.

"I know, Heather. I'm sorry, but that's ridiculous. It was *just* a dream. I'm not going anywhere, I promise! How could you let a stupid dream ruin your whole day?"

"It's not the dream, Ryan. It's the sad feeling I woke up with that won't go away. It's hard to explain." *Maybe I'm getting my period.*

"Well, stop it! Everything is fine. Now, let's get back into the school before we both get in trouble."

"Ok," I reply, taking one last drag of my cig before we get out of the car and head back toward the school. It's the beginning of February, and it's freezing outside. I'm glad Ryan came out here. Even though I'm scared to death to face my fate, I don't know if I would have made it out in the cold the rest of the day.

I give Ryan a quick kiss before going into the school, and we go our separate ways. I start walking toward the principal's office, wondering what's going to happen to me. I start to feel scared again. *Fuck, is she going to kick me out?* I'm so sick of always being afraid of getting kicked out of wherever I'm living, and this time has been the worst. She knows how much I love Ryan and that I'm happy at school. I don't have a million friends like I did in Ohio, but I'm ok with that. I've been able to focus on my work more.

I'm getting good grades for once, and I'm even getting a "B" in math. Keeping up in math has been hard with moving around all the time. Every school I go to is always working on something different than the last school, so none of it has ever made any sense to me. I'm starting to understand it now. English hasn't been so bad, either; that's another one of my weak areas. *Why the hell do I need to learn how to dissect a sentence? How can a sentence have so many rules?* It's always seemed so stupid and senseless to me.

We had to do a speech in front of the class for public speaking in English. It was really hard. We could do it on anything we wanted. I chose to talk about the foster care system—what I think is wrong with it

259

and how I think it could be better. I got choked up talking about it. It was embarrassing because no one here gets it like I do, but the teacher gave me an "A" anyway. All my friends had a million questions that I didn't really want to answer afterward, but that's what I get for opening that door, I guess. *What was I thinking?*

As I approach the office, I can see Donna standing on the other side of the glass door. *What the hell is she doing here?* I wonder. She's my new mentor. They quit sending the young speechless girl to see me. I think the drive was becoming too much for her, and Donna lives really close to me. I like her better, anyway. Donna is older and has been through more in life, so she gets me more than the other girl. She's not Robin, but she's nice and always honest with me. She doesn't fake her way through her time with me like a lot of people have, and she is never afraid to give it to me straight. I feel I can trust her.

"Why did they call you?" I ask her as I walk through the door. "Heather, where have you been?" asks Donna. "Everyone has been worried about you," she adds with less anger in her voice.

"Is Bethany kicking me out? Is that why you're here?" I ask quickly. "No, of course not," she replies. "She asked me to come get you because it's a closer drive for me, and she has to be home for the little ones to get off the bus. Are you ok? What happened today?"

"Why don't we take this into my office," the principal butts in. We go into his office and he shuts the door. "Why don't you both have a seat," he says, pointing at the two chairs in front of his desk. "Heather, what happened today?" he asks. "You've been a good student with minimal issues since you've been here. What set you off?"

I explain what happened in the driver's ed class and how I didn't want to go back to class because the teacher embarrassed me in front of the other kids in the car. After so much time had passed, I figured I was in trouble anyway so what was the point in coming back in.

"You should have come straight to me so we could have figured it out together," he says.

"I know. I'm sorry. I promise next time if something happens, I'll come here first."

"Ok. I'm not going to suspend you this time. Just go home for the rest of the day. Get plenty of rest this weekend, and we'll start over Monday morning, ok?"

As I say ok, Donna and I head out of his office.

On the twenty-five-minute drive home, I wonder how much trouble I'm in. "So, she isn't going to kick me out?" I ask Donna.

"No, Heather. Why do you think she's going to kick you out?"

"Because she's always hanging things over my head...like she's waiting for me to screw up badly enough so she can finally do it."

"You know, Heather, not everyone is always against you."

"I know, Donna, but *she* is," I say with certainty. I don't trust anything Bethany says or does. She will say one thing to my face, and then, I'll catch her talking about me behind my back and doing things that I know aren't right. She's sneaky and conniving. I know she's even taken it as far as reading my journals. I have them set a certain way in my closet so I can tell when they've been moved around. I don't know why she treats me like she doesn't trust me. *What have I done to deserve that? I have nothing to hide.*

I miss living at Ellen's. She would never invade my privacy the way Bethany does, and she had reasons to think I was hiding things from her. At the end of my stay there, I was hiding things, lots of things. I've wanted to call her so many times since I've been here and beg her to let me come back, but my fear of rejection stops me. I called her a few times when I first left, but I knew it would make moving on too hard, so I stopped calling. I hope she doesn't think I don't love her, but the phone works both ways, and she hasn't called me, either. I know it's for the best that I just move on.

When I get home, I get a phone call from Dad telling me that my great-grandfather died. I'm sad for Dad more than anything. He was always close to his grandparents growing up, and he used to spend summers at their house. I barely knew my great-grandfather, but what I did know I loved. He was sweet but very quiet. *What is it with the men in my family?* He was 89 years old and lived a very long life. I know people can't live forever, but it still makes me sad.

Dad says he's going to pick me up for the funeral, but then my case-worker calls and says I can't go because of what happened at school. "You think you deserve to go after what you did?" she says.

Since when is going to a funeral a privilege? I don't understand these people half of the time. They're always trying to make me feel like I'm the one with all the problems, but most of the people I have to deal with are crazier than I'll ever be.

The weekend has been hell. I'm grounded, so I can't go anywhere or call anyone. Bethany has been acting extra strange, and she won't even let me call my mom. I'm pretty sure she's not allowed to stop me from calling my own mother, but what can I do? I'm out in the country in the middle of nowhere, and the nearest house is a half a mile away. It's not like I could run away even if I wanted to.

I keep sneaking out to the garage pretending to smoke, but I'm really using the phone. I've been trying to call Ryan since I left school Friday and I can't get a hold of him. I can't help but feel like he's avoiding me on purpose. It's starting to feel like my dream all over again, but that's not possible, right? To dream something that comes true? *No way!*

Between not being able to be with my family, wondering if they're all ok, and Ryan not talking to me all weekend, I feel a pit in the bottom of my stomach the size of the Grand Canyon. I can't shake the desperation I'm starting to feel. I feel like I've been walking around hyperventilating for the last two days, and no matter what I do, I can't seem to catch my breath.

Chapter Eight

"How did you end up in foster homes?"

"I don't know, probably the same way you did," I reply.

"Well, why did you come here? What happened at your last placement? Did you get in trouble?"

This stupid girl and all her questions! I just want to sleep and be left alone, but she won't shut the hell up.

"Yeah, something like that," I reply with a yawn and roll over to face the wall.

She can't seem to take a hint. As she keeps running her pie hole. "I've lived here for six months. My last foster dad molested me, and I never knew my parents."

WOW! This girl has issues. She doesn't even know me, and she's blurting out all her business.

"That really sucks, but I'm tired and just want to sleep. Can we talk about this tomorrow?" I ask, annoyed.

I really don't care what her problems are. We all have them. Maybe that makes me heartless, but all I care about right now is sleeping my pain away. Besides, I've heard her story a thousand times before. I just don't want to hear it again—not right now, anyway.

"Ok. I'm sorry," she says quietly as she shuts off the light.

Oh, hell. Now I feel bad. Damn her!

As I lie there trying to sleep, all I can think about is Ryan and everything that's happened in the last few days. My heart fills with an overwhelming amount of sadness. I can't fight the tears, so I lie in bed, crying silently. I just want to sleep as long as it takes to forget about him. I know I'll never forget him. The heartbreak I feel is suffocating. I can barely breathe, much less think straight. Now that I'm far away from him, there's no way to fix it. I'll probably never see him again.

I feel so stupid for the way that I acted, but what else could I have done? He ignored me all weekend. When I saw him at school, he acted like he didn't even know who I was. I gave him what he had coming and slapped the shit out of him...twice. I slapped him so hard that my hand hurt, and I left a welt on his face. He asked for it. *Asshole!*

He was standing in front of me, screaming, "Come on, you big tough girl. You know you wanna hit me, so hit me!"

So, I hit him—hard. I've never seen him act like that before. When he was screaming at me, his face was as red as blood with snot shooting out of his nostrils as he yelled. Something is wrong with him, and I hate that I don't know what it is. Ryan is quiet and funny, never mean or temperamental. *Maybe that's the real him, and it took a while for me to see it.*

After I slapped him, he ran away. Literally! I chased after him like a crazy person, but my smoking addiction only got me four blocks away from the school, and I just couldn't run anymore. I refused to go back to the school because I knew I'd be in deep shit. Instead, I called Donna from a pay phone and she came and picked me up. Already feeling the tension building at Bethany's, I knew she was going to kick me out for sure, so what was the point in calling her?

I was right. She was definitely kicking me out and didn't even want me to come back to pack my stuff. My caseworker wouldn't let her do that, so I avoided Bethany while I was there getting my things. I didn't even say goodbye. She is a coward and didn't want to tell me to my face that she was done with me. What I did wasn't personal against her. There was no reason for her to get angry about it.

I don't miss her or her house in the least bit. My only regret is Ryan and not knowing what I could have done differently. I wonder where he is and if he misses me as much as I miss him. I've tried calling him in the last few days since I've been here. Unfortunately, his mom keeps answering the phone, so I have to hang up. He doesn't know where I am, so he wouldn't know how to call me back if he wanted to.

I'm living in my hometown again. At least I'm back where things are familiar. But I don't know where I'm going to end up, and the foster home I'm in now is only temporary until my caseworker can find me something permanent. There's no guarantee it'll be around here, and that scares me.

I've lived with this woman before. They brought Mal and me here once when we were running away a lot after I came back from Ohio. Mal didn't like the lady at all, but I think she's ok. I know I don't want to live here for long, but at least she's not mean. I have a feeling she makes extra money doing phone sex because I can hear her late at night through her bedroom door, talking dirty and giggling. Maybe she's talking to a boyfriend? Although, the outgoing message on her answering machine is pretty raunchy. Sometimes, I wonder where DCFS finds these weird people.

Everything happens for a reason, though, right? What does that even mean anymore? No matter how much I hear that or try to convince myself that it's true, it still doesn't make sense. Sometimes, I think it's just a coping mechanism or something to get me through all the bad shit. Does everything *really* happen for a reason? Or is it all just random and things just happen by chance and coincidence? Do some people have great lives with minimal to no tragedy while others get slapped with more tragedy than any one person should ever have to endure all out of luck? Is there really a God controlling everything that happens to us? *I hope that there is because without a God, none of it even matters, and we're all doing it for nothing.*

While I lie there, pondering doubts about my existence, I remember the dream I had and how real life played out almost exactly the way it had in my dream. It gives me a glimmer of hope. No matter how much I wish it wasn't true, it makes me realize that there has to be something more. Maybe it was God letting me know He is there and that everything is going to be ok. Or the universe was preparing me for the pain I was going to feel.

I had to go to court today for a review since I lost my placement. I swear, I feel like l live in that courtroom sometimes. Every time I go in there, I'm scared as hell that the judge is going to lock me up with my sister or send me back to another group home. He didn't this time, though. *Thank You, God!* He ordered my caseworker to find me another foster home. Mom was there, too. She comes to all of my court dates no matter what and always asks for them to send me home, but they never do. However, she's not even living at home right now. I'm sure she knew it was a long shot, but at least she still tried.

Mom brought Artie, the guy she's been staying with, to court with her, and it's the first time I've met him. He seems nice enough, but he's not Dad, and I can tell he likes to drink. It's something about the look in his eye. Maybe it's the same glassy look Mom and Dad always have. I didn't get mad like I used to when I was younger about her being with someone else. I don't know why. I guess I realize there's no point in being pissed off about something I can't change.

When I was leaving the courthouse, we hugged tight, and I couldn't let her go. I stood there forever, hugging her. With my nose buried in her hair like I used to as a kid, soaking in the smell of her White Diamonds perfume and cigarettes, I was having flashbacks of the times in my childhood when things weren't always so bad. I told her I loved her and missed her. We both got tears in our eyes as we hugged, but I really don't know why because we have said goodbye a million times before. Something was different this time. I could feel it.

When we parted ways, she was in the car next to me, driving down the street. She didn't see me, but I stared at her, almost in a trance. There was something different about the way she looked at that moment. I can't quite figure out what it was, but I have never seen her look more beautiful. The way the late morning sun was glistening on her long blonde curls, the way her lips moved as she talked, and something about the sunglasses she was wearing. They made her look almost glamorous. Someone I wanted to know so badly, but she was just out of my reach.

A stranger could have seen her at that moment and thought, *Wow, I have to know her.* They would never know all the pain and sadness she carried behind those sunglasses. At that moment in time, I was mesmerized. Although it was brief, it made my heart long for her like it never had before, and something inside of me wanted to yell out for her not to go.

If I had only known that would be the last time I would ever see her, hug her, or smell her, I would have never let her go. I would have begged her to take me with her. I would have told her I loved her a thousand times and how sorry I was for always acting like such a pissed off little girl. I would have told her that I have forgiven her for all her mistakes. I can't help but think that if I had said everything I've held in my heart for so long, maybe she wouldn't have abandoned me that one last time.

The next morning after I have my breakfast, the foster mom tells me that Dad called while I was sleeping and wants me to call him back. I avoid my roommate as much as possible. Terrified she's going to corner me with her tales of woes, I rush off to the living room to call my dad.

"Hey, Dad, it's me. Did you call?"

"Yeah...uh, I'm gonna be coming to get you this afternoon so we can go see your sister."

"Today? But it's only Wednesday. I thought we were going on Friday?" I can hear Dad breathing on the other end of the phone, but he's not answering me. "Dad? Did you hear me?"

"Yeah, I heard ya, Heth. We're going today instead, ok?" he replies with a weird tone in his voice, but I instantly dismiss it in the excitement that I don't have to wait another two days to see my family.

"Is Mom still here? Is she still going to come with us?"

"No, Heather, I don't think so."

"Why not? I thought she was coming too?" I ask, feeling disappointed.

"I don't know, Heth," he says with a sigh. I can tell by his tone he's getting annoyed with my questions, so I don't push the issue.

"Well, when are you coming? I have to go to counseling in a little bit."

"I'll be there by the time you get back from that. Pack a bag because you get to come home for a few days."

Huh?

"What? Really?" I ask with such excitement my hand starts to tremble. "What made them decide that was ok? We haven't had weekend visits in a long time, and it's not even the weekend yet."

"I don't know, Heth. I asked them if it was ok, and they said it would be fine."

Something seems weird about this, but I'm certainly not going to argue with him. "Ok, I'll see you in a little bit," I reply anxiously. "I love you, Dad." He hesitates again. "Dad?"

"Yeah, love you too." *Why is he acting so weird?* I wonder after hanging up the phone.

"What's going on? Is everything ok?" asks the foster mom as I linger by the phone.

I shake off the uneasy feeling as I turn to answer her. "Yeah, everything is fine. He was just acting kind of weird, but that's how my dad is sometimes. I'm sure it's no big deal. Did you know they were going to let me go home for a few days?"

"Yes. Sandra called me this morning and told me," she replies.

Ok. Just last weekend I couldn't even go to a family funeral. Now, I suddenly get to go home for a few days in the middle of the week?

"It seems strange, but oh, well, I get to go home, so who cares," I say as I rush off to shower and pack.

At counseling a few hours later, I talk to Kyleen about the usual things, but I'm having a hard time focusing because I can't wait to get done so I can go with Dad. I'm not really into talking when she's asking me about all the things that have happened recently, so I give her short answers.

"Heather, why are you so distracted today? What are you thinking about?" she asks.

"I don't know. Dad is coming to get me when I'm done, so I'm excited to see everyone. I can't wait to see my sister. I haven't seen her in almost a year. I'm sad over everything else, but I'm happy right now because I get to go home for a few days and forget about it all. I guess I'm just not in the mood to talk about anything. I know my mom isn't living there right now, but I hope I see her while I'm home."

Kyleen seems distracted today, too. She's not saying much either, and we end our session fifteen minutes early. She takes me out into the waiting room where my new mentor is waiting for me. I can't see Donna anymore because she lives too far from here.

"Heather, you know Judith. I'm sure you two are going to get along just fine."

I know Judith pretty well. She's good friends with Robin. She's a short, stocky Black woman with a big personality. She's loud, funny, honest, and her laugh can carry on for miles. I like her a lot, and I agree with Kyleen. We're going to get along just fine.

Judith takes me back to the foster home where I grab my garbage bags full of my things and we wait for my dad outside. We make small talk until he pulls up. I packed everything I have just in case. For all I know, they might have something permanent for me when it's time to come back. I've learned my lesson about leaving my stuff somewhere I'm not familiar with. My roommate, Miss Chatty Cathy, seems nice, but I don't trust that she won't get sticky fingers while I'm gone.

The drive is long and boring, so I pull a book from one of my garbage bags to make the time go faster, but my mind won't stop racing. It's impossible to read.

"Dad, where is Mom?" I ask, breaking the silence in the car.

"I don't know, Heath."

"What do you mean you don't know? She was here yesterday for court. Did she go back to Iowa already?"

"No, I don't think so."

"Well, where is she then? Why didn't she come with us?"

"I don't know."

"She was supposed to stay with us last night when Dad went to work, but she never showed up," Theo pipes in from the front passenger seat.

That's weird. I hope she's not using drugs again.

"Where is she staying while she's here?" I ask Dad. I can see his eyes from the back seat in the rear view mirror as I interrogate him, but he doesn't make eye contact with me.

"She's been staying in a motel not far from the house," he replies, clearing his throat and reaching for a cigarette.

"Is she going back to Iowa, or is she going to stay here?" I persist.

"I don't know, Heather. I don't know what your mom's plan is, ok?" he says sharply.

Excuse me, grouch! I don't know why he's being so quick with me. I just asked a question.

The silence grows in the car with only the low sound of Dad's classic rock music playing in the background of my thoughts. Normally, I would be bugging him to change the station, but right now, I'm thinking too much to listen to it anyway. I can't get Mom off my mind, and I find myself reminiscing on all the good times.

"Hey, remember when Mom was freaking out about who spilled the bread out into the bread box, and she was so mad because none of us would admit to it?" I ask, laughing.

"Oh, yeah, that was funny!" Theo laughs.

"Then months later, we caught Johnny on a home video doing it while Mom was the one videotaping him!" I add, and me and Theo start to laugh harder.

"Shut up, you guys," laughs Johnny from the back seat. "I didn't know I did it! I was taking the bread out, and Mom called my name and it fell out as I was turning around to look at her. It was all Mom's fault the whole time!" he chuckles.

I remember it like it was yesterday. We were all sitting around, watching home movies with Mom one day when we saw it, and we all started cracking up laughing. She was so furious about who dumped the bread into the bread box. For days, she walked around pissed off, mumbling under her breath, "Nobody around here ever does anything, do they?" The whole time, the answer was right there in front of her face and she didn't even realize it. I'll never forget the way she laughed about it while we all demanded an apology, laughing with her, and all she would say was "oops."

For the rest of the drive, we laugh about the good old times. We don't do it very often, and it feels good to get along with my brothers, remembering the good things instead of all the bad. Dad remains quiet while we all laugh. Every once in a while, one of us tries to include him in on the laughter, but he seems distant and uninterested. I wonder what's with him today. *Maybe he had a late night drinking or not enough sleep after work.*

After two and a half hours of driving, we finally make it to the place where Malory lives. It is huge, and there are bars on all the windows. *Scary.* I don't know how Malory deals with living in a place like this, but she's not cowardly and weak like me. She's tough, and nothing seems to ever scare her or defeat her. I rarely ever even see her cry.

As we're buzzed into the building, the door slams shut behind us with such a loud bang it echoes in my ears. I realize at this very moment that I could never be locked away in a place like this. I don't care what DCFS asks me to do. *I'll do it!* The thought of ending up here scares the shit out of me.

I turn sixteen in a little less than two weeks. I don't have that much time left before I will finally be free from everything, but I know the next two years will drag by slowly. Malory is so lucky. She turns eighteen in a few months, and she can get out of here, away from the system forever. *Maybe she'll get her own place, and I can go live with her until I'm emancipated.*

The guards seem mean and cold as we're escorted into the visitation room. The room is cold and bright from the neon lights that are making flickering sounds above us. There's a big round table in the middle of the room that we sit around, waiting quietly for Mal.

"Where's Mom?" Malory asks as she sits down at the table next to me after giving us all a hug.

"I don't know," Dad mumbles. That seems to be the question of the day, and he doesn't know anything.

"Well, she was supposed to come see me today, so I was confused when they told me you guys were coming and she wasn't," she says.

Wait, what?

I look at Mal confused and then back at Dad. "I thought we were all supposed to come together Friday?"

Dad just sits there, not responding.

Mal looks back at me. "Well, I talked to Mom the other day and she said her and Artie were coming today. I didn't know you guys were supposed to come at all."

The subject gets dropped in the assumption that Mom is just being Mom. For the next ten minutes, Mal and I make small talk trying to catch up on all the time we've lost while the boys and Dad sit talking quietly.

"Girls?" calls Dad, trying to get our attention. "I know you've all been through a lot, and you girls not living at home has been hard on all of us, but it's important we always stick together as a family. You all have to learn how to be there for each other and back each other up."

Oh, brother. Here we go with the lectures. Malory must be thinking the same thing because she elbows me in the side, and we look at each other, sigh, and roll our eyes.

"Girls, I'm serious; this is important. You need to listen to me," he says, dropping his head. He hesitates before he lifts his head again, and when he does, he's crying.

Oh, God! What the hell is going on? I look back at Mal, and her eyes are fixated on him. I can tell she's starting to worry, too.

He clears his throat and rubs his eyes before saying the worst thing I have ever heard him say. The worst thing I have ever heard anyone say. All the pain I've ever been through in my life could have ever prepared me for the words he mutters next.

"It's none of your guys' fault. None of this has ever been your fault, but your mom died last night."

WHAT? Are my ears playing tricks on me? He didn't just say die? He couldn't have!

Suddenly I can't feel my legs or my arms, and as the numbness travels through my entire body, my heart begins to pound, and I feel rage like I have never felt before. I do the only thing I've ever known how to do when something bad happens. I run. I jump to my feet as fast as I can with such force that my chair goes flying backwards. *Get away! Get out of here now! Run away as fast as you can, and it'll be like you never heard those words.* I storm out of the room and start jogging down the hall toward the main entrance.

When I reach the door, I'm already out of breath. My hands and arms are shaking so badly that I can barely hold my arm out to push the button. I push it repeatedly until someone finally answers.

"Can I help you?" asks an annoyed female voice on the other end of the intercom.

"Let me out of here," I gasp out, barely able to talk.

"If you go out, you can't come back in," she replies with an attitude.

"I don't care, lady! Just open the door and let me out of here!" I demand.

The door buzzes, and as soon as I open the door, my feet hit the pavement. I start running as fast as I can through the large parking lot toward the van.

I try the door handle, but it's locked, so I fall down on the curb at the back of the van and wrap my arms around my knees tightly. I pull them as close to my body as I can and begin to rock back and forth. I can't get Dad's words out of my head. They keep playing over and over.

"Your mom died last night. Your mom died last night. Your mom died last night." I shove my fingers into my ears and bury my head into my knees to try to silence the sound of his voice, but it doesn't work. I want to scream out at the top of my lungs, but when I open my mouth, nothing comes out.

Why, God? Why? Why did you do this to us? Why did you take her away? When I realize not a single tear has fallen from my eyes, I try to force myself to cry, but I can't. *Why can't I cry? What's wrong with me?* I wonder, and I begin to shake almost uncontrollably when I feel an arm gently wrap around my shoulders.

"Honey, you should come back inside now," says my sister's counselor softly.

"I don't want to," I reply with my teeth chattering, continuing to rock back and forth with my forehead pressed tightly against my knees and my eyes squeezed shut.

She holds me tight for a few minutes before saying, "You really should be inside with your family right now. It's not good for you to be out here alone. You all need to be together right now."

Oh my God, my family. My poor family. Oh my God...poor Johnny, poor helpless Johnny, who has been glued to Mom's side since the day he was born. My poor dad, my dad who has been head over heels in love with her all of these years. The man who would do anything for her no matter how much she didn't deserve it and would always take her back no matter what. Theo, who always defended her even when she was wrong. My poor sister, who is stuck in a cell and can't have any contact with the outside world. How is she going to deal with this?

I know she's right. I have to get back in there. "But they said I couldn't come back in," I say, lifting my head.

"It's ok. You can come back in."

We stand and start walking back toward the door, and I can feel my knee's shaking and all my muscles feel like Jello. I think I might fall.

When I walk back into the room, everyone is crying, and I hesitate by the door. I consider turning back when Dad lifts his head and looks at me. I can see pain in his eyes that I have never seen before, and it makes me want to crumble to the floor. Suddenly, the tears start pouring out of me like they've been backed up for centuries. I drop down at the table, bury my head, and cry so hard my body shakes. I cry so hard I can barely breathe, like I have never cried before. I can feel what's left of my heart shatter right here in this room. I know there is no way I will ever be the same again.

Chapter Nine

The next week is such a blur I can barely think a clear thought. I feel like everything around me is spinning out of control while I'm stuck in slow motion. It's like a nightmare where you're trying to run away from a monster, but your feet will barely leave the ground.

When all the crying slowed down that day at the detention center, we all wanted to know why and how. Dad said it was an accidental overdose. The anxiety medication that she'd been taking for a long time was not supposed to be mixed with alcohol. He said she'd been mixing them for years, and he supposed that it finally caught up to her, and her body couldn't take anymore.

I hate pills! I don't care what's wrong with me, I will never take them. I remember when she was sober and the stupid doctor put her on all those different medications. I was angry because even though she wasn't drunk, she still wasn't Mom. All I ever wanted was for her to be normal. I know no matter how weak she was sometimes; she wanted the same thing. She fought so hard for so long. And in the end, look where it got her. *What was the point of any of it? What was the meaning to her life if everything happens for a reason?*

We are having the service in Ohio at the Catholic church Mom was raised in. She will be laid to rest in the same cemetery as her family that has passed away before her. Her burial will be on Valentine's Day, a day that's supposed to be about love and happiness. *Why can't they pick another day?* Valentine's Day will never be the same for any of us, and Mom, being the hopeless romantic she was, would really hate this.

The wake is huge. I had no idea Mom knew so many people. There must be hundreds of people here. I refuse to go inside when we first arrive. Dad tells my aunts to let me be while he and my brothers go inside. Mal isn't here. It's so unfair. The warden of the detention center claimed that since the funeral is so far away, they don't have the staff it would take to transport her. None of it makes sense. *Don't they let murderers out for funerals?* They act like she's committed some horrible crime. She should be here right now. Maybe then it wouldn't be so hard for me.

As I stand on the sidewalk near the entrance, I'm greeted by numerous strangers walking toward the door who stop and stare. They are crying and saying things like, "Oh my goodness, you must be Lorynn's daughter. You look just like her. Come here, you poor thing." Then, they hug me like they've known me for years.

I'm finally saved when I see a familiar face walking toward me. "Jack! Oh my God, what are you doing here?" I ask as I meet him halfway and go in for a hug.

"Heather, I'm so sorry about your mom. I wish there was something I could do. I heard about what happened, and I had to come show my respects," he says softly.

"Thank you so much for coming. It means a lot to have a real friend here," I say, hugging him tightly and starting to cry.

We walk around the block, talking for a little bit, catching up on lost time. For a brief moment, my mind actually goes somewhere else, and it's nice. I love Ryan, but seeing Jack makes me remember how special he was to me when I lived with my aunt. It helps to have someone here who knows me so well. For a moment, I don't feel so alone.

When we approach the entrance again, I see Aunt Phoebe standing by the door, smoking a cigarette. I turn to Jack and explain to him that I haven't been inside yet.

"Heather, you should really go inside now. You know you have to do it."

"I know, Jack, thanks so much for being here," I say, hugging him again before I turn to walk toward my aunt.

"Oh, honey, come here," she says, holding out her arms with tear-filled eyes. Even now, with her mascara running down her face, she's still so beautiful. Looking at her is almost like looking at a twin of my mom, and I start crying hard again as I hug her. "Come on, baby girl. I'll walk up there with you. It's going to be ok. I promise," she says as she sobs.

When we first walk in the door, I see a table full of pictures. One is a large picture of my mom, another is a collage, and there are numerous other family photos. I linger by the table for a while, trying to avoid the inevitable when I feel my aunt's hand on my shoulder.

"Come on, honey. It's time."

If I walk out of here now, can I just pretend this never happened? As soon as I turn to my right, I see her, and nothing in the world could have prepared me for how hard it really is to see her lying there like that. *It doesn't even look like her; that can't be my mom.* My knees start to go weak, and I begin to shake. I don't want to walk any further, but my aunt has me hugged tight to her side. And I know there is no running away from this.

After standing in front of the casket and sobbing like a baby with my aunt for what feels like forever, I turn and look at her. "I wrote her a letter. Do you think it would be ok to put it in there with her?"

"Oh, honey," she says, sobbing harder. "Of course you can."

I know I can't bring myself to touch her or reach my hand inside the casket, so I hold the folded-up letter out to my aunt. "Can you please do it for me?"

"Oh, baby," she says, crying. "Anything you need, I'll do it."

"You can read it if you want to," I add quickly and walk away.

I can't stand up there staring at her crying like that for too long. It's too hard. I don't want to leave her, either, so I find a spot on a couch nearby where I can still see her if I want to. I only get up every once in a while to use the bathroom or to sneak off to have a cig.

I think about the letter I wrote to her last night when I couldn't sleep. I wonder if there is any way she can really know what's in my heart now that she's gone. I told her how sorry I was for not saying I was sorry enough and for not trying harder to be a better daughter when I had the chance. I told her how much I loved her and how much I wished I could take all her pain away so life wouldn't have been so hard for her to live. I promised her I would always try to do the right thing and not ever travel down the same path as her. I told her that I have forgiven her for being weak, and I begged her to forgive me. I told her that I understood why she was always so sad, even though part of me still doesn't. I don't know if I ever will.

As the hours pass, the more I stare at her, the more numb I become. I can't cry anymore. I feel completely empty. *I hate the lipstick they put on her. I wonder who picked it.* It's really bright; Mom would never wear that color. I wish I could go up there and wipe it off of her. *She would hate it.*

I'm still amazed how many people have been in and out of here and the amount of people who have approached me. They know by looking at me that I'm her daughter. I never knew how much I looked like Mom until now. Part of me feels proud of it, but the other part of me hates being a reminder to the people who are crying for her.

I can't believe the stupid things people say in these situations when they don't know what else to say. I've heard so many people say, "I'm so sorry for your loss, but she's in a better place now." *Really?* She was only forty-one years old, and her youngest child is only eleven. How could anywhere but with us be a better place for her? She will never see any of us graduate, go to college, or get married and have kids. *How on earth is this better for her or for any of us?*

My cousin, Ashley, sits down next to me for a while, and all I want is for her to go away before I hit her. Nothing is making me angrier today than she is. She's been walking around the wake, talking about the baby she's a few months pregnant with. The whole time, she is laughing, smiling, and showing off an ultrasound picture. I have not seen her shed one single tear, and it makes me want to rip her eyes out. When she sits down next to me and continues to brag about her pregnancy, I literally get up and walk away from her as fast as I can in the middle of her sentence.

Ashley and I had a big fight once when I lived at my aunt's. I can't even remember what started it now, but looking back at it, I find myself getting angry all over again. During that argument, she made the comment, "Your parents don't even care about you, and that's why my mom had to take you in!" In return, I called her a bitch. And the second I said it, she hauled off and slapped me.

I didn't have a chance to react because Christopher was standing there and tackled me down on the bed. No matter how much I screamed for him to let me go so I could beat the shit out of her, he refused to get off of me until I calmed down. He finally told her if she didn't leave the house, he was going to let me up so I could finish what she started because she continued to stand there and run her mouth.

Afterward, I was glad that he did that because God only knows what would have happened if he hadn't. Now, when I think about what she said that day and the way she's been acting today, I wish I could go back in time because I would have torn her up. *If she knows what's good for her, she will stay away from me the rest of the day.*

I walk into the smoking room where my aunt is and sit down next to her. "What's wrong, Heather? Your face is beet red. Did something happen?"

I hesitate to tell her because after all, Ashley is her daughter. But I'm so angry right now that I could spit nails. I quickly blurt out why I'm mad and start crying a little.

"Oh, honey, I'm so sorry. God, I don't know what's wrong with Ashley sometimes. I'm so mad she's acting that way, but please, don't let it bother you, ok? She did love your mother. She just doesn't know how to handle all of this," she says as she hands me a cigarette. "Here, Heather. It's ok, take it."

Huh? Is she serious?

I look at her dumbfounded. "But what if my dad comes down here?"

"I'm sure he won't care. He'll understand. We're all going through a hard time right now," she replies. I reach out to take it from her as she adds, "If he gets mad, I'll take the blame."

I haven't even smoked half the cigarette when my dad walks through the door as I'm blowing smoke out of my mouth. *Oh, shit!* Before I have a chance to react, he takes a quick look at me, turns, and walks right back out of the room.

My aunt nudges me. "I told you. It's fine," she says with a sniffle.

I have never seen my aunt so distraught before, and it breaks my heart. All the anger I had toward her when I left her house has disappeared. I know that none of it matters anymore. As much as she and my mom fought, they loved each other just like Malory and I do. I can't imagine how I would feel if I lost my sister. It makes me miss her even more, and I wonder if she's ok. There is no way she can be. I'm sickened that there's nothing I can do to be there for her.

My cousin is nowhere to be seen in the crowd of people when I leave the smoking room, so I find my place back on the couch. I'm confused and scared. I have never needed my mom more than I do right now. *Irony sucks!*

I keep wishing she were sitting here next to me, making me feel better. I want to be mad at her for leaving us and for not thinking of us when she swallowed those pills down with a bottle of booze. I want to be mad at her for never thinking of us all the times before when she could have killed herself. But no matter how hard I try, I can't hate her for this final knife she has jabbed into all of our hearts.

All I can feel for her right now is sorrow and pity. I feel sorry that she had to live such a tragic life. In the end, she never got what she wanted. It seems so unfair that she had to suffer through so much. *For what? I thought everyone's life was supposed to have meaning? What was the meaning of hers?*

I'm trying not to be angry at my grandpa, so I avoid as much eye contact with him as possible. I can't help but sit here and think about all of the stories I've heard about how bad her childhood was and all the bad things he did. Part of me wants to scream at him and tell him that it's all his fault that she's dead.

As I sit there thinking about everything and wondering how it all ended up this way, it suddenly hits me. *That's it! This is the reason for my pregnancy and the way it had to end! Finally, something that makes sense! I can finally find a reason for something in this screwed up life!* If I wouldn't have gotten pregnant, none of that horrible stuff would have ever happened. As much as I wish I could take it back, I know now that I wouldn't. Not for anything! I would have never gotten as close to my mom as I did in the last six months without that happening. If I had the baby, I would be sitting here, ready to give birth at any time. There is just no way I could have handled that without my mom. *Thank You, God, for giving me that brief moment of closeness to my mom.*

I've been telling myself since I was little that I will never be like my parents. I have never felt it as strongly as I do right now. I owe it to my mom and to myself to make sure I don't falter on the promises I've always made. No matter how hard life gets for me, I will never use drugs, and I will never become an alcoholic. Even if the temptation becomes strong, I know I will be too damn scared to end up like her to ever go back on my word.

Chapter Ten

After we came back from Ohio, I stayed with Dad for a few extra days before finding out that the judge has requested another hearing for our case to be reviewed today. My mind is swirling with questions about why he would request another hearing so soon. I'm scared of what will happen when we get there. The judge has never requested a hearing like this before. The hearings are usually because I've run away again or lost my placement. Otherwise, it's a normal periodic review that was already scheduled at a previous hearing.

On the hour drive to court, the silence between Dad and me is deafening. My insides want to burst from not being able to say the things I know need to be said. I know he is drowning in sorrow. We all are. Instead of talking about it, we've been walking around like zombies, trying to figure out what to do next on our own.

The boys went back to school today, and I'm worried about them. I think it's too soon for them to go back. I know there is no way they could be thinking about school right now. I hope there is someone there they can talk to about it. Although Dad is probably right; going back to school might help take their minds off of everything that has happened.

To top it off, the thought of what Malory must be going through makes my stomach turn. She'll be at court today, too. I hope they let me hug her and talk to her this time. The last time we were both there together, they brought her through the back of the courtroom in shackles. We couldn't talk to her or touch her. However, I knew they would be taking her down the elevator that day, so I waited close by, hoping I could tell her that I love her. The guard yelled at me, but I didn't give a shit. What was he going to do, lock me up with her? Malory wasn't allowed to say anything back or she would be in trouble. But I could tell by the look in her eyes that she was saying she loved me, too.

"Heather, did you bring all your stuff with you when you came home?" Dad asks, interrupting my thoughts.

"Yeah. I don't want my stuff to get stolen again, and who knows where I'm going today after court."

"Well, I'm hoping they will just let you come home with me today," he adds.

"Really, Dad? You think they'll let me?"

"Well, we shouldn't get our hopes up just in case they say no, but that's the plan," he replies.

I feel a little of the hope that's drained away from me in the last few weeks slowly start to return.

I know he's right and that I shouldn't get my hopes up. We've been down this road a million times since we were taken away, but I can't help it. I have to have hope. Without it, I know I wouldn't have made it this far.

My thoughts return to Mom. *Please, Mom, be there to watch over us today. We need you now more than ever. If you could help send us home, I promise I will try harder than I ever have. Without you there, Dad and the boys need us home. I would give anything to be given the chance to start over.*

As I pray, I picture her face and how beautiful she looked that day in the car when I last saw her. I struggle to swallow the huge lump in my throat and fight back the tears as we pull into the courthouse parking lot. I turn to my dad before opening the car door, and my eyes fill with tears. "Dad, if they let me come home, I promise I'll be a better kid."

He doesn't respond, but I know by the look he gives me that he knows I mean it.

While sitting on the bench outside of the courtroom, waiting to be called in, we're approached by a woman I've never seen before. She's beautiful with long blonde curly hair and pretty, kind blue eyes. She's short and thin, wearing a black skirt suit with shiny black high heels. When she opens her mouth to speak, she talks with a sweet, low Southern accent.

"Hi, Heather. My name is Charlotte Cope, and I'm the new GAL for your case. If it's ok with you, I'd like to speak with you and your sister alone before we head into the courtroom."

"Malory is here already?" I ask anxiously.

"Yes. She's waiting for us in the conference room."

"Ok," I reply, somewhat confused. *What the heck is a GAL?*

I follow behind her, and just before entering the conference room, I ask, "What's a GAL?"

She turns and looks at me with surprise. "Are you kidding?"

"No," I respond shyly.

"Oh, sweet baby, come on. We have a lot to talk about," she says as she opens the conference room door.

"Malory!" I cry out as soon as I see her. I rush over to hug her, crying and not caring what the guard behind her has to say about it. *I dare her to try and stop me!*

"Are the handcuffs really necessary?" Charlotte asks the guard sharply.

"I'm sorry. It's policy to keep them on her at all times," replies the guard.

"Well, if I have anything to do with it, she won't be leaving here in them," snaps Charlotte.

Whoa! I like her already.

"Ok, girls," she begins as she sits down and opens a large file in front of her. "Do either of you know what a GAL is?"

"No," we both respond almost simultaneously.

"You don't know who your GAL is? He stood on the same side of the courtroom as you at every court date you've ever had. Did he ever speak to you?" she asks curiously.

"We know who he is, but we've never talked to him before. He would always agree with whatever the state recommended, so we figured he was there for them," I respond knowing my sister feels the same way. We've had plenty of conversations about that man and always wondered who he was.

"Oh, honey," she says touching my hand from across the table, "he was your old GAL, which stands for Guardian Ad Litem. He's an attorney who is supposed to represent you in court. He should have been talking to you both, fighting for what was in your best interests."

Malory and I look at each other, and I know we're thinking the same thing. She quickly looks back at Charlotte and says it first. "So, the last four years, we've had our own attorney and didn't even know it? That's fucking bullshit!" she says angrily as a tear falls down her face.

"Poissant! Watch your mouth!" snaps the guard.

"It's ok," says Charlotte looking up at the guard. "She's right. It is bullshit, and she has every right to be angry." She turns back to us. "I'm so sorry he didn't do more to help you, but let's look forward, not backward. I WILL help you. I will fight for you and your needs and wants as long as it's what's best for you. I've spent a lot of time looking through your file," she says, sifting through the pages in front of her and pausing before looking back up at us. "I couldn't be sorrier that more wasn't done to help your family. I'm so sorry for the loss of your mother. My heart aches for your entire family."

"So, what do you think is best for us?" I ask curiously, wondering how she will be any different than the mysterious man who watched us go through hell for the last four years. He never did more than glance over at us every once in a while.

"I am recommending that you be released from the care of DCFS and be returned to your father immediately."

"Really?" Malory asks with excitement and tears in her voice.

"Yes, really," says Charlotte with a smile on her face.

I reach over and grab my big sister's handcuffed hand and squeeze hard. *Things are going to be different at this court date.* I can tell by the way this woman talks that she knows what she's doing. I wonder where she's been all this time. I can't help but feel sad. I wish we would have met her before it was too late. Mom would have loved her. They have the same feisty personalities.

Once everyone is settled in the courtroom, the judge announces that Malory wrote a letter addressing the court. Before the hearing is to begin, he wants her to read her letter. I look up at my dad before she even starts reading it, and I can tell he's going to burst into tears at any moment. I wish that I had the courage to reach out and grab his hand. I would give anything to be able to show more affection toward him right now.

Malory begins to read. "I wrote this letter because it's the only way I can express my grief locked away in this cell while my family is at my mom's funeral, saying goodbye to her without me." She stops reading to wipe her eyes and catch her breath, but then continues in the saddest, most tear-filled voice I've ever heard. A voice that makes everyone in the courtroom cry. I can even see tears in the judge's eyes as she reads on.

"It's not fair that I'm stuck in here while my mom is being put into a box and buried in the ground, and I'm not even allowed to say goodbye to her for the last time. I hate everything right now. I hate the state for never doing what they should have done to help my family. I hate my mom and dad for not trying harder to get us home. I hate the court for locking me away and taking the last year of my mom's life away from me. More than anything, I hate myself. I know I'm the only one I can blame for missing out on so much time with my mom. If I could take it back, I would." She stops again, unable to read through her sobs.

I see Charlotte touch her shoulder and whisper something in her ear.

After a few minutes of silence, the judge looks at our caseworker and says, "Please, tell me it's not true that she wasn't allowed to go to her mother's funeral?"

"Your Honor, we tried everything we could to get her out of there for the service, but the warden wouldn't allow it," she responds.

"Obviously, you didn't try everything, or she would have been there!" he barks.

Holy shit!

"For crying out loud, they transport adult prisoners to funerals who have committed much worse crimes. There is no acceptable reason for her not to have been there," he adds.

"I'm sorry, Your Honor. We did everything we could," says Sandra, lowering her head.

"Why didn't you petition for an emergency hearing so I could handle it? Don't tell me you tried everything!"

The courtroom fills with silence as I sit in shock over how upset the judge seems. I've never seen him this mad at anyone other than us.

"Mr. Poissant, Miss Heather, please approach the bench," he says looking over at Dad and me.

My heart starts to pound as I walk toward the front of the courtroom and find a place next to my sister. I link my arm inside of her cuffed arm and hold on as tight as I can.

"What are your recommendations, Mrs. Cope?" asks the Judge.

"Your Honor, I think this family has suffered enough blows for this entire room, and what's in their best interest is clear. They need to be together so they can work through this tragedy as a family. I strongly recommend you reunite this family today."

I can feel myself start to shake and I can't control the tears that are falling down my face.

The judge looks up at us with sorrow in his eyes and says, "I can't help but feel responsible for how much this system has failed your family, and I can't tell you enough how sorry I am. I wish I would have done more to force DCFS to follow my orders. The system is supposed to help bring families together. I can't help but feel like it's done nothing but tear yours apart." He pauses and lowers his head.

Holy crap, is he going to cry?

When he looks up again, he looks over at Sandra and the prosecutor. "Do either of you have an issue with the recommendations from Mrs. Cope?"

"No, Your Honor," they both reply.

Oh my God, we're going home!

"Good, because it wouldn't have changed my mind anyway," he says as he looks back up at us. "I'm so sorry for your loss, and it is my wish that you are able to come together as a family during this terrible time. Go home, girls. You need to be with your family," he says with a hard thump of his gavel.

Holy shit! I can't believe what just happened. As happy as I am to have finally heard him speak those words, my heart breaks at the same time because Mom isn't here to share the joy with us.

"Your Honor?" calls the guard that brought Mal. "Yes?" he replies.

"I can't just let her leave today. I have to take her back because there's paperwork that needs to be done before we can let her go."

Oh, no! I look over at Mel and see the blood drain away from her face.

"Excuse me?" asks the judge with a hint of sarcasm. "Well, it's a process, Your Honor."

"I don't see why she has to be there for you to get your paperwork in order. I said she's being released today, so she's being released today, and that's final."

"With all due respect, Your Honor, I could lose my job if I don't follow procedure."

He looks at her as if he's about to bite her head right off. "I think your procedures have caused enough damage, so I couldn't care less about them. What I say goes, and that's that."

"But Your Honor," she begins to plead, but he doesn't give her a chance to finish.

"But nothing! Let me ask you this, who am I?" She just stares at him as if she doesn't know how to respond. "Don't just stare at me. I asked you a question. WHO am I?"

"The judge, Your Honor," she cowers.

"And WHO put her in your facility in the first place?" he asks.

"You did, Your Honor."

"That's right. I did, and I am taking her out. Today! So, you go tell your warden if he has an issue with it that he can take it up with me. I also expect that all of her things will be mailed to her in the condition she left them in and that nothing will be missing. Do you understand?"

"Yes, Your Honor."

I am completely blown away right now. I can't wait to hug my sister as soon as they take those stupid cuffs and shackles off her. I don't know whether I should cry or jump up and down. I look up at my dad and smile. For the first time in a week, he smiles back at me. *Maybe there is hope for our family after all.*

Chapter Eleven

My eyes suddenly open, and I realize I'm not dreaming. *Damn how could this be happening?* I roll onto my side and see the cold steel toilet two feet in front of my face.

Gross! Only animals live like this, and I am not an animal. Tears start to form in the corners of my eyes. I know I don't belong in this hell, and I don't know if I will ever forgive Dad for sending me here.

I sit up and rub the sleep from my eyes so I can stand and look out of the tiny window that's between my bed and the toilet. As I long to be out there with the rest of the free world, the pit in the bottom of my stomach grows bigger. *How could he do this to me?*

The loud buzzing of the door startles me away from my self-pity. "Poissant," calls the guard as she opens the door, "time to eat."

Eat? That's something I've barely been able to do in the last two days. The food is disgusting, barely suitable for wild animals. But I know without it, I'll be sicker than I already am, so I eat enough to keep my hunger pains away.

As I sit down at the table, I stare down at the slop in front of me. I feel more out of place than I ever have.

"Hey, white girl," calls out a Black girl from the other end of the table, "what you do to get put in here?"

I look up at her and have to force the tears back. "Nothing," I mumble, picking up my dry, hard toast and cramming it into my mouth. I chew extra hard, hoping to relieve myself of some of the anguish built up in my chest. I feel like a caged lion ready to explode and attack at any moment.

"Yeah, none of us did nothing! We all innocent in here," she laughs, and the other girls chime in with laughter. "No, really. What you do?"

"Really. I didn't do anything," I reply with a firm face. "I'm on house arrest. My dad and I had a fight. He kicked me out of the house and refused to let me back in, so I went to stay with my boyfriend. After a day, my boyfriend's mom, who is a real bitch, caught him hiding me there and called the police knowing I would get arrested. So here I am. Like I said, I didn't do anything."

"Oh, girl, they gonna revoke your house arrest and make you stay here the rest of your probation time."

Fear hits me like a ton of bricks as her words linger in my ears. "But how could they do that to me? What was I supposed to do? Where was I supposed to go? He kicked me out! I didn't wanna leave. I sat on the porch, begging him to let me back in because I knew I'd be in trouble, but he wouldn't let me in!" I say with half fear, half anger.

"I don't know, girl. That's just the way it is when you on house arrest and probation. They ain't gonna care what you have to say."

I know she's right. That's exactly what happened to Mal when she was on probation, but this is different. He kicked me out. What other choice did I have? There's no way they can punish me for something I couldn't control. How could they? I dump what's left of the slop on my tray into the garbage, and ask the guard to let me back in my room.

"You know this is your only rec time until later? You sure you wanna go back to your room early?"

"Yeah, I'm sure," I mumble through clenched teeth as she opens the door to let me back in my cell.

I lie back down on my bed and cover my head with my pillow. I just want to sleep until it's time for me to go to court in the morning. It's Sunday, and I've been here since Friday night. I'm praying my case will be called in tomorrow and that it's not dragged out until Tuesday. I don't know if I can make it here another day.

What if that girl is right? What if they do make me stay until my probation is over? Or worse...until I'm eighteen! I start sobbing at the thought of it and say a prayer to Mom. *Please help me, Mom. You know I don't belong here. I'm not like Malory. I won't make it.*

I try hard to fall asleep, but I fail. I've slept at every given opportunity since I got here trying to make the time pass faster. My mind is spinning as I think about everything that's happened in the last seven months, and I start to feel homesick. I would give anything to be at home with Dad and the boys. As hard-headed and clueless as Dad can be sometimes, I still want nothing more than to be at home with him.

Living with him has been hard at times, but I've also been happy there. I'm so torn with my feelings; I don't know which way is up. We got along great when I first moved in with him. He was extra attentive, and in some ways, he even spoiled me rotten. I suppose he was trying to overcompensate for losing Mom. Dad, being the way that he is, doesn't know how else to show his love.

Malory didn't last a whole week living at Dad's before she left to move in with Tony. I begged him not to let her go. But he knew the fight wouldn't be worth it; she would be turning eighteen in less than two months. She received her GED while she was in the detention center, so school was no longer keeping her grounded anywhere. Dad's words ring in my head. "Well, I figure if I give her enough rope, eventually, she'll hang herself with it." I know he was right, and he couldn't really stop her, but I can't help being angry that she didn't care enough about the rest of us to stay.

She got pregnant within months of living with him. Then, she married the stupid asshole. I can't believe that's the life she wants to live. I'm angry at her for not realizing how much more she could have become. She was so good at softball. I know she could have gotten a full ride to college. I could even picture her going to the Olympics. When we were kids, all she talked about was becoming a veterinarian. She's so smart. I know she could have done it. Now look at her. She's basically still living in prison. She goes from one jail to another. *How can she stand it?* Being locked away like this makes me want to jump out of my skin. I hate being controlled by anyone or anything.

Tony barely lets her see or talk to Dad. He never lets her see me or the boys. He tells her that she's not allowed to talk to me because I'm a bad influence, and he doesn't want her to become a whore like me.

Whore? I'd show that bastard what I really think of him if I could. Then they'd have a reason to lock me away like a monster. I know I'm not a whore, but he knows I'll try to influence her to get the hell away from him. That's really what he's trying to stop.

She didn't even tell us she was getting married. We only knew because Dad stopped by to see her unannounced, and she was all dressed up. Of course, he questioned why, so she told him. Even though he wouldn't say it, I could tell he was heartbroken when he told me about it. I was in shock that she settled for a courthouse wedding. But I guess looking back now, it doesn't surprise me. He controls everything she does, says, and even what she wears.

I don't ever get to talk to Mal, but I know more about what's going on than she thinks. Lynne, one of the counselors at PSG, lives across the street from them. We've known Lynne since our days at Anchusa because she used to work there too. I've always been particularly drawn to her. She was always so nice at Anchusa, and when we crossed paths again, I latched on to her. At PSG, she does music therapy, but we spend all of our time together talking instead of doing music. I'm not really interested in learning to play an instrument these days.

Talking to Lynne and finding out what goes on is as close to my sister as I can get. She never has anything good to tell me and shares stories about the fights that go on outside. I know she's worried about Mal. Lynne thinks Tony is abusing my sister. *Duh!* She says she tries to say hi and talk to Malory whenever she sees her. But if Tony is standing there, Malory keeps her head down and won't even look up at her.

I have a hard time imagining my sister living that way. She's always been the strong one. So why can't she stand up to him? She's never had an issue standing up to anyone before. I don't understand this hold he seems to have over her, and it makes me angry. I love her, and I miss her more than anything. I want to be a part of her life. She's my sister; how could I not? *How could she do this to our family? How could she choose him over us?* Maybe if he wouldn't have taken her away from us, she would have been there to protect me when Dad couldn't. And I would have never ended up where I am now. The thought makes me hate Tony even more. I have to stop thinking about this because I can feel my blood beginning to boil.

I know, it's partially my fault for being here, but I don't think I did anything bad enough to land here. *It's so unfair.* Dad thinks he's teaching me a lesson, but being in baby jail is taking it too far. I learned my lesson the first time he sent me here. That was all I needed. This time, though, it is total bullshit. I hope wherever he is that he feels bad for it. He's probably sitting in a bar, drinking himself into oblivion. That's all he has done since Mom died. I know he's trying to deal with losing her the best way he knows how, but what about me and the boys? He's not thinking about what's going on in our lives. I tried telling him, but I didn't know how to get through to him.

He took us to see a family counselor when I first moved in with him. His insurance paid for it. I wasn't required to be there or anything. He actually decided to do it on his own. I know at first, he was really trying, but that didn't last long. We only saw the counselor one time before Dad gave up. He has a hard time talking to anyone, much less a stranger. I don't have a hard time talking to anyone except him. The irony twists my stomach into bigger knots. *Why can't I talk to him? Why won't he listen to me when I do try or ever open his eyes to what's really going on?*

While living with my dad, the school year started off good. But like most of them, it eventually took a turn for the worse. My first day of school was my sixteenth birthday, and my first-hour class was art. As soon as I walked into the room, everyone stopped what they were doing and stared at me. It's a very small school, so it's not easy to pretend you're not the new girl like some of the other schools I've been to. A girl sitting at a table close by saved me from embarrassment by pulling me down into the empty seat next to her and instantly befriended me.

During the morning announcements, just when I was beginning to feel at ease with my new friend, they announced my birthday over the loudspeaker. I have never been more embarrassed in my life. The whole class stopped what they were doing and once again stared at me.

Marcy, being the friendly and outgoing person that she is, couldn't help but shout out, "Oh my God! Today is your birthday? It's her birthday, everyone!" I know she had the best of intentions, but I was mortified. For the rest of the day, whenever I was near her, she made sure everyone around knew it was my birthday. She's sweet in that way. It was embarrassing, but it was the most attention I received all day, and it made me feel good.

Marcy is smart, pretty, soft-spoken, outgoing, and naïve (but in a good way). She has a smile you can see a mile away, and she's innocent. When I say innocent, I mean *innocent*. She's a year older than me and still a virgin. I envy the strength she has when it comes to her virginity. She has boyfriends, but her will is so strong that nothing could break it. She has grown up in such a good home. They go to church every Sunday, and her parents are amazing. The relationship she has with her family is inspiring. I know it's too late for me to have those things. But I pray that if I ever have a family of my own, it's like hers. *I wonder if I can ever be the sort of mom she has or if I'm just too broken now.*

I shock the hell out of her with my stories all the time. I don't mean to, but sometimes I forget who I'm talking to until I see her mouth dropped to the floor. *Now look at me.* She's probably in church right about now, and I'm locked away in a cell, lying on a cot with a toilet next to my head. *God, why is she even my friend?* I know I don't deserve her friendship. I would give anything to have her life. I know she knows how lucky she is, too, and she's thankful for it. Only a good person can take a broken, damaged girl like me under their wing the way she has. I really miss her.

The first week of school was the "Turnabout Dance" when the girls ask the guys. Marcy begged me to go with her. At first, I said no way. I didn't even know anyone. How could I ask a guy to go with me? She told me that I didn't have to worry about that part. Her date had a friend who'd already been eyeing me. When she pointed him out, I thought, *Ugh...not my type.* She convinced me that it didn't matter and that going to the dance would be a good chance for me to meet new people so I could make more friends.

At the time, I thought she was right, and I knew going with her would be a blast. Who cares if my date was a huge dork? I didn't have to date him afterward. She said he was one of the popular guys in school, and that shocked me. *That's what they consider popular?* I mean he was ok looking and not a total dog or anything, but definitely not my type. He was not what I would see as "popular," either. I realize now after everything I've gone through that being "popular" isn't what it's cracked up to be. It certainly isn't important in the real world.

It didn't take long to realize going to the dance with Mr. "Popular" was a huge mistake. I tried to tell him afterward that I only wanted to be his friend, but he wouldn't let off. He's on the track team and loves to run. So, he started running almost a mile to my house every day. He was ok in a dorky sort of way. I thought it was sweet that he thought so much of me that he tried hard to impress me. All of his efforts to charm me started to pay off after a few weeks. One night while Dad was at work, I let him come into my room. When he tried to kiss me that night, I didn't stop him, but boy, I wish I would have. It was a pretty heavy make out session that went a little further than it should have, but I was smart enough not to let it go all the way.

Within a week, I realized I shouldn't have messed around with him at all. I wanted to end it before he expected more. As much as I tried to force myself to be attracted to him in that way, I just couldn't, so I told him we could only be friends. It wasn't long after that the rumors started to circulate. He told all of his "popular" friends in school that I took his virginity! I couldn't believe it. I was horrified. I've never had a guy spread rumors about me before. *Guys do that?*

For the most part, I've kept to myself at that school. I haven't traveled very far outside the circle of friends I have with Marcy, and there are only a few of us. Marcy feels bad that she ever talked me into going to the dance with him, but it's not her fault. I should have slammed the door in his face the first time he ran to my house. I knew there was something weird about him. As sweet as the gestures seemed at the time, it was pretty desperate on his part, begging for me like a little puppy dog. *Loser!* I should have known better. I really need to learn how to listen to my gut.

I tried to ignore the scrutiny I took from all the boys at school after that, but it was so hard. Instead of being tortured by a group of mean girls, it was the boys. Which, in a way, is so much harder to deal with. *How do I defend myself to a group of boys?* It's not like I can beat the hell out of one of them.

I wanted so badly to tell my dad what was going on. I wished I could go to him crying, and he'd be the kind of dad that would go after them, demanding that they leave his little girl alone. I longed for him to threaten to tear them apart and make them too scared to ever even look my way again. I knew that wasn't realistic, though. Instead, I tried to keep it to myself and handle it on my own. I kept praying they would find someone else to harass.

BUZZZZZZ! I jump from my thoughts. *Fuck!* I'll never get used to that sound.

"Poissant! Time to shower."

Ughh! This makes me feel more nauseous than the food here. I want to cry at the thought of showering in front of all these strange girls with the guards watching. *God, get me out of here.*

Chapter Twelve

I finish my crude, invasive shower, eat lunch, and attempt to sit in the day room, distracting myself for a while by watching TV. As much as I just want to sleep the day away, maybe the TV will pass the time more quickly.

"Hey, white girl!" calls out the familiar voice from breakfast this morning. I turn around and see her with a few other girls sitting at a table playing cards. "Wanna play some spades with us?"

What the hell, why not? Daytime TV sucks, anyway.

"I don't know how to play," I say, sitting down at the table.

The girls snicker at me. "What do you do on the outside if you don't even know how to play spades?" asks a rundown looking white girl sitting next to me.

"I don't know. Hang out with my boyfriend on the weekends. Go to school and hang out at the beach during the summer." *Damn, the thought of the beach and Ryan make the pit in my stomach grow even bigger.*

Black girl laughs. "I thought you looked like one of those innocent *Beverly Hills 90210* type of girls. You ever been locked up before?"

"I've been in and out of foster homes, group homes, and residential homes since I was little, but I've never been to juvie until recently. I was locked up once for two days and then put on house arrest, but if I have anything to do with it this time, I won't be here more than a few days. And then, I'm never coming back," I reply with confidence.

She nods her head at me and smiles. "What's your name, white girl?"

"Heather," I respond, throwing down a spade.

"Damn, you even have a Beverly Hills name," she says, snickering. I smirk. "Did I throw down the right card?"

She laughs again. "It's all good, white girl. Spades is a jailhouse game. You won't learn that at the beaches," she laughs.

I feel stupid never having played this game before. I can't even remember the last time I played cards. I guess I've been a little busy trying to reach my eighteenth birthday.

"So, white girl, I'm just gonna keep calling you 'white girl' if that's cool. Where you from?"

"I don't give a shit as long as you're cool with me calling you 'Black girl,'" I say with a smile and a bit of sarcasm.

She nods her head and smiles. "Ahh...shit, someone's got jokes," she says, still laughing.

I like her. She reminds me of my old friend Shaniqua. We could definitely be friends outside of here.

I tell her where I currently live, but explain where I'm from in Illinois. *Indiana is not my home.*

Her eyes widen, and she half laughs. "You're from the ghetto, girl! That place is almost as bad as Gary, Indiana. I have a cousin who lives there. I guess you're not so *90210* after all, are ya?" she laughs.

"Nope. I can hold my own," I say with confidence. There is one thing I've learned in situations like these- even if I'm crumbling on the inside and feeling like a total coward, I can't let anyone see that. That's when people take advantage and trample all over you. *I have to be tough, even when I feel like I'm anything but.*

The rest of the afternoon and evening isn't so bad. I guess being around the other girls where I can talk, watch TV, and play cards is better than being locked away in my room with only my thoughts to keep me company. At first, I was scared to be around them, not sure if I would be surrounded by bully criminals or not. They want to get out of here just as bad as I do, and fighting won't get us there.

I'm growing tired of hearing all their opinions on how I'll be here until my probation is over. It's a relief when it's time for lock down and lights out. The dark brings me closer to going to court, and my potential release from this baby jail.

Once I'm alone in the dark, my heavy thoughts return. I can feel the sting in the back of my eyes where the tears are sitting, ready to fall any second. Ryan's face flashes through my mind, and that's all it takes. I'm crying like a baby again. No matter how hard I try not to think about everything, it's impossible sitting in this tiny, cold, quiet cell. There's nothing here to drown out the chaos that's twirling around in my head.

Once my tears slow down, I realize that I haven't had a panic attack for the last few nights I've been here. *That's odd.* I've been getting them for months now. Every night when I try to go to sleep, I jump out of bed in a panic as soon as I start to doze off. It feels like something is smothering me, and I'm convinced I'm going to die in my sleep just like Mom did.

I was fine when I first moved to my dad's, but as soon as school let out for the summer, it hit me with a vengeance. It has been a complete hell ever since. After suffering through it for the first few weeks, not knowing what was wrong with me, I figured out how to avoid having an actual attack. I decided it would be better if I stopped trying to sleep at night altogether. I've been forcing myself to stay awake every night, watching the same old TV programs I used to watch with Grams. That brings me peace. As soon as the sun starts to show her shining face, I know it's safe to fall asleep. *I wonder why it's suddenly stopped.* I haven't had a peaceful night's sleep in three months. Now, to be able to sleep in a pitch-black room without the TV in a place like this shocks me.

I guess it makes sense why I started having them. Mom dying in her sleep has to have something to do with it. Watching Mom go through panic attacks made me an expert, so I knew what it was when it started. I can't believe I used to roll my eyes at her for it and thought she was faking them. I feel so bad now. I wish I could go back in time, wrap my arms around her, and tell her everything was going to be ok. Instead, I acted like a complete asshole. I couldn't see the pain that life had caused her. All I could see was what it was doing to us. I guess I thought it should have been easier for her to figure all her shit out. Nine-year-old Heather is in the back of my subconscious mind, waving a finger at me with one hand on her hip. I am reminded of how selfish I was, and the realization rocks me, filling the pit in my stomach with regret.

Dad is never home when I have panic attacks. He's either working midnights or in the bar. Who knows, maybe it's partly his fault that I started getting them too. I haven't been able to talk to him or anyone else about them. I keep trying to handle them on my own by telling myself it's all in my head. For the most part, it's been working. I guess I'm afraid if I tell someone that it's happening, they will want to dope me up on the same medication that played a part in taking my mom away. That's the last thing I want. *I have to stop thinking about the attacks or I'm going to make myself have one.* This is the last place on earth I want to have one. At least at home, I know I'm safe.

Toward the end of the school year was when everything between Dad and I really started to go to shit. He was never home, and the torturous boys at school were becoming too much for me to handle. I decided I had enough. One day at school, I was walking down the crowded hall to my next class, and one of the boys passed me. He bumped into my shoulder so hard that he almost knocked me over. I knew he did it on purpose because he was looking right at me with disgust in his eyes when he did it.

I yelled at him to watch where he was going. And he turned, yelling out for everyone to hear, "Hey, Heather! Why don't you go fuck Adam again?"

As soon as he said it, he bent over to pick up a pencil he dropped on the floor. I had reached my boiling point, so I charged over to the wooden door that he was standing in front of, grabbed onto it with both hands, and swung it toward him as hard as I could. It hit him so hard in the head that he went flying backwards on his ass. I giggle a little at the memory. *Asshole got what he deserved.*

When I got home that day, I told my dad that I was done with school. I was sixteen, and it was now my choice to drop out, but he wasn't hearing any of it. He told me that school was the only thing he expected me to do. He wasn't going to allow me to live with him if I dropped out. I wished I could tell him why I was so unhappy, but it's too hard to talk to him. He probably wouldn't have listened to me, anyway. It took all the courage I could gather just to tell him that he couldn't possibly understand how hard it was to always be the new kid at school all the time. He was always so popular growing up and didn't have a care in the world. Everyone loved him.

I had hoped he would ask what was going on. Maybe then I could have told him. He didn't ask. Instead, he yelled at me. When he couldn't get through to me the next morning, he called the police. I listened in on the other line while they told him there was simply nothing they could do to force me to go to school because of my age. He told them he was going to kick me out, and they said he couldn't do that, either. I guess looking back now, I understand why he was so frustrated. I felt bad for putting him in that position. But maybe if he would have stopped and listened to my pain, he could have helped me get through it.

The dispatcher on the other end of the phone said one final thing that sealed my fate. "I'm sorry sir, there's nothing we can do if she isn't doing something to disrupt your home."

He responded with, "Well, about a month ago she broke a mirror in my bedroom."

That's all it took, and they were on their way, arresting me and charging me with criminal mischief. I still can't believe they could arrest me for something that happened that long ago. Besides, the damned mirror was already broken from Dad shoving Mom into it during a drunken brawl not too long before she moved out of the house. I can't even remember now why me and Dad were fighting the day

I damaged the already broken mirror. That's how silly it was. I think he took my car away for smoking or something of that nature. I was acting like a spoiled brat (which he's partially responsible for turning me into), threw something at it in my tizzy, shattering it a little more than it already was. *Stupid!*

I sat in this hell for two days after that. When they let me out, they put me on house arrest. Not the kind where I have to wear an ankle bracelet or anything, more like intensive probation. I couldn't leave the house other than to go to school unless Dad gave me permission. He had to call me out to the probation hotline, letting them know where I was going, and call them again once I returned home. It's really not so bad. I could still do anything I wanted, as long as Dad was in a good mood and ok with it, which he usually was.

My mind wanders to a happier time at Dad's when I first moved in with him. Just a few weeks after Mom's death, I turned sixteen and got my license. Despite how much the asshole driver's ed teacher hated me, I passed his class with a "D." Dad took me to take my test on the day of my birthday.

The feeling of having my license is indescribable. Funny how a small piece of plastic can hold so many big possibilities. I've been ready to be free for so long. Even though I've never driven further than the Lake Michigan beaches on the Indiana dunes, knowing that I can go a lot further someday soon is liberating.

Dad bought me a car. Well, it was supposed to be my car. After I got my license, he told me to start looking for one but to make sure I didn't go over $1500.00. I was ecstatic. Fifteen hundred dollars is so much money, and I couldn't have been more thankful.

Every day on the way home from school, I passed a car lot that sat on the corner of one of the major intersections in our small town. Right out in front of the car lot facing the road sat a pretty little red car with my name written all over it. A 1995 Grand Am GT with a moonroof and dual exhausts. Everyone in school with a license wanted that car, including me. I knew it was probably out of my reach, so I didn't mention it to Dad. But one day, he asked if I had found anything yet. I really didn't have time to go looking. How was I supposed to do that without a car to drive around in? *It's not like he was taking me to look for one.*

I gathered the courage and told him about the pretty red car.

"Yeah, I've seen that car, Heather. I can tell ya right now, it's a lot more than $1500," he said, laughing at me sarcastically.

He surprised me a few days later when he said we could go take a look at it and take it for a test drive. Well, *he* test drove it. I could tell by the expression on his face while he was racing it down the back roads outside of town that he was falling in love with it, too. Dad has always had a need for speed and an eye for sporty cars, especially red ones. I wonder how he's been satisfied driving a minivan all these years.

When we left the lot, he told me how much the car cost. I realized it was way out of the price range he gave me. As much as I longed to be the envy of the school, I accepted that it wasn't meant to be.

A week later when I came home from school, I was sitting on the couch watching TV.

Dad called out from his bedroom, "Hey, Heth! Go in the garage and get me the Phillips screwdriver, will ya?"

I remember wondering what the hell he wanted a screwdriver for. We're lucky Dad can screw in a lightbulb. He's never been a handyman. His only tools are the absolute necessities: a hammer, some nails, a few screwdrivers, a wrench, pliers, and duct tape. Fast cars and sports have always been Dad's thing. Fixing things has never been in his interests.

When I opened the garage door, I almost peed my pants—literally! There sat that pretty red car. My insides were jumping up and down while I stood there with my mouth dropped to the floor in shock. It took I don't know how many minutes before I could finally gain enough composure to react to it. I'll never forget the look on his face. It was pure pride for making his little girl happy. A look that said, "Yes! I succeeded! I'm the best dad in the world!" And he was and he still is, no matter what his flaws are.

It started with the car, but he did other things to show his affection in the only way he knows how. I'd ask for five dollars, and he'd hand me a twenty. Part of me knew what he was doing, and I felt bad because I didn't need that much. He would insist that I take it anyway, and I'm no fool. I enjoyed the attention he was showering me with.

Looking back, I know he was overcompensating for Mom being gone. Also, he doesn't know how to express how he feels with words, so he shows it with material things. I know how messed up that is, but I also know it's the only way he knows. Even though I wish he could open his mouth sometimes instead of his wallet, I understand him more now than ever.

Since I was little, I've had this dream of becoming a model. It is ironic because my self-esteem is piss poor. I really don't know why I want it so bad. Maybe I just wanted people to finally notice me in a good way, and I won't have to take anyone's shit anymore.

All of the people who have doubted me over the years and tried to beat me down could sit back and think, *Damn look at her. She made it. I'm an asshole for treating her like garbage.*

Yeah that's what it is. I know it now, and the yearning inside of me to be able to hold up my middle finger for the whole world to see is so strong that I could explode.

I snap back into reality when I remember how short I am, taking after Mom. I really don't have the confidence to be a model, anyway. I envy Mal for getting all the height from our dad. I had my chance over the summer, and I blew it. That's it for me. I'm done trying. My dreams of becoming a model are no more.

I filled out an application for the Miss Teen of Indiana beauty pageant and sent some pictures along with it. I didn't tell Dad I applied for it because I never thought I would get a response. I was on cloud nine when they responded, telling me I had been voted in as one of the contestants to compete.

I was in shock, but excited and eager to tell my dad about it. I felt as if I had already succeeded in some small way. He was happy that I was so excited. Even though being in the pageant was going to cost him a lot of money, he was willing to do what it took for me to go. We had to travel to Indianapolis and stay in the expensive hotel where they held the pageant. I didn't want to be included in the talent contest. *What talent do I have to show them? How to smoke, cuss like a sailor, and run away?* Instead, I entered myself into the Miss Photogenic contest.

The second night we were there, it was time for me to get all dressed up in my formal wear and get on stage. My confidence and excitement turned into complete horror. The thought of being on stage for everyone to stare at me made me feel vulnerable and exposed. I thought everyone would be able to see through my fake smile somehow, and the thought made me physically ill. Seeing all the other girls didn't help. They had their moms and other females there to help them get ready, and that sent me over the edge. I knew I didn't have what it really took, and I was a fool for ever thinking I did.

I couldn't get my hair to do what I wanted it to do because I have never been good at primping myself. I'm a wash-and-go kind of girl, so getting it up in some luxurious style was impossible. My heart ached for my mom, and I know my dad probably thinks I was just acting like a spoiled brat when I said I wanted to give up. He asked me if I was sure at least ten times before we finally packed up and left.

He didn't act like he was mad at me, but he was quiet as ever. I could see the disappointment in his eyes. I wish now that I would have sucked it up and gotten over all of my fears, even if it were just for him. I want so much to make him proud, but no matter how much I try, I keep falling flat on my face.

What did I do? The normalcy I shared with Dad for that brief time in the beginning didn't last nearly as long as it should have. Lying here, I realize how much I miss it and how much I need that back. The pit in my stomach is a reminder of where I am right now and what I've lost. There's nothing liberating about these feelings at all.

I know Dad tries in the best way he knows how, and he always has. I've never been able to hate him the way I did my mom when I was younger. I want to hate him right now, but I still can't. I know in his own messed up universe, he thinks he's teaching me some grand lesson.

I swear I've learned, God. Just let me out of here before it kills me.

Chapter Thirteen

In the morning, I wake from my restless sleep, saddened that another night has passed where my mom didn't visit me in my dreams. I've begged her every night since she left to come to me in my sleep, but she still hasn't, not once in seven months. I want so badly to wrap my arms around her, nuzzle my nose into her hair, and breathe in her smell just one more time. *Why, Mom? Why don't you come see me?* I can't help but feel like she must be mad at me, and it brings a tear to my eye. Dark questions creep into my mind. *What if she can't come see me? What if there is no heaven? What if there is no God at all, and her life ended the day I watched her get lowered into the ground?* I have to shake these morbid thoughts from my head. They are my biggest fears. If I think about them too long, I am sure to send myself into a panic attack.

I turn my thoughts to Ryan and our last moments together before I was brought here. The thought makes me smile. Ryan is everything to me, and I would move heaven and earth to be with him. He's the only boy I don't feel guilty about being with. I know sex has been a problem for me. I have thought that I have to give myself to someone so they'll love me. I've been so damn stupid with boys. I know that's my biggest demon, but with Ryan, it's different. We dated for months before he even considered it. He was determined to make sure that I knew I meant more to him than that. In the end, it was my overactive teenage hormones that finally convinced him it was time.

We got back together toward the end of the school year after Mom died and I came back from the funeral. I was finally able to reach him over the phone. He told me for months how much he missed me and still loved me. Before we could try again, he told me he had to get through his own issues.

Back then, he wouldn't explain why he acted the way he did when we broke up. I learned everything later, and it was devastating to hear. The new discovery didn't make me love him any less. I learned that he became addicted to cocaine when I was living at Bethany's. He knew how I felt about drugs, and he didn't want to drag me through it. *I guess that explains the short fuse he had toward the end and the way he acted in school that day.*

I was blown away when he told me. How did I not know? He said he was doing it even when we were together by sneaking off to the nearest bathroom to get his fixes. As much as I know about substance abuse, it amazes me how naive I still am when it comes to drugs. *I feel so stupid for not seeing or recognizing what was going on right in front of my face.*

I still worry that he will go back to using, just like my mom, and I find myself questioning everything now. I'm trying to trust him, but it's hard. I love him so much, and I don't want to give up on him. I know what it's like to be doubted, judged, and have people toss you to the side like a piece of trash. I will never do that to him because he's been the only constant in my life. I need to be the same for him.

Aside from his mom still being the nasty wench she is, things have been amazing between us. Even with all the miles that separate us, our love is stronger than it's ever been. He's graduated now, so when he's off work, Dad would let him stay the weekends at our house. Since he's eighteen, his mom can't stop him. It's not an idea that Dad was really jumping up and down over, but he was more lenient because of the two hours Ryan had to drive one way to see me. He wouldn't let him go anywhere near my room when he was there. So, he would sleep on the pull-out couch in the living room. Dad really likes Ryan, and I can tell he trusts him with me.

Without Ryan, I don't think I would have made it this long at Dad's. His drinking has been intense. Many nights, I lie awake in a panic. I worried myself sick about him, knowing that he was out drinking himself to death. When the bars would close, if he didn't walk through the door shortly after, I would beg Ryan to take me looking for him. I'm always worried I'm going to find him in a ditch or smashed into a tree. Too many times, we have found him passed out in the car on the side of the road or in some stranger's driveway.

He totaled the minivan drinking and driving shortly after he bought me the car. That turned my car into his car, and I could only drive it with special permission. He took me to the impound lot to show me the van. He also showed me the car he smashed into, and the sight of both made me want to throw up. I can't believe so much damage can be done while both people walk away untouched. I wish he would stop drinking.

What would we do if we lost him, too? I wonder if he ever thinks about that. He has a bad problem, but his pride and stubbornness keep getting in the way of him getting help. Or maybe it's pure stupidity and selfishness. He's convinced himself that help isn't unnecessary, and he says that when he's ready to quit, he can do it alone, but I know better. *Damn the stupid old man! Has losing Mom taught him nothing?*

BUZZZZZ! My heart leaps for joy at that sound this morning, knowing I could be getting called into court and possibly leaving. My stomach is extra queasy from skipping breakfast today. My stomach is in knots. I couldn't bear the slop again.

A heavy-set Black woman with dark red lipstick appears in my doorway. "Poissant, time for court."

Oh, thank God!

After waiting over an hour outside of the courtroom, my name is finally called. *Here it goes,* I think, standing up and walking toward the courtroom door. As I walk through the doors I keep my head held high. I picture nine-year-old Heather curled up in a ball in the corner of my mind, scared as hell. *You're going to be ok,* I assure her. *No matter what happens, you're a survivor.*

As I approach, I'm surprised to see my caseworker and Dad standing toward the front of the room. I didn't know either of them would be here because I've been unable to use the phone.

"Hey," I whisper to them with a smile as the guard walks with me past them, standing me on the opposite side. *This is weird. I've never stood on the opposite side of Dad in court. Why is he on that side with her and not over here with me?*

The judge begins. "Set before us today is the case of a minor child, Heather Poissant."

Child? I'm far from a child and have been for a very long time.

"Said minor child was picked up on Friday, September 18th, 1998, on charges of disobeying the terms of her probation that is due to expire on October 20, 1998." The judge pauses, looking almost bewildered. Then, he looks up at me. "Why in God's name would you do this right before your probation is about to expire? You've made it all these months with no problems. What happened, young lady?"

My eyes fill with tears, but I want to be strong, so I don't let them fall. I manage to choke back the lump in my throat as I respond, "Your Honor, I didn't want to leave the house, but my dad kicked me out. I sat outside, asking him to let me back in, but he wouldn't. So, I went across the street to my friend's and called my boyfriend to come and get me. I didn't know what else to do or where else I was supposed to go." I lower my head and wipe the tears that I can no longer control. *Damn you, Heather, suck it up. Why do you always have to be such a baby?*

The judge's eyes suddenly fill with what looks to me like shock. He turns to Dad, lowering his head and peering at him over the top of his glasses. "Sir, please tell me that you didn't really kick your sixteen-year-old daughter out on the street, where God only knows what could have happened to her?"

Oh, shit! His reaction gives me a glimmer of hope. *Maybe he won't make me stay after all.*

Dad lowers his head, and from where I'm standing, I can tell he's going to cry. He chokes back his tears as he raises his head to answer. "Yes, Your Honor, I did," he replies, clearing his voice. Dad does that voice-clearing thing a lot when he's trying not to cry. He offers no explanation of why he did it.

I suppose he's tired of fighting with me all the time.

"I'm sure you're well aware that typically when someone disobeys the terms of their probation, it's standard for the probation to be revoked, and they spend the rest of their term here?" he asks, turning back to me.

Oh my God, no, please! I think to myself as he continues.

"But this case is different. I am certainly not going to punish you for something you couldn't control."

I let out a huge sigh of relief, and I can feel the pit in my stomach begin to ease.

"With that said," the judge adds, "I also cannot send you back to a house where I can't trust that you won't be kicked out again. I need to know that you will be safe, so I am forced to release you back into the care of the state of Illinois. I am also going to release you from probation in the state of Indiana. I do not see a threat of letting you off early when you will be under the care of another court."

The pit in my stomach returns with full force, and I feel like I could throw up right here in the courtroom.

"Is that going to be a problem, Ms. Blackburn?" he asks my caseworker.

"No, Your Honor."

"Ok then, I wish you the best of luck, Miss Poissant. Case dismissed." With that too familiar bang of the gavel slamming down, it's over just like that.

Now what?

My tears have returned, and I turn to look at my dad. He's not looking at me. He's wiping his eyes with his head lowered. I want to run to him, hug him, and beg him to please take me home with him. I want to stay with him no matter how screwed up our family may be. I wish we could figure it out together somehow. *Why does the answer always have to be for me to be taken away? Who's going to make sure there's food in the house and that my brothers are eating? They need me there and I need them too.*

Sandra lets me ride with Dad to the house to pack my things as she follows closely behind us. We don't talk on the ride home. The silence speaks for itself. I know I'm sorry, and I'm sure he is, too. *What else is there to say, anyway?* I only have a year and five months left until I turn eighteen so I'm sure this is the last time I'll have the chance to live at home. It's a hard pill to swallow, but I have to do it somehow.

In no sort of a hurry, I pack everything up, and I call Ryan to tell him what's going on. He doesn't seem worried. I know this means the drive to see me will be closer for him. That's the last thought on my mind right now. I hug and kiss my dad when I leave, and we say I love you like we always have. I tell him I'll call him when I know where I'm going. *I wish I could say goodbye to the boys.*

"Where are you going to take me?" I ask Sandra as we head off toward the highway back to hell.

"I don't know, Heather, you've been to almost every foster home in the county."

So, what's your point?

"We're going to have to go back to the office so I can make phone calls to try and find you a place. I'll try my hardest to find you somewhere close, but you know nothing is guaranteed."

"Can you please call Ellen and ask her if I can come back there Please, Sandra?" I plead with desperation in my voice.

"No, I don't think so, Heather. I know her beds are full."

How the hell does she know that? Maybe she placed someone there recently. I know she always has a house full, but I had to at least ask.

Dear Diary,

This foster home is hell, and I hate it! The lady is such a weirdo. You must be getting sick of me only writing in you when I'm alone and miserable. I'm sorry I do that. I guess I was just a little busy while I was living with Dad trying to pretend life was normal, even though it's been everything but that. Why am I apologizing to you? You're paper in a book. You couldn't care less. Wow, I must be losing my mind, and it's this house that's making me that way. I've only been here for five days, but it feels like an eternity in hell! The only thing that brings me relief is Ryan coming to see me every day when he gets off work.

I'm in some lame-ass country town that I never knew existed. The town consists of a post office, one park, a church, one gas station, and only a handful of houses. They don't even have their own school. The crazy lady took me to the high school a town over to register me for classes today. I don't know anyone from there. All I know is it's really small. From my experience with small schools, I know I don't want anything to do with it. Everything in this town is corn fields. I know I was around way less when I lived with Bethany, but it was different living on the farm. I enjoyed it. Something about this place just creeps me out. I'm sure it's partly to do with the demonic woman under the same roof as me.

I knew as soon as I met her, there was something off about her. But now, I know for sure I was right. For starters, she knows I smoke and she says she doesn't care. She's even given me packs, but then she will take them away from me for no reason at all for hours at a time. She gets this twisted smirk on her face when she knows I'm craving one, and she'll laugh with an evil laugh. She's getting off on it in some sick way. Ryan has been giving me packs so I don't have to ask her for them, but she will even take those away!

A few days ago, while I was having a nicotine fit, she came to me and handed me a cigar and said, "Here, you can smoke this if you need one so bad." Then the crazy lady stood outside and laughed at me while she watched me try to smoke the damn thing. It took everything in me not to stick it in her eye. Then, one night, she kept me up really late telling me crazy-ass stories about her and her family. I learned about her brother, who is in prison. You're not going to believe what for, either. Killing his girlfriend and her parents!!! How nuts is that, Diary??? And get this, he's *getting out of prison soon, and she can't wait for me to meet him!!! What is wrong with DCFS? Do they not screen anyone they give a license to? She could be making the whole thing up just to scare me, who knows. Either way, she's insane! I don't care what anyone says. I'm not staying here. I can't! Why? So her murderous brother can off me next? I can't do anything in private. I'm sure writing in you is a mistake because she will probably read this when I'm not looking. I wouldn't be surprised if she stands over me and watches me sleep! I can hear her breathing on the other end of the phone anytime I've tried to call anyone, so now I know to keep my conversations to a bare minimum. When Ryan is here, she won't let us leave her sight. If we go outside to smoke, she follows us. God, she is sooo weird!!! It's driving me insane not to be able to talk to anyone without her psycho ass lurking over me.*

When Ryan came to see me today, I gathered the courage to ask her if we could walk down to the park. I figured she should let me since it's close enough to see from the window but far enough away that I can have a private conversation. To my surprise, she said yes. Ryan and I joked on the short walk that she was probably watching us with binoculars. You're not going to believe this, but she actually was! When we walked back in the door, there were binoculars on the table in front of the window! I was frozen solid and elbowed Ryan in the ribs to look. He couldn't believe it, either. She is taking things way too far. I mean...what the hell am I going to do a block away in the broad daylight?

I had to go to the high school football game with her, her husband, her son, and her daughter tonight. I couldn't believe it, but my judge was there! We walked right past each other on the bleachers. We were so close to each other that we could have reached out and shook hands. We made eye contact, said hi, and quickly kept going. It was awkward seeing him outside of the courtroom.

As I sat there watching the football game, I wanted so badly to run to him on the bleachers and beg him to take me away from this mad woman's house. I don't know what I'm going to do. I can't live here. I won't!! I've tried to tell Sandra, but she won't listen. She just keeps telling me my next option is another group home or worse. As much as I love him, Ryan is no help, either. He understands why I hate being here but tells me to just deal with it so I don't end up somewhere worse.

Nothing could be worse than here! I'd almost rather go back to baby jail than be in this house any longer! This lady really scares me. And what does Ryan really know, anyway? As crazy as his mom is, at least he gets to live with her. I keep trying to tell myself to suck it up, but she is unbearable, and I just can't do it. I swear, the next thing she does to me that's messed up, I'm outta here!

Scared for my life, Heather

Chapter Fourteen

I'm sitting outside of the courtroom, waiting patiently on the bench, more nervous than I've ever been. Aside from our brief encounter, I haven't seen the judge but once after my mom died.

I'm so afraid of disappointing him. I've stood in front of him at least a hundred times since I entered the system, and I've never felt like I do right now.

After his big heartfelt speech when Mom died, I know things are different. I see now just how much he cares about our family, and the last thing I want to do is make him regret sending me home. I ran into him just yesterday, and now, here I sit on a Saturday without a home again. *Oh, God, what if he says "screw it" and sends me away like he did my sister until I turn eighteen?* I've never been to court on a Saturday, and I didn't know they could even do this. Charlotte called it an emergency hearing, and she says they can call them at any given time. She's the one who petitioned for it after receiving my phone call today.

I left the foster home this morning and walked to the pay phone at the gas station. I called her, collect. I told her everything that was going on and begged her to get me the hell out of that woman's house. I'm still amazed that I have my own attorney who I can call collect on a Saturday morning. She answered the phone right away and didn't hesitate to accept the call. *Man, she wasn't lying when she said I could call her at any time.*

I've been on edge since I moved in with this nut case. And in my opinion, I have done a great job biting my tongue. I couldn't take it anymore. This morning, she informed me that I was going to have a whole new set of rules in her house: no smoking, no calling Ryan or seeing him, and no calling or seeing any friends at all. *I mean...what the hell is that?*

Ryan has been coming to see me every day since I moved in with her, and now, all the sudden and for no reason at all, I can't see him or talk to him? I'm not allowed to have any friends at all? *Who does she think she is?* I understand that I'm under her roof and I have to follow her rules. But Christ, her rules and the way she treats me is unreasonable. *Bipolar witch!*

I bit my tongue yet again and said ok. I told her I wanted to call my caseworker, but she refused to let me use the phone at all. That was it for me. I know my rights. She can never deny me a phone call to my caseworker. I finally told her where to stick it, and I walked down to the pay phone.

Trying to understand that crazy lady and the way she does things is beyond anything I've ever had to try to comprehend. She hasn't done anything too insane yet. But given everything she's done in such a short period of time, how long will it be before her twisted head games go even further?

As I look up while I am still patiently waiting for the judge, she is standing across the way by the railing that looks down onto the first floor, talking to my caseworker. Crazy lady's lips are moving at an alarming rate, and I wonder what she's saying. How could she have anything to say at all? The only rule I haven't followed is smoking in my room. The first night I was there, she refused to let me have a cigarette even though she told me I was allowed to smoke. I snuck one after everyone went to bed, but I haven't smoked in there since.

She has jet-black hair that comes right above the back pockets of her jeans, and dark, evil eyes that I can see right through. I don't care what anyone says, there is something wrong with this lady. She doesn't have me fooled. *Why the hell is she even here?* I have never had any of my foster parents come to my hearings before, especially when I'm refusing to live with them. They can't force me to stay somewhere. *Why does she even want me there? So she has someone to manipulate and torture?* I refused to go back to her house when I called Charlotte, so I stayed at the gas station until Sandra came and picked me up.

Her husband is here, too, but he is standing far enough away from her that he's not a part of whatever conversation they're having. *Poor bastard, I wonder how he does it.* He seems nice, but he barely ever talks. It's obvious who's in control in their house. He's probably scared to death of her just like I am.

Crazy lady walks away from Sandra. She joins her husband, and they walk to the other end of the lobby.

"Heather, can you come over here please?" calls Sandra still standing by the railing with her back to me.

I get up and walk over to her. "What's going to happen? Please, don't make me go back there," I plead. "I'm telling you, something is wrong with that lady. She scares the hell out of me."

"Yeah, she's something that's for sure," she replies almost under her breath while looking down at my open file that she has resting on the railing.

"What is that?" I ask, noticing her reading something that looks handwritten.

"Heather, what I'm about to tell you is going to be very upsetting, so I need you to stay calm, ok?"

Oh, boy, what now?

"Uh...ok," I reply, confused and afraid of what's coming next.

"This is a letter that she wrote, and it's seven pages long," she says, motioning towards my file.

"WHAT?"

Holy hell, she IS crazy. "What could she possibly have to say about me for seven pages when I have only been there for five days? What does it say?" I ask, feeling my blood begin to boil.

"This is your copy to read before we go into court," she replies, handing me the letter.

"This is going to get read in court?" I ask, becoming even angrier. "Heather, I tried to talk her out of it but she's insisting the judge

read it. You know how it goes; everyone gets a copy." I snatch the letter from her and begin to read.

By the end of the letter, I'm crying uncontrollably; my tears are that of anger more than sadness. I cannot believe the garbage that she's saying about me. I'm shocked, and I feel sick to my stomach that the judge is going to read all of these lies she has made up about me. Where does she even come up with this stuff? Only a very sick, demented person could try to destroy someone the way she is me.

She goes on for seven pages about how horrible of a girl I am and how I need to be locked away. She rambles on for at least three of the pages about my "sexual tendencies." *I want to beat the lying bitch senseless! What sexual tendencies?* I've barely even been able to give Ryan a kiss hello and goodbye because she's always watching us.

She says I've been trying to seduce her husband and her son! I have barely talked to or even looked at either one of them since I moved into her house, much less come on to them. The thought of it disgusts me! Her husband? Give me a break! He's about the same age as my dad, and he's not even remotely attractive. *Gross!* I would never, and the thought of it makes me shudder. Her son? He's fourteen years old, and he's only an eighth grader. He's just as unattractive as her husband. Anyone who knows me would know that I would never act in such a trashy manner. I know I'm not an innocent virgin, but holy hell, her words make me out to be some sort of a devious harlot.

She also rambles on about how I'm sneaking out of my bedroom window at night to go have sex with random guys. *REALLY? Now I know why the bitch moved to the other end of the lobby! If she knows what's good for her, she will stay clear away from me.* How can her husband go along with this knowing none of it is true? *Cowardly bastard!*

"Sandra, this is all lies! Please tell me you know that and you don't believe any of this?" I say, crying and visibly angry, pacing back and forth, trying to control the rage I feel. I am ready to tear that crazy lunatic apart.

"Heather, I know, trust me! I've known you long enough to know you would never do any of this, and believe me when I say, I will NEVER place another child in her home again!"

Her words ease my mind, but only a little because...what about everyone else who has to read this? What will they think? The embarrassment I feel knowing the judge is going to read it makes me want to throw up.

"It's going to be ok," Sandra says as we walk toward the courtroom with crazy lady and her husband following behind us at a distance that's safe for her.

"Sandra, why is she even allowed in the courtroom?" I ask in a whisper once we're inside. "I'm not going back to her house. What happens to me next is none of her business!" I snap.

"I know, Heather. Don't worry about her, ok?"

Yeah...easy for you to say, lady.

After everyone gets settled in the courtroom, I stand there for what feels like an eternity while everyone reads her god-awful letter. My tears won't stop no matter how hard I try. It's impossible to stand here and be strong. I feel broken; I may as well have been run over by a Mack truck.

My attorney is standing up in front of the judge, looking fidgety and waiting patiently for things to begin. I haven't noticed her reading the letter. She must have read it before we got called in. I haven't had a chance to talk to her yet. She turns around and we make eye contact. She winks at me and gives me a small smile as if she's trying to say, "Don't worry, I've got your back."

"Ok, is everyone finished?" asks the judge, settling back in his chair and straightening the papers in front of him. "Ok, first things first," he begins, clearing his voice. "Mr. and Mrs. Smith?" he calls out, looking toward the crazies who are seated in the benches behind us.

"Yes?" responds Mrs. Crazy with a smirk as they both stand to address the judge. *Psycho!*

"I think it's quite clear that there are no intentions for Heather to return to your home, correct?" he asks.

"Yes, Your Honor, but if I can I'd like to add some things."

What? What else could she possibly have to add? Hasn't she come up with enough lies about me? Now she wants to add more? The audacity of this woman. I swear. It's taking everything in me right now not to shout out all the things I'm really feeling right now.

"No, that won't be necessary. I think you've said enough," replies the judge with disdain in his voice.

Whoa! Did her letter make him angry, too?

"She is no longer going to be in your home, so your presence here today isn't required. You are dismissed from my courtroom."

Holy crap! Tell her, judge!

Once they leave the courtroom, he turns to me. "Heather, I'm sure you have things you would like to say regarding this letter? When someone presents something of this manner during court proceedings, you have the right to defend yourself."

"Yes, Your Honor, and the things I really want to say will get me in trouble, so I'll keep it simple. Lies! Everything in her letter is a lie!" I say, trying to keep the anger in my voice in check but failing miserably. "Where she found the time to come up with such insanity is beyond me, but I beg you not to believe any of that. It makes me sick to think that anyone could believe those things to be true about me," I add with my voice starting to crack. *Shit, I'm going to cry again.*

He looks at me with a relaxed look on his face and a bit of a smirk but says nothing.

"Ok, what about you, Miss Cope? Anything to say?"

My attorney, beautiful and strong as ever, says in such a matter-of-fact way, "Your Honor, the ideas that she states in this letter are just completely preposterous. I haven't been on the case long, but I've spent a great deal of time studying Heather's file. She has never been accused of such things before. To think her personality has done a complete transformation in the five days that she lived there is ridiculous."

Whew! Thank You, God, for sending her to me.

"Ok, enough said on that matter; let's move on," says the judge.

Thank God! The knots in my stomach begin to untangle. I think he must know it's all lies. At least, I hope he does. *They should take the crazy lady's foster license away!* No kid, no matter how messed up they are, should ever have to live in her hell.

"Where are we now, Ms. Blackburn?" he asks my caseworker.

She steps away from me and moves closer to the bench. When she opens her mouth, I am in shock. My stomach is instantly tied back into knots.

"Your Honor, there are simply no homes left to place her in. She's been in almost all of the foster homes we have available in this county. In total, she has been placed in over thirty-five foster homes, three group homes, two residential homes, three hospital stays, and was recently sent to a juvenile center twice while living with her father. There is just simply nowhere else to go from here. I am recommending that she be sent to the detention center until she can be emancipated on her eighteenth birthday."

Wait, what?

I cannot believe what I am hearing. *How could she stab me in the back like this?* She was being so nice to me outside of the courtroom, and now this? *Thanks for the warning, bitch!* I always thought she was on my side. God, I have never been so wrong in my life. You give someone your trust, and look at what they do with it. *Backstabber!*

"Let me get this straight, Ms. Blackburn. You are suggesting that we all just give up on her, lock her up, and throw away the key?" he asks with a sarcastic laugh that brings hope back to my heart.

"Well, Your Honor, I don't know where else she's supposed to go," she replies.

"Well then, I suggest you do your job and find somewhere for her to go!" he snaps. "She is not a criminal, Ms. Blackburn, and unless she has broken some law that I am not aware of, a detention center is out of the question completely! Do I make myself clear?" he doesn't give her a chance to respond. "We are not in the business of throwing kids away like they are trash. We are supposed to be helping them."

As he continues to snap at my back-stabbing caseworker, I realize how much I love and admire this man. I have never been more thankful that he is in my corner. "She doesn't belong in a detention center, Ms. Blackburn! She belongs in a good home with someone who will take care of her. If sending her away would make your job easier, I can arrange for you to be relieved of your duties permanently and get her a new caseworker who will help her. Is that what you want?"

"No, Your Honor," she says quickly, visibly shaken.

"Good to hear. I think we have made enough mistakes with this case. Let's get it right this time," he adds. "Does anyone else have anything to say?"

"No, Your Honor, I think you've said it all," boasts Charlotte with a smile of pure pride on her face.

"Ok then, that's it for the day." He looks at me and adds, "Good luck to you, Miss Poissant. I hope I can trust you won't prove me wrong."

Unsure if it's a question or a statement I respond quickly with a smile on my face, "No Your Honor, I won't. Thank you so much."

He's right. I won't prove him wrong...I can't! This is it for me. And I know that wherever I go, I have to make the best of it, and not screw up this millionth chance he has just given me.

It's been a long time since I've felt so many different emotions in one day. I'm exhausted. I can't even look at Sandra when we leave the courthouse. I can't believe her. I will never trust her again. *How could she? Am I really that bad? Ok, maybe I am sometimes, but still!* I know I can be a handful, but I'm not the horrible person she just tried to make me out to be. I'm certainly not the things that crazy lady claimed in her letter of lies either. I am shocked. I never knew how many placements I lived in before. I lost count years ago. I can't believe I've been to so many. The realization is an eye-opener, to say the least.

"Well, what are we going to do with you?" asks Sandra in a humdrum tone.

I can tell she feels like an ass over what just happened. *She should.* *It serves her right for backstabbing me.*

We've been sitting in her office while she goes over the list of available foster homes in the area. "Can you PLEASE just call Ellen?" I beg. "I swear, Sandra, if you get me back over there you will never have to deal with me again! She is the only person I've ever lived with that has cared about me. If I can go back, I will never leave."

"Ok, fine," she says with a sigh. "But you're the one calling her!"

My heart leaps in my chest from the joy her words bring, but my nerves are shot. *What if she says no?* I don't know if I can handle more rejection today.

"Mom?" I say when she answers the phone. "Heather, is that you?"

"Yeah, it's me," I say quietly.

"Where are you?" she asks.

"I'm at the DCFS office with Sandra."

"Oh, yeah? What's going on?" she asks curiously with a hint of worry in her tone.

The sudden panic I feel over possibly being rejected is overwhelming. I can't handle it, and I start crying hard.

"Mom, can I please come home?" I don't let her answer before I quickly continue, crying and tripping over my words. "I know I screwed up when I was with you before, but if I could take back hurting you, I would. There's nowhere else I want to be. Please, give me another chance. You're the only foster mom I've ever had that has ever cared about me, and I'm stupid for ever screwing that up."

There's a brief pause of silence on the other end of the line that makes my heart stop. "Of course you can come home," she responds, and I can tell she's crying

My heart starts to beat again, and I cry unfamiliar tears of happiness. "Thank you so much! I swear, Mom, it will be different this time!"

"I know, Heather, but we're going to have to sit down and have a long talk. You know you're going to have to earn back my trust."

"I know, Mom, and I will. I swear. I'll do whatever it takes. I promise!"

Chapter Fifteen

"**H**EATHER!" Ellen yells from the top of the basement stairs. "PHONE!"

"Hello?"

"Heather?"

Oh my God, why does he keep calling me?

"What do you want, Shane? Why do you keep calling here?"

"Chill out, girl, she doesn't know it is me calling. I told her I was someone else."

"Shane, she's not stupid. I'm sure she knows it's you, and I'm not going to lie to her. I have told you a million times that I have a boyfriend and I love him."

"I know, girl, you need to calm down. I just wanna be your friend."

Friend? Who is he trying to fool?

"Shane, it's not just that," I reply, becoming extremely irritated. "You know if Ellen thinks I'm talking to you again that she's going to kick me out. I'm not losing my home again over you!"

"Damn, girl! Alright then, I'll talk to you later."

"No, Shane! No later! You have to stop calling me!" I bark before slamming the phone down on the receiver next to my bed.

I can't win for anything. No matter how hard I try sometimes, it seems like trouble always hunts me down. Ellen laughs at me and calls me a drama queen. I know I bring it on myself sometimes, but not this time. I'm going to kill Darius for telling him that I live here again. He swore to me he wouldn't tell him. And like an idiot, I believed him. We've kept in touch all this time. He has never given Shane my number before. Why now that I'm back here? Shane knows exactly where to find me, and Darius chooses to tell him? *Screw him! I'm done being friends with him.*

"HEATHER!" calls Ellen's voice again.

Oh, shit! She knows. My heart starts beating faster. "Come up here, it's time to eat."

Oh, thank God maybe I'm in the clear. Why am I scared, anyway? I haven't done anything wrong. Maybe I should just tell her so she doesn't think I'm hiding anything from her.

I avoid all eye contact once I'm upstairs just in case. I swear I feel her burning a hole in the back of my head as I stand at the counter, making my plate when suddenly the phone rings again. *I swear to God, if that's him again, I'm going to freak out.* I watch her as she walks into the living room and answers the phone.

"Heather, it's for you," she says, and I sense irritation in her voice.

What the hell does he want?

She gives me the look of death as I take the phone from her. I know she knows.

"Hello?"

"Why did you hang up on me?"

Oh, for the love of God!

"I can't talk to you. I'm eating," I say quietly, and I quickly hang up, handing the phone back to Ellen.

"Heather, dare I ask who that was?"

Crap! My heart is pounding again as I stand there, staring at her like an idiot, not knowing what to say. I know I can't lie to her. *Don't lie, Heather, just tell the truth.*

"Well, girl? Don't just stand there staring at me. Answer me, and don't you lie to me, Heather. You know how I feel about liars."

Shit, just spit it out.

"Mom, he keeps calling. I keep telling him to stop, but he won't! I swear to you, I want nothing to do with him. Darius told him I was back here, and now he won't leave me alone."

"What did I tell you about trusting Darius? He's no good, Heather. For crying out loud, you've only been back here a month."

"Mom, I know that now, and I'm done being friends with him I swear."

She looks at me through squinted eyes as if she's peering into my soul, but I think she knows I'm not lying to her. She knows I can't lie to save my life, not to her. "Well, if he keeps on calling here, I'll sick the cops on his ass. He doesn't wanna screw with me," she adds in a huff.

No one in their right mind wants to screw with her.

"If he keeps calling, let me know, and we'll handle it legally if we have to. I'll take you to get another protective order against him."

Whoa! I hope we don't have to take it that far.

"Is he the one who keeps calling here, giving a different name every time they call?"

"Yes," I say quietly.

"I knew it was him. I ain't no damn fool. You should have told me."

"I know, but I was afraid of getting kicked out. It won't happen again," I reply.

"It better not," she adds before dropping the subject.

The weekend is quiet with no more phone calls from my stalker. Thank God! Ryan is here, and he would flip out if he knew he was calling me. I haven't been able to bring myself to tell him that he's been bothering me. There's no point in getting him all worked up over something he can't control. I'll just handle it myself.

On Saturday night, Ryan and I drive out to his house for the night. I love being at Ellen's, but we never get any privacy there because there are always so many people at the house. Ryan's parents went out of town for the weekend, so we'll have the house all to ourselves.

"What do you want to eat, woman?" Ryan asks, kissing me on the forehead.

I'm not really that hungry. "I don't care, nothing big."

"Ok, soup it is then," he replies, getting up from where we're sitting at the breakfast bar in his parents' large kitchen.

This house is so big and nice. It's a newer house that his dad built for them not too many years before I met Ryan. His mom doesn't work, and his dad is a union electrician. By the looks of his house, he must make good money. My dad's income can't be too different, but it makes a big difference when you're not drinking all your money away. I wish I had grown up in a house like this. But then again, I wish a lot of things were different about the way I grew up.

As I sit, waiting patiently, I watch him as he pours chicken soup from a can into a pot on the stove. I catch that old familiar smell from behind me, and I turn to look into the room that's off of the kitchen. The glass French doors are partially propped open, and I can see the hospital bed where his grandfather was until he died a few months ago. "Is your mom ever going to get rid of your grandpa's things?" I ask, rubbing my nose. "I can still smell the hospital smell. I hate that smell. It reminds me of when I lived in the hospital."

He sits back down on the stool next to me and pauses as if he's remembering something. *I hope I didn't upset him.*

"I don't know. I guess she's having a hard time letting go. You know how it is to lose a parent, ya know?"

It took Dad a long time to finally go through Mom's things. Actually, I was the one who had to go through them. He came to me one day when I was living there and said, "Well, I guess it's time we go through your mom's stuff. Why don't you go in there and take what you want to keep? I'm going to drop the rest of it off at Goodwill."

I was appalled at the thought of any of her things going to Goodwill. At first, I protested the idea. Leaving all her clothes hanging where she left them made me feel like she might come back someday. I'm sure it made Dad feel the same way, but I knew he was right. It can't be healthy to hold onto that idea for too long.

I finally brought myself to go through all of it one day when Dad wasn't home. It was a lot harder than I thought it would be. I sat on the floor, smelling her clothes for hours, crying. Her smell still lingered on them like she had worn them the day before. Among her things, I kept a black leather coat that she cherished. I always begged her to let me wear it, but she never would because she was worried that I would ruin it. I kept the blue dress that she wore to her youngest sister's wedding. That was when she was sober and in great shape. She looked amazing that day. Although I know I will never wear the dress, I can't part with the memory of the time when she was normal and happy.

In the bottom of her side of the closet, I found boxes where she kept her most personal belongings. I was shocked to find huge notebooks that were filled from front to back with diary entries. I had no idea my mom kept journals. Reading them was almost unbearable. Most of it was written during the time that she was sober. I'm guessing it was a part of her recovery process.

She talked about her childhood a lot in them, and those parts were hard to swallow. Reading about the abuse brought back all the anger that I had shoved in a locked closet in the corner of my mind. I kept wanting to believe it wasn't true. It made facing my family easier over the years. But having it shoved back in my face like that forced me to finally accept it and deal with it.

On a certain level, it helped reading those things. I got to know my mom better even after she was gone, and I was thankful for that. It also filled me with a lot of guilt because I learned of all the pain she suffered over losing me and Malory. She wanted so much to be a better mother to us, and not knowing how to make things right tore her apart piece by piece.

I realize now how lost she was and how much she wanted things to be different. The idea of forgetting her scares me the most. I am afraid I won't remember her face, her smell, her smile, her quirky laugh, her anger, her fear, her failures, her triumphs, her hopes, and her dreams. I want to keep it all with me, the good and the bad, forever.

"Earth to Heather," Ryan says, waving his hand in front of my face.

"Sorry," I say, shaking my head as if to shake the memories free. "Where did you go?" he asks.

"I don't know. I was thinking about my mom."

"Oh," he says with a frown. He never knows what to say to me about her. "I'm sorry, babe. That's gotta be really hard for you. Are you ok?"

I lean over, wrap my arms around him, and rest my head on his chest. "Yeah, I'm gonna be."

I pull away and look up into his brown eyes, remembering something. "Did I ever tell you about the Navy paperwork I found when I was going through her stuff?"

"No. What are you talking about?" he asks curiously.

"She enlisted in the Navy when she was eighteen but then never went."

"Really?" he asks, his eyes wide.

"Yeah, and she had to ask to be let out of it because she had already signed all the papers. I found the letter that she wrote to them explaining why she wanted to be discharged. The letter made me sad."

"Why? What did it say?"

"It said that she enlisted for the wrong reasons. She said she was trying to escape her past and realized it was the wrong reason to go. That she felt like going would be running away from everything instead of dealing with it. She went on to explain how she got engaged to be married, and she felt like her new husband could help her get to where she needed to be. They let her go with an honorable discharge."

His eyes widened more. "Wow, Heather. That's kinda crazy. Is that when she met your dad?"

I laugh. "No. That was when she met her first husband, Dick." I laugh louder. "It's funny how back then people would actually call their kids that. Why wouldn't they just call him Richard?"

"OH! I didn't know she was married before. You never told me that," he replies, looking sad like I kept it from him on purpose.

"No. It's not like that, Ryan. It's just that there's so much to tell, I can't keep up with what I've told you and what I haven't. It was no big deal. She wasn't married to him for long. I don't know if she even loved him. I think *he* was the escape, not the Navy. I think going to the Navy scared her, and he was her way out. She was always trying to run away in one way or another, so it makes sense. Kind of scary how familiar that sounds, huh?" I add with a chuckle.

"Yeah, Heather, but you're not like her," he says, pulling me closer. "Heather, you're stronger than she was, and you know it."

Am I? More times than I can count, I have run away from my problems, just not always in the same way she did.

Later that evening after watching movies, we decide to head to bed when his sister comes in looking as bitchy as ever. *I wonder if she and her boyfriend had a fight.* I scurry off to the bedroom, not knowing if she's going to make some smart remark about me being here. Sometimes, she doesn't say anything. If she's in a bad mood, she'll give Ryan a hard time about it.

She's twenty years old, and she is a really pretty girl, but she has a bit of an ugly personality sometimes that ruins her pretty face. She's like Jekyll and Hyde. I have a hard time keeping up with her sudden mood swings. She can be so sweet sometimes with her soft innocent voice, and then other times be a raging, snotty wench. She acts like a spoiled daddy's girl. If she doesn't get her way, watch out!

"Ryan, you know she's not supposed to be here! Why is she here? Mom is going to kill you when she finds out!" I hear her say in her evil Hyde tone through the cracked bedroom door.

Great, here we go.

"Shut up, Dana! Mom isn't going to find out because YOU are not going to tell her! Why do you have to act like such a spoiled shit all the time? God, I hate you!" Ryan snaps with an angry and fierce tone. *Whoa!* He can be so scary when he gets mad. I hope she has the good sense to shut up before he gets even angrier.

"I'm calling Mom!" I hear her pout as she stomps off down the hall toward her bedroom.

What is she, ten?

"No, you're not, Dana!" yells Ryan, following her.

He must have caught up to her because then I hear her squeal, "Ow! Ryan, let me go right now!"

Oh, this is just ridiculous. I hurry to the door and pull it open to see them at the end of the hall by her bedroom door. He has her pinned up against the wall.

"Ryan!" I shout. "Let her go! Just take me home. It's not worth this," I yell.

He lets her go. Next, she comes stomping down the hall, glaring at me with the most pathetic pouty face I've ever seen on a grown woman. "This is your entire fault, Heather!" she says as she passes me and stomps off toward the kitchen.

I quickly grab my things and head toward the door slipping on my shoes. As I'm pulling the door open, Ryan grabs my arm. "Where are you going?"

"Oh, are you going to manhandle me now, too? Let my arm go and take me home, now!" I see Hyde off in the distance behind him, crying, and on the phone with someone. *What a baby!*

"I'm sorry, Heather. I'm not mad at you," Ryan replies, quickly releasing my arm.

I hurry out of the house as he follows closing the door behind him.

"Heather, it's going to be fine, just come back inside. It's late. We shouldn't drive all the way back there tonight," he says, sounding concerned.

"Ryan! She's calling your mom! We can't stay here!"

"So what! My mom is not going to drive all the way back here tonight just because you're here."

Who knows with that crazy lady. She probably will.

"I don't want to stay, Ryan. I just want to go home," I say, starting to feel even more agitated. "What the hell have I ever done to your family, anyway?" I ask, feeling the sting in the back of my eyes.

"Heather, you know you have never done anything, so stop it."

I know it's just because I grew up in foster homes and my family isn't as perfect as his. *God, I'm so sick of being judged.*

The door suddenly opens and Dana appears. "Lannie is on her way here, and you're both gonna be in trouble!" she says, still pouting.

What the hell am I going to be in trouble for? Wow, she's such a child. I think to myself, not able to hold back a chuckle.

"What's so funny?" she asks in her snotty tone.

"Uh...you are!" I say just as snottily. *I can play her game, too.* "God, grow up Dana!" I shout at her. I look at Ryan. "If you aren't going to take me home, I'm walking!"

I don't want to stick around and wait for his even older sister, Lannie, to get here. I don't know her but she seems just as scary as his mom. I turn and start to walk down the driveway toward the road, and he follows behind me, begging me to come back.

"Where do you think you're going, little girl? You get your butt back here right now!" Dana yells out, leaving her place at the doorway and following behind us.

Wow, she's got some nerve!

I can't help but laugh as I stop walking and turn to face her. She stops dead in her tracks. "Who do you think you are, talking to me like that?" I ask sarcastically. "Who are you, my mother?" I add, laughing. *She's pathetic!*

Her lips curl up into a twisted, sadistic smile, and the look she gives me couldn't possibly be uglier. With her eyes squinted and evil, she pauses before she responds, "No! Because your mom is DEAD, remember?"

I'm suddenly blinded by the color red, and I can feel the vein in my neck starting to pulsate hard. I realize I've stopped breathing. I quickly look at Ryan. He takes a step back. Then he holds his arm out toward his sister as if he's presenting me with some grand prize. "What the hell are you waiting for, Heather? Get her!"

The anger I feel doesn't give me a chance to think before I react. I lunge at her, grabbing her by the hair and slamming her face into my knee multiple times while screaming every profanity that comes to mind. I throw her to the ground and pin her shoulders down with my knees so she can't move her arms. I completely lose it and punch her so many times in her face and head. While all of this is happening, I am thinking about all of the things I have kept pent up inside of me for so long.

"Get off of me!" Dana screams out, crying and shaking her head back and forth to try to avoid the blows.

"You wanna remind me again where my mom is, you evil bitch?" I scream back at her, continuing to punch her. My chest is starting to burn; my knuckles hurt; my throat is on fire from screaming and breathing so hard.

Ryan finally pulls me off of her. "Ok, that's enough, Heather," he says as he drags me away.

Dana gets up and runs into the house crying.

"Babe, you fucked her up!" he cries out laughing and doing some little jumpy thing like I just did the world a great service.

Dork! I force a smile, bend over, rest my hands on my knees, trying to catch my breath. *Wow, that felt good.* I feel bad because I know I unleashed things on her that weren't all her fault.

"Ryan, it's not funny. Stop laughing. Your mom is really going to hate me now."

"Aw...fuck it, Heather. Who cares! She deserved it for saying that to you. Are you ok?" he asks, rubbing my back.

I flash back to the time Ryan's mom threw my mother's death in my face. We had just come back from her funeral, and I tried calling Ryan. When his mom answered, I hung up. She got my number from the caller ID and called back. When I answered, she started screaming crazy shit at me saying things like, "Nobody wants you. You're no good. My son doesn't want you, and your own parents don't even want you. And guess what, now your mom is DEAD!" She said it with such an evil laugh. When she heard me gasp, she continued to laugh and said, "How's that feel? Payback's a bitch baby!" Then, she hung up the phone laughing her ass off. *Sick bitch!*

"Ryan, what's wrong with the women in your family? Why are they so evil?"

"Heather, I don't know. I'm so sorry," he replies, grabbing me and hugging me tight. "Heather, I'm going to move out of here. I'm done with them. If they don't want to accept us, fuck em'! You know how much I love you, right?" he asks gently, grabbing me by both cheeks and looking into my eyes.

I nod my head at him and start to cry.

"Baby, please don't cry. Everything's gonna be ok. I promise," he says, taking me in his arms.

For a moment, I believe him.

Chapter Sixteen

"Oh my God, Ryan, what the hell are you doing?" I cry out in panic. "Where did you get a gun?" I sit up as fast as I can in bed.

He's standing at the foot of the bed, holding a handgun to his head.

"Why don't I just do you and everyone else a favor and blow my fucking brains out all over this room right now?" he yells out, crying and shaking uncontrollably with the gun held to his temple.

Oh my God, what should I do? I think about lunging toward him and trying to take the gun from him. But I'm too afraid, it will accidentally go off. I'm frozen still with fear racing through my veins. My hair is standing straight up on the back of my neck, and my entire body suddenly feels numb.

I've only ever seen this look on his face one other time. It was that day at school. His face is beet red with tears streaming down and snot is coming out of his nose. He screams at me, "Fuck it, Heather, I'm just gonna do it! Fuck everything!"

"Ryan, please don't!" I beg, starting to cry. "I didn't mean it, I swear. I don't want to break up, ok? Just please, for the love of God, put the gun down." *Holy shit, this is what he'll do if I want to break up?*

After what feels like an eternity in hell, he lowers the gun.

"Where did you get a gun?" I ask, terrified, still crying but he doesn't answer.

He walks toward me with the gun still in his hand but lowered by his side. I don't recognize the look he has in his eyes. *Oh my God, is he going to shoot me?* I close my eyes and brace myself for whatever is coming next. *Dear God, please save me. This can't be the end of my life.*

When I open my eyes, he's standing next to me, looking down at me with the saddest eyes I've ever seen. I'm not breathing. My heart feels like it's going to jump out of my chest. He slowly sets the gun down on the table next to the bed. *Oh, thank God.*

He plops down next to me, puts his arms around me, and buries his face in my chest as he starts sobbing. He is crying so hard that even I'm shaking. "I can't lose you, Heather," he says through his crying with his head still in my chest.

I place my hand on the back of his head to comfort him but I am still frozen solid. I let out a deep sigh of relief. "Ryan, please get the gun out of here. You're really scaring me."

He looks up at me with bloodshot eyes. "There's no bullets in it, it's fine."

"*What?*" I ask through gritted teeth feeling my fear instantly turn to pure rage. "What is this, some kind of sick twisted joke?" I cry out, pushing him away from me.

"Heather, I'm sorry," he replies, still crying.

"I can't believe you would do that to me, you monster!" I scream at him, running from the room.

I storm out of the house and go to the side of the garage. Pulling my cigs out of my coat pocket, I sit down and light one. After that crazy shit, I could probably sit here and smoke the whole pack. *What was he thinking?*

Things have been going to shit in the last month since the fight with his sister. His mom is on even more of a mission to destroy us. I don't have to deal with her, but I know she's been putting a lot of pressure on him to dump me. I don't expect her to understand since she said something equally as evil as Dana.

What is wrong with these people? I wonder as I take a long, hard drag from my smoke. His mom walks around, acting like she's some goody-goody church lady, but I see right through that. That's why I don't go to church. What's the point when half of the people there are nothing but hypocrites who pretend to be all God-worthy? They have such deep, dark secrets that they hide from the rest of the world. I'm the bad one because I don't go to church every Sunday and fake it with the rest of them. At least I'm not a phony; I don't hide who I am. What you see is what you get. I really don't give a rat's ass what anyone thinks about me anymore.

All of this has made us bicker with each other lately. That's how it started today. It was such a stupid fight. Look what it turns into. I got frustrated. So, I told him I was done and that I didn't want to be with him anymore. I didn't mean it. I was just mad and threatening to run, which is my classic reaction to most problems. He knows me well and should have realized that I didn't mean it. After the stunt he pulled, I *should* be done with him. But how could I ever leave him now? How will I ever be able to trust that he won't hurt himself? I know I need to tell someone, but who can I tell that would really help him?

Dear Diary,

After the gun incident, Ryan moved in with his friend down the street. He said it was a wake-up call to get away from his mom. He thinks if he's out of there that we won't fight as much. But unless he moves across the country from her, I know she will always be up his ass about me. He keeps promising me that he's not suicidal and tells me not to worry. How the hell is that possible after what he did?

You're not going to believe this, but he told me a few days later that he was going to pull the trigger just to mess with me even more, and then he realized later that there was a bullet still in the chamber. What the hell is wrong with him? He can be such a good guy one minute, and the next minute act like a crazed lunatic. I know what's wrong, his crazy-ass mother!!!

I haven't had a panic attack since I moved out of Dad's. But ever since that happened, I go into panic mode when I'm with him. When he's sleeping, I'm constantly checking to see if he's still breathing out of fear he has taken something. I'm always checking his car and his belongings to see if he has the gun with him. He says I'm being paranoid, but what the hell does he expect? I'd like to see how he would act if I did that to him. Part of me is still angry that he put me through all of that. I don't know if I will ever be able to get over it. I have no trust in him anymore at all, and I question everything constantly.

Needless to say, we are definitely not fighting less. We are fighting a whole lot more. I'm already an insecure person, and this has sent me over the edge. I question if he's using drugs again, and if he's cheating on me. I know I'm driving him nuts, but I can't help it. I feel like I lost the person I once knew. Hell, maybe I never knew him at all. I still love him more than anything. I just wish I understood him. He says he has problems too, and that I'm not the only one. Hello. It's not like I think I'm the only person on the planet that has a fucked up life. I just think he doesn't realize how fortunate he's been. He makes things worse for himself. Maybe I should practice what I preach, but I don't do stupid shit like drugs or put guns to my head! He swears he's not using again. But honestly, I don't know.

I gotta go the phone is ringing.

Heather

"Hello?"

"Hey, girl, whatcha you doin'?"

Oh, great...here we go.

"Nothing," I reply. I offer nothing more and don't ask what he's doing. I'm getting used to his phone calls. They seem harmless. No matter how much I tell him to quit calling, he won't. So, I keep the conversations to the point, trying not to linger on the phone with him for too long. *Maybe I'll bore him into not calling anymore.*

"Where are you?" I ask curiously, noticing the sound of loud traffic in the background.

"I'm at the payphone at Walgreens." *Oh, geez, he's right down the street.*

"Why are you there, Shane?"

"Heather, can you please meet me in the alley so we can talk?"

"No, Shane! There's nothing for us to talk about. For the gazillionth time, I have a boyfriend!" I reply annoyed, and I quickly hang up the phone. *What the hell is he doing by my house?* This is getting creepy. He's never going to take the hint, and he's really starting to bother me. Maybe Ellen was right? Maybe a restraining order is the right way to go? The phone rings again. *Holy shit!*

"Hello?" I answer, irritated.

"Heather, please don't hang up," he says quickly as if he's preparing for me to hang up right away.

"Hello?" answers Brook on the phone upstairs.

"Brook, I got it. Hang up." She's still there. I can hear her breathing. "Brook! Hang up the phone!" I snap.

"Whatever, Heather!" she says as she slams down the phone. *Ugh...I can't stand the little brat anymore.* We got along so much better the first time I lived here. But now, she's fourteen and has gotten her period, which makes her a raging witch half the time.

"Shane, I am not meeting you out back. I can't see you, ok?"

"Heather, please," he begs in the most pathetic voice I've ever heard. "I just wanna talk to you, that's all."

"Shane, what could you possibly have to say to me in person that you can't say over the phone?"

"Heather, please just let me say what I gotta say. And then I swear, I will never bother you again."

Hmm. That sounds tempting, but I don't know if I believe that he will actually leave me alone.

"Yeah, right, Shane! You're just saying that to get me out there."

"No, Heather. I mean it. I really will leave you alone if you just hear me out."

"Ugh...fine, Shane, but you need to be quick. I don't know when

Ellen will be back. Give me ten minutes," I say, hanging up the phone without waiting for a response. *What am I doing?*

I'm really getting tired of this guy. If letting him say whatever he has to say to my face will get him to finally leave me alone, it will be worth it. It's the middle of the day. If he tries anything funny, I'll just scream.

I walk upstairs to scope out what everyone is doing before heading out the back door. Ellen is at the restaurant she goes to every day with her sister and whoever else wants to join them. They sit around drinking coffee, smoking, and talking. She shouldn't be back for another few hours.

"Where's Brook?" I ask David, who's in his usual stance when he's in trouble, which is almost always when Brook is babysitting. It's a form of punishment Ellen came up with for the younger kids that Brook uses excessively. They are to stand up straight with a can of vegetables in each hand. They have to raise their arms up and hold them there. Mom usually only makes them do it for a few minutes at a time. Brook will make them stand there until they are sweating, shaking, and crying. If they cry or drop their arms, she makes them stand there longer. It's cruel and unusual punishment. Whenever I can, I save them from it.

David looks at me with tear-filled eyes, and his arms shaking. "She's in the bathroom," he says in a low muffled voice. I can tell he's choking on his tears.

"Put your arms down. She's not out here, and she can't see you. How long have you been standing there like that?" I ask.

"I don't know. A long time," he replies, wiping the tears from his eyes with the back of his arm.

"Jesus, give me the cans," I say, taking the cans from him and setting them on the counter as Brook comes walking out of the bathroom.

"Why did you let him out of punishment? I didn't say it was time!" she says with her usual attitude.

"I don't care, Brook. I'm older than you, and I say that's enough! You don't have to be so damn mean to them all the time!" I look at

David, who looks thankful to have been saved. "Go play, David," I order. Then, I quickly shoot a "don't mess with me" look at Brook.

"You can't do that, Heather! I'm telling Mom!"

"Go ahead. Tell her! What are you gonna say? That I stopped you from torturing him?"

I don't have time for her shit right now. I need to go take care of my stalker, so I ignore her attempts at an argument and walk out the back door. I don't see his car, but I can hear his loud music as I make my way toward the alley, walking alongside the garage. As I turn the corner at the back of the garage, he's standing outside of the car, leaning against the driver's side door.

"Shane, turn the music down before someone sees you back here and tells Ellen!" I snap.

"Damn, girl. Ok, sorry," he replies as he leans into the open window to turn it down.

The neighbor is a nosey Rosey, and I'm sure she'd love to tell Ellen what I'm doing back here if she notices me.

"Whatever you need to say, hurry up and say it before the neighbor sees us." I say, crossing my arms and standing a safe distance away from him. With the garage at my back, I am not making direct eye contact with him.

"Heather, it's not that simple," he says with his head lowered as if he's being bashful.

What the hell? I have never seen this side of him before, and it almost makes me feel bad for being so cold towards him. All I ever saw when we were together was a lying, two-timing, cocky asshole. I quickly remind myself of what he put me through and shake the guilty feeling away. *This man can't be trusted. He's just trying to manipulate me.*

"You look pretty as always."

Oh, please! He needs to drop the innocent boyish act. I know what he's up to. I'm not the naive girl I once was.

"Is that all you wanted, Shane? To try to weasel your way back into my pants? Because it's not going to happen!" I bark at him.

"No, Heather. That's not it. I swear. I just wanna talk to you."

"About what, Shane?"

"Why don't we sit in the car? It's chilly out here," he suggests.

"Are you crazy? I'm not getting in your car!" *He's right, though, it is getting cold out.*

"Heather, I promise I won't drive anywhere. We'll just sit in the car and talk."

What does he want to talk about so bad?

"Heather, I know you don't trust me, and I don't blame you. I don't deserve your trust after everything that happened, and I'm sorry for that. But if you will please just listen to what I have to say..." His voice trails off.

What does he want...to apologize? Why can't he just do it and go? It's been so long since it all happened. I don't even care anymore. He no longer has the effect on me that he once did.

"Shane, I'm over you. I have been for a long time. I don't need an apology from you."

"I know you are, but please just hear me out," he says desperately.

Somehow, I know I'm making a mistake, and my gut is screaming at me as I walk to the other side of the car. "Fine. But you need to be quick, Ellen will be home soon," I say, lying through my teeth, knowing it may be a while. I just want him to get it over with and leave so I can be stalker free.

Once we're in the car, he turns on some song and claims it makes him think of me.

Yeah, ok, manipulator!

"Heather, you really do look good, girl," he says, squinting his eyes and getting that sexy look on his face that used to work on me so well. Seeing it now makes me wonder what the hell I was thinking, and I can't hold back my sudden laugh. "What's so funny?" he asks, frowning.

"Nothing. I just knew you were up to no good. It's not going to work on me anymore, Shane. I'm not the same stupid little girl I used to be."

I reach for the door handle to get out of this mess, and he gently grabs me by the arm. "No, Heather, please don't go. It's not like that."

"Then what's it like, Shane? I shouldn't even be talking to you! What do you want from me?" I ask, quickly looking down at my arm as if to tell him to get his hands off or else.

"I just wanna be friends," he replies, removing his hand from me. "What? There is no reason for us to be friends. We cannot be friends after everything you did to me."

Before I know it the car is moving, and he starts to drive away.

Oh, crap!

"Shane, where the hell are you going? I can't go anywhere with you! Stop the car now!" I yell.

"Heather, I'm not going to hurt you. I promise. I just wanna spend some time with you and talk."

Oh my God...what the hell was I thinking getting in his car? I should have known better. My gut warned me. *Shit! When will I start listening to my gut?* My heart begins to race as I wonder where he's taking me. I think about jumping from the car, but he's rounding the corners without stopping as if he knows what I might do.

I picture my mom, turning in her grave and pointing her finger at me while scolding me, "You should have known better, Heather." My stomach suddenly feels sick. If Ryan could see me now, he would never talk to me again. I don't want this man. I want nothing to do with him. I just want him to go away and leave me alone for good. *Oh my God, I'm such a fool.*

"Shane, you need to take me home. Ellen will be there soon and wonder where I am. I didn't even tell Brook I was leaving."

"Chill out, girl," he says in a relaxed tone. "I'll get you home soon, don't worry. I just wanna show you something."

Show me something? Whatever it is, I couldn't care less to see it.

I sit in silence as he drives down Court Street, heading east, and to my shitty luck, every stoplight is green. If I wanted to get out, I can't. He babbles on about random things, telling me what he's been doing the last few years. *As if I really give a shit.* He tells me he's sorry to hear about my mom. He acts like he's concerned for me, but I know better than to buy into his act.

"What's wrong with you, girl?"

What do you think, stupid?

"Nothing Shane, I just need to get home."

"Wow, you really have changed."

I don't think I've changed that much. I'm just not hanging on to his every word, and falling at his feet like I used to.

"Where are you taking me?" I ask suddenly, feeling afraid because it seems as if he's heading out of town. *Oh, man, what if he's taking me where they find dead bodies?* As the thought crosses my mind, I flash back to how afraid I was that day in his car.

"Girl, stop worrying. I just want you to meet someone."

First he wants to show me something, and now he wants me to meet someone? Which is it? He's lying, and I'm afraid of what his real plan is.

"Shane, take me home now!" I demand.

"Heather, why are you freaking out?" he asks, laughing. I shoot him a look, and he knows exactly what I'm thinking. "Heather, I'm not going to hurt you. You need to relax."

"Shane, how can I relax? If Ellen finds out I'm with you she's going to kick me out, and the next step for me is juvie!"

"She's not going to find out unless you tell her."

"I can't lie to her, Shane, and what about my boyfriend? What if he finds out? He'll never talk to me again, and all for what?"

I know I need to calm down. Making him angry is definitely not something I want to do. Maybe if I'm nice, my chances of getting home safe will be greater. I know where he's headed, even though he doesn't tell me exactly where we're going. Where else would he be going in this direction?

We're outside of town now, and the car is moving way too fast for me to jump out. I swallow the lump in my throat and say a silent prayer to my mom. *Mom, I know you're mad at me right now, and I'm sorry. My intentions were good, I swear. Please, watch over me, and make sure I get home safe. I don't want to die today.*

Chapter Seventeen

I was right about where we were going, and I've never seen anything like this. It's so isolated from everything else. There is nothing but dirt roads and double-wide trailers that are spaced really far apart. It looks like something out of a scary movie, and I just want to go home.

"Shane, where are we going, and why did you bring me here?"

"Girl, chill. I want you to meet my family."

Meet his family? What the hell for? He didn't want me to meet his family when we were together. The only time he mentioned his family to me is when he threatened to bring me out here to have his brothers kill me. I'm not sure if I should be scared or if this is just some desperate attempt on his part to get back together with me.

"Did you grow up here?" I ask nicely as he pulls into the driveway of a really dumpy trailer. I try to be as nice as I can so he won't hurt me, but I'm dying inside.

"Yeah, girl. You knew I grew up here."

Yes, I know, I'm just distracting you from killing me, asshole!

Wow. I know I had it bad, but this is beyond bad. How does anyone actually grow up in this place? There is literally nothing out here but hilly fields and dirt. I don't even see any grass, just random patches of it. Everything that should be green is dead and brown. I know it's fall, but I have a hard time picturing it ever looking any different than this. I imagine that the summer heat probably keeps everything dead with no trees around to shade anything.

I stand frozen in a terrified daze at the bottom of the old metal stairs as he heads up in front of me, surely thinking I'm following behind him, but I can't move. There is something about this place that makes the hair on the back of my neck stand up. The trailer is a dingy white with brown shutters that are half falling off. The windows are covered in plastic. The patio and stairs are so rusted that they look like they could give way at any moment. It looks abandoned, and part of me starts wondering if it is. *Is this where he brought me to do whatever it is he plans to do with me?*

He turns to face me once he's at the top and smiles. "Girl, what are you doing? Come on!" he says with a chuckle.

"Shane, who lives here?" I ask.

"Heather, why are you acting so crazy? It's my ma's house."

"So someone lives here?" I ask again.

"Of course someone lives here! Why else would I bring you here?" he replies, walking back down the stairs toward me. He stops on the bottom step. "What's going through your head right now?" he asks, looking down at me sadly, but I just shrug my shoulders. "What do you think I'm going to do to you?"

I look at him blankly without answering and shrug my shoulders again.

"Wow, you must really think I'm some kind of monster, don't you?"

Duh! Again, I shrug my shoulders.

He reaches out and hugs me, burying his head into my hair, but I don't hug him back. "Heather, I'm sorry I scared you so bad before. I'm not going to hurt you. I promise. Please, just come meet my mom."

Why?

He pulls away, grabs my hand, and turns to pull me up toward the stairs, but my legs feel like weights underneath me, and I can't move.

"Heather, come on please?" he pleads, tugging at my hand.

I know I can't win out here in the middle of nowhere. I have no choice, so I take a deep breath in as I follow his lead. *God, please let me make it home today.*

"Ma!" he calls out as he slowly opens the door.

Oh, thank God! His mom does live here.

"Damn, boy, you don't have to yell. I'm sittin' right here," she replies.

As I walk in the door behind him, I see his mom sitting at the table in the kitchen. I suddenly feel more relieved than scared. Surely, he isn't going to have his mom kill me. Although she looks like she's capable of it.

His mom is a small-framed older Black woman. But I can tell right away by her demeanor that she's scrappy. She has dark skin and dark eyes. Her hair is covered with rollers and a clear shower cap, and she's wearing a robe.

"Why didn't you tell me you were coming over here, boy? I woulda got dressed!" she snaps at him. "Who's the pretty little white girl hiding behind you?"

He introduces us, and she actually seems like she might be nice. *Too bad he's doing this a little too late.* I wonder if this is his ploy to get me back. It's not going to work.

Slowly, one by one, I meet his dad, one of his brothers, and a female cousin. As poor as they may be, his parents seem like decent people, but I'm really confused. He looks nothing like any of them. They all have really dark skin. Their facial features are not the same or even similar. Was he dropped off at their doorstep?

After we leave his parents' house, I tell him I really need to go home. He's really pushing his limits with me when he pulls up in front of some burger joint that looks more like a shack. The building is small, dingy, and as old as the dirt in this *Twilight Zone* town.

"I know you're hungry, Heather. Let me feed you before I take you home."

"Ok, fine," I sigh as I get out of the car. I notice him smiling in the

355

corner of my eye. I know he thinks he's won, but he has never been more wrong. I am hungry, and I'm relieved to know I no longer need to be afraid for my life.

He makes small talk with the nice older man at the window. I can tell he's known him for years. I'm sure it's not hard to know everyone out here.

"Ew! What the hell is this?" I ask after taking a bite out of my burger.

"You never had it like that before?" Shane asks, laughing.

"No! What is it?"

"Girl, that's a ghetto burger," he replies, cracking up laughing "It's got relish on it," he adds.

"Relish?" I ask, dumbfounded. "Relish is for hot dogs, not cheese-burgers." I can't help but laugh.

After moments of silence, he gives me that smoldering look again.

Oh God, I hope I haven't done anything to give him the wrong impression.

"Shane, I have a boyfriend, and I have no intentions of breaking up with him or cheating on him."

His look quickly vanishes. "Damn girl! Why do you keep saying that? I know!"

"Well, I don't know why you kidnapped me and brought me out here or what it is that you want from me."

"Kidnap you? Ha! You're funny, girl. Come on, let's go for a walk," he says standing up and reaching for my hand.

"Shane, I have to go home."

"I know, Heather, just a few more minutes. I promise."

"Shane, you've been making me promises all day and haven't kept any of them."

"I know, I'm sorry. After this, I swear I'll take you home."

He leads me up a hill behind the burger joint that has a lone, scraggly tree at the top of it. It might be the only tree out here. Every-thing else is all brush. The hill could be pretty if it was grassy and not all dirt. This moment might even be romantic if I was with anyone other than him. He's talking to me, but I'm not really paying attention. My mind wanders to my old friend, Lisa. As I look around, I wonder where they found her body. Now that I've actually seen this place, I can see how it would be easy to hide a body out here. The thought sends a chill down my spine.

"You ok?" he asks, trying to get my attention.

"Yeah, I'm fine. Come on, let's go. I really have to go home. Ellen is going to freak out."

"Ok," he replies, but I sense the hesitation in his voice.

Before he can say or do anything else, I head back down the hill toward the car.

Once we're in the car heading back toward normal civilization and green grass, I start to feel more at ease. My relief comes a moment too soon when Shane suddenly pulls off the dirt road into the middle of a field with tall weeds.

"What are you doing, Shane?"

He doesn't answer. He keeps driving until the car is completely surrounded and covered with weeds. It's obvious he has really thought this through or this is not the first time he's done this.

What the hell is he doing?

I look around, and all I see are dead weeds that are taller than the car on all four sides. There's no way anyone can see us here, and I can't see out. My heart starts pounding. "Shane!" I yell as the car comes to a stop. "What the fuck are you doing?"

"Come on, girl. Stop pretending like you don't miss it," he replies as he puts the car in park. He turns toward me and puts his arm around me, trying to pull me closer to him.

"Shane! I have told you so many times. I have a boyfriend, and I love him! This is not going to happen!" I shout as I try to pull away from his grasp, but he's not letting me go.

He has his arm wrapped securely around my neck. He pulls me toward him and turns my face with his free hand to make me look at him. Oh no, he's got that mean look in his eye. *There's the old Shane. I knew he couldn't be far away.*

"Shane, please let me go," I beg quietly.

His face is so close to mine that I can feel his warm breath on my face. He's not letting go. He pulls me even closer and forces a kiss on my lips while I'm trying to resist using my hands to push him away and pull backward at the same time. *He's too strong.*

He pulls away from his abrasive kiss. "Come on, Heather. Don't you miss it?"

"No, damn it, I don't!" I say grabbing his head with my hands and trying to push him off me. "Shane!" I gasp out, already exhausted, and my neck feels weak from trying to pull away. "Please," I beg with a whimper in my voice. "I love my boyfriend, and I'm not a cheater."

He suddenly lets go and settles back in his seat face forward with a look on his face that tells me he's thinking hard about something.

"Please, take me home, Shane."

He turns to face me. "So, you don't cheat on *any* of your boyfriends or just this one?" *Where the hell is he going with this?*

"I don't cheat on anyone, Shane, but this one is different, too. He's good to me, and I'm not going to hurt him."

"So you didn't cheat on me?" he asks with doubt in his voice. "No!" I reply.

"That's funny, 'cause I'm pretty sure you and Darius had something going on," he says with spite in his voice.

Oh, geez!

"You know it is possible to be friends with someone without sleeping with them. I never touched Darius, and I can't believe you would think that. Not everyone is like you, Shane!" I snap back at him.

After minutes of silence, he leans over the center console so far he's almost on top of me, and he's in my face again. "Heather, I want you," he whispers in my ear.

"Shane, no!" I say, trying to push him out of my face again, but he won't move.

Before I know it, he has completely climbed over the center council and is on top of me pinning me to the seat.

"Please, Shane, stop!" I beg, feeling the tears starting to form in the back of my eyes.

He's kissing on my neck and breathing heavy in my ear, and the feeling is giving me the creeps. I think I could throw up. I don't know what to do next. *Do I scream? Do I fight him? Have I made it clear enough that I don't want this? God, I'm so scared.* I'm terrified that if I fight back he'll hurt me. I'm in the middle of nowhere in a field of weeds, and he knows no one knows where I am. *Is this why he brought me here?*

Suddenly, he reaches over on the side of the seat and pulls the lever so the seat falls all the way back.

Shit! This is happening, and I can't stop it. "Shane, I said no!" I cry, trying to push him off me again. "I love my boyfriend. I don't want this!"

He stops and stares at me. Tears are streaming down my face. "Why are you crying?" he asks.

As if you don't know!

"Because I don't want to do this. I love my boyfriend."

He stares at me for a moment, and I think he might listen to me and stop. I couldn't be so lucky as he continues where he left off, kissing my neck, fondling me wherever he can put his slimy, dirty hands.

I don't know if I have ever felt this gross before. The memories of my thirteen-year-old self at the elementary school park flash through my mind, and it occurs to me that he is undoubtedly going to rape me. I can't fight him. I'm too scared he'll kill me and leave my body in these weeds. So, I quit trying to push him off me, and I lie there in the seat, stiff as a board, crying the whole time while he has his way with me. He looks at me a few times, seeing the tears coming down my face, but he keeps going anyway.

My body is in survival mode. My instinct is not to fight him but to give him what he wants so I can make it out of this alive. I did my part. I said no a million times, and my tears should be enough to enforce that. Without even thinking about it, I say out loud a few times through my tears in a quiet voice, "I love my boyfriend," but he keeps going anyway.

When he finally takes me home, I have him drop me off a few blocks away from the house. I get out of the car without saying a word to him, and he says nothing to me. I cried the whole car ride back, and he remained quiet. I know he realizes what he did. *What could he possibly have to say to me?*

I continue to cry on the walk home, anxious to get there so I can take a shower and wash his filth off of me. I know what he did was wrong; it was rape. I'm old enough and smart enough to know the difference now, but I won't go to the police. I can't. The sorry piece of shit deserves to rot away in a jail cell for the rest of his pathetic life. But I know if I go to the police, I will never be able to get away from him, and I just want him out of my life. He didn't say it. He didn't have to, but I know he will never bother me again. *He got what he wanted.*

Ellen still isn't home. *Thank God!* I take a long, hot shower, go down to my room, climb into bed, and turn on the TV for background noise. Ever since the panic attacks started, I can't sleep without the TV. It's a force of habit now to turn it on. I'm just going to stay down here the rest of the night and avoid Ellen at all cost. I can't tell her either because she'll go crazy. Maybe not on me, but definitely on him. I can't have the police involved in this. *Who knows, she may kick me out for being stupid enough to get in his car in the first place. She'd never trust me again.*

I lie in bed, crying, wondering what the hell I'm going to do about Ryan. I have to tell him. He's the one person I can't hide it from. He needs to know. He has the right to know. I just don't know how I'm going to do it. I know what happened isn't my fault, but getting in his car was. I won't blame Ryan if he never wants to talk to me again.

At least he had the good sense to wear a condom. When we were dating, he never even thought about putting on a condom, but this one time he did. *Thank God! Who knows what he's carrying these days.* The fact that he even had it with him tells me what his intentions were. Whether it was to avoid the nightmare of another pregnancy or cover his tracks from the police, it doesn't matter. I need to get past this, but I know I can't even begin until I tell Ryan.

As I lie here, staring at the TV, I am not paying attention to what's on because I'm too busy crying. I am worrying myself sick about how Ryan will react to this. I realize how truly exhausted I am, and I roll over to face the wall. *I'll sleep away my worries for now.*

With my eyes still half open, I slowly start to doze off when I suddenly feel a presence around me. My eyes shoot open. I don't move. I'm frozen solid. The presence feels like a warm blanket wrapped around me as if someone is lying behind me with their arms around me and is holding me tight. A tear comes to my eye. I'm unsure if I should be afraid of the feeling, but I feel more comforted than scared. I imagine my mom's arms around me and her telling me everything is going to be ok.

"Please, don't leave me," I whisper, starting to cry harder as I hold my body perfectly still, afraid the feeling will go away.

When I finally fall asleep, I dream about my mom for the first time since she died. She's standing in the middle of a crowd of people with her back to me, and I know in my heart it's her. I would recognize her hair anywhere. I start running toward her, crying and calling out to her, afraid she'll disappear before I reach her.

When I get to her, I reach out and grab her shoulder. "Mom?"

She turns and smiles. I grab her and hug her as tight as I can, crying and telling her how much I love and miss her. I beg her to come back with me. While I'm hugging her, I have my hand in her hair. I can smell her perfume. It's all so real that I never want to wake up.

She backs away from my hug to look me in the face. "Heather, I can't stay. I'm sorry, but I promise everything is going to be ok. I'll always be with you."

She looks so beautiful and peaceful. Something about her is different.

"No, Mom! Don't leave me! Please!" I beg her, crying, but she slowly disappears.

Chapter Eighteen

As I sit on my brand-new couch in my new apartment, beaming with joy, I am overwhelmed by the excitement of my newfound independence. I look around, wondering how the hell I finally got here. After all the things I've been through, I never thought I'd see the day. Mom was right. Time really does fly by. *It sure didn't seem like it at the time, though.* I couldn't wait to be on my own. And now that I'm finally here, I couldn't be happier.

Well, these boxes aren't going to unpack themselves. I find a spot on the floor and pull one off the boxes over in front of me to open it up. The first thing I see is the wooden frog that Mom made for me during one of her hospital stays when she was attempting to get clean. I flip it over and stare where she wrote "To: Heather" on the bottom of one leg and "Love, Mom" on the other. It brings a tear to my eye. *I miss her so much.* I know if she were here that she would be proud of me. I don't know if the bitterness I feel over losing her will ever go away. Knowing she would be proud isn't enough sometimes. I want to hear her say it and see it on her face. There are so many firsts that she's missed and a million more to come. *How will I ever deal with all of them?*

I set the frog to the side and continue to rummage through the box.

At the bottom sits my latest journal. *Hmm...I should write or maybe I'll read a little bit first.* As I flip through the pages, most of my entries are about some stupid boy breaking my heart. The most recent one is Greg. *Geez...I was pathetic over him.* I had been dating him for a little over a year, and I finally just cut him loose for good this time.

The beginning of our relationship was perfect, like they always are in the beginning. Before long, he showed his true colors. He wasn't a woman beater or anything like Shane, although the bastard did slap me once. Ellen happened to be looking out the window and saw him do it. I thought she was going to kill him. When she came running out the door, screaming at him, he was terrified, and he took off like a little coward. He never touched me again, and he was no longer welcome at Ellen's. Even though she hated him after that, I was dumb and stayed with him anyway.

Now when I look back, I can't believe I ever even dated him. He was a jerk, and it didn't really sink in until recently. And now, I want nothing more to do with him. Now that I'm finally on my own, this is where I'm going to stay. On. My. Own. Completely. I'm done letting boys hurt me and walk all over me. For the first time ever, I have no interest in having a boyfriend or being tied down. I realize now how much I let boys affect my life, and I'm totally over it.

Who knew a little independence could change your outlook so much? It's my turn to think about myself, what I want, and where I'm going. I don't have time or patience for anything else. And someone tying me down will only get in my way.

I flip back through my journal to the days before Greg, and there's more entries about another stupid boy—Kevin. The eighteen-year-old weirdo from my childhood who is now twenty-five with five daughters all from different mothers, and he doesn't take care of any of them.

God, how did I ever think he cared about me back then? I was such a stupid little girl. No wonder my mom went crazy about my relationship with him. I'm glad I ran back into him because I don't know if I would have ever realized how truly messed up he was otherwise. I needed to see it. What he did was wrong. I think it was normal for me to have a crush at eleven years old. What wasn't normal is that he took advantage of that. *Yuck!* The memory of it gives me the creeps.

A few pages before my run in with Kevin, there's a happy entry, and it makes me smile.

Dear Diary,

I'm so excited! I am finally finishing high school! It's not the way I imagined it, but it's happening! I'll be able to start taking classes at college a year sooner than I was supposed to, and I can't wait!! Since I'm not seventeen yet, I had to go to court today and ask for the judge's permission. I was really nervous because I had to explain to him why I wanted to drop out of school to get my G.E.D. The explanation was simple. It's not like I wanted to drop out, but I'm so far behind on my credits that there is no way I'm going to graduate on time. I'd end up spending an extra year in high school. As long as I'm in high school, I have to live in a foster home. I am sad that I'm going to miss out on all the normal things other kids get to do, like prom and graduation. I'll never go to a high school reunion...but since when has my life ever been normal? I know I've missed out on a lot of things growing up. But now, I just want to succeed so I won't miss out on the important things later. Getting my G.E.D. gives me a head start on college, plus, I can move out on my own as soon as I turn eighteen. There's no way in hell I want to wait an extra year to be able to do that.

I love Ellen to death, but being on my own means finally being away from the system. There's nothing I want more than that. I was surprised by the judge's response. He went into a big, long speech about how he always knew I was different, which is why he kept giving me chances. He said he was proud of the bright, strong, young woman I've become. He also said it gives him great pleasure to be a part of me succeeding. If he can help me reach my goals, he will. It felt good to hear him say those things. I couldn't be more thankful that he didn't give up on me. Because God knows, there were many times he probably should have. So next week, I get to go take my pre-test to see if I need the study classes. If not, I get to take the test right away. Yah! I get to start college in the fall!!! All the people who have ever doubted me along the way or tried to hold me back can go suck it!

The Soon-To-Be High School graduate! Heather

I can't help but giggle with excitement and smile as I remember the judge's speech. It was the last time I saw him. Looking back now, I think he knew it would be. There was no need for me to see him when I wasn't moving around and getting in trouble. Going home was no longer something I was fighting for. I knew I needed to stay grounded where I was to get through the rest of my time in the system.

I flip the pages back a little further, and I find my Ryan entries, remembering how all of that went terribly wrong. I thought the rape was going to be the end of us, but he was surprisingly supportive about it. Naturally, he wanted to kill Shane. But I didn't know how to find him. Even if I did, I wouldn't have been crazy enough to tell Ryan. I was right about Shane, too. He left me alone after that. No more phone calls or anything. *Thank God.*

Shane got what he deserved in the end. He screwed up his intensive probation and was sentenced to four years in prison. He's already served some of his time and will be released soon on good behavior after only a year and a half. The piece of shit deserves to spend the rest of his life in there. But there's no doubt in my mind that he'll be back there someday. I've been staying updated on the department of corrections website of his release date, terrified that he'll hunt me down when he gets out. I hate how much I fear him. *I wonder if that will ever go away.*

I read the entries about my pregnancy with Ryan and the miscarriage. I still can't believe I got pregnant again. I thought we were being safe. I don't know how I could have been that stupid again after what I went through the first time.

The whole thing changed our relationship and there was no going back. He was distant and cold while I was terrified and angry. I didn't want a baby, but I knew abortion was not an option. I could never do that again to a baby or to myself. I spent a lot of time praying to God in those few months to take the pregnancy away, promising Him that I really did learn my lesson. Eventually, my prayers were answered.

I've never felt so conflicted about anything before. I was sad, but I was also relieved. Nothing can describe the guilt I feel for wishing it away like I did. I don't know if I'll ever have kids. I always thought I wanted them, but I just don't think I deserve them. If it does ever happen, I'm going to make sure I do it the right way. I'll finish college first and then worry about marriage and kids. Right now, the thought of that couldn't be any further from my mind.

Moving on to another diary entry, I find one about my sister.

Dear Diary,

Malory is such an evil BITCH! I tried to call her today, but Tony was home so she put on her usual act. I wonder if it's even an act anymore. If he's there when I call, why doesn't she just hang up on me? She takes it too far. She told me today I'm a dirty, nasty slut, and that I'm not her sister. She wants nothing to do with me. I'm dead to her and to never call her again! I was so mad and hurt. I called her back and cussed her out. I know she's going to call me tomorrow and pretend like she didn't mean any of it. She always tells me she only says those things because he's standing there. She has to pretend like she hates me so he doesn't think we talk to each other. But why does she have to be so mean about it? She must actually think those nasty things about me or she wouldn't say them, right?

Ellen got so mad today after it happened because I was upset, and I couldn't stop crying. She keeps telling me that I need to walk away from her. "Sister or not, you don't deserve to be treated that way." She's my sister! How could I give up on her? I know I probably need to. All she has ever done is hurt me. But ever since Mom died, I feel stronger than ever that we have to stick together. Something is wrong with my sister. It's like she has two personalities. I don't understand her at all. How could we be so different? She always tells me I'm a stuck-up bitch too. How could I be a stuck-up bitch when I love someone like her!? She only says that because I dress and act like a girl. Tony has her thinking and dressing like a damn boy! She even talks like she's a gangster! She didn't used to be like that. How could anyone let someone change who they are? She's so two-faced! What's wrong with her? I think she secretly hates me for something that isn't even my fault, but she won't come out and say it.

After she left Ohio and got caught on the run, I sent her a letter once she got to her new foster home. I mailed her my school picture and the homecoming picture of Jack and me. When she moved in with Tony, she had to hide them from him so he didn't know she cared about me. I guess he found them and pretended like he threw them in the garbage. A few weeks later, while she was doing his laundry, she found my school picture in the back pocket of his jeans. When she asked him why he had it, he said, "Because your sister is fine." She asked him why he didn't keep the other one and he said it was because he didn't want a picture of me with some dude in it! What a creep! Is that why he always pretends like he hates me? Because he has a crush on me? Ever since that happened, I can't help but think she hates me because of it. How is that my fault? I would never like him like that! He is disgusting! How can my own sister hate me so much when I have never done anything to her but try to love her?

Betrayed,

Heather, the nasty slut!

That happened a few years ago. And today, nothing is any different. I still keep trying to love her and be close to her. The outcome is always the same. She constantly calls me a slut or whore when she's mad at me. She knows it's what bothers me the most. I have obviously been with more guys than her, and sometimes, I start to believe those things about myself.

I wish I could take back the mistakes I've made. But I can honestly say, I'd rather be a "slut" and date different guys until I find the right one than be with one guy who abuses me and treats me the way Tony treats her. I can only pray that someday she will open her pretty eyes.

Malory has a son now, and I pray that he doesn't have to grow up the way we did. It's not fair for him to be born into that mess. I have to sneak around to see them, and I hate it. For now, I have to live my life for me and not let her hurtful words drag me down. No matter how much it kills me that I don't have my sister. *Have I ever really had her?*

I turn to an entry about my dad...

Dear Diary,

I had an argument with Aunt Phoebe today on the computer. I feel like I could scratch her eyes out right now. She told me I was no longer her niece at the end of it. Oh, well, good riddance!!! So typical for her to disown me. What else is new in that family? I don't understand why disowning someone is always their answer to everything. I think I understand now why sticking together as a family was always so important to my mom. She knew what it was like to be abandoned. Although she did it to us countless times, she always tried to teach us differently. Such a contradiction, I know. Aunt Phoebe got mad at me because I went off on her after she talked trash about my dad for not helping pay for Mom's funeral. I guess everyone in Mom's family thinks he lied about not having life insurance on her. They are even talking about taking him to court and suing him! If that happens, I will never speak to any of them ever again!

I called my dad after I talked to her, and he laughed about it. He said let them. They won't get anything out of him. I asked him if it was true, and he said no. He had Mom taken off his insurance some time before she died. Not the smartest thing for him to do given how she lived her life, but I believe him. He kept telling me not to be so upset over what anyone else thinks, but I can't help it. They are supposed to be my family. Aunt Phoebe also talked trash, saying how they always go to the cemetery all the time while none of us ever do. I'm seventeen years old! What does she expect me to do, fly to Ohio in my jet? Dad doesn't go because he's not ready. They have no idea how hard it's been for him or the rest of us because they're not around. I'm so tired of their opinions and accusations. They just need someone to blame for her death, so they're choosing Dad. I am the wrong person for her to vent to.

Maybe if they came to see us more than one time in all these years, they would know how much my dad loved my mom, and that it's not his fault she had so many problems. They're in denial. That's what it is.

369

They don't want to take any blame for anything they did to hurt her, so they're putting it off on him to cover up their own guilt. What do they expect from me? How can they expect me not to defend him? He's my dad and the only parent I have left. I'll be damned if I ever let anyone talk bad about him. I know he's not a perfect man, but he tried harder than Mom ever did. Her problems started way before they ever met! Her problems started with those hypocrites!

Confused & Pissed Off Heather

Remembering that now still makes me a little angry. Aunt Phoebe went six months without talking to me. We're ok now, but we don't talk all that much, anyway. Maybe someday, things can be different, and the blame game will finally end. I've been guilty of blaming other people, too, always putting it off on her childhood. The reality is, Mom is the only one who can really be blamed for how her life turned out. I know she was dealt a crap hand, but so was I. I know I haven't always made the right choices, but I have tried so hard to learn from my mistakes. Most importantly, I learned from watching her mistakes. And I know that I will never live the same life she did, no matter how bad things may get.

Chapter Nineteen

I worry about my dad all the time. His drinking has spiraled out of control, which makes me also worry myself sick over the boys. He's so lost without Mom. I kind of understand him, but my brothers don't. Theo seems so angry all the time. I see the kind of hate boiling inside of him toward Dad like the hate I used to have toward Mom. I try talking to him, but all he'll ever say is, "You don't know, Heather, because you're not here. You'd rather live in a foster home than be with your own family."

Yeah, right, that's what it is. I hope someday he understands and stops being so angry all the time.

Christmas and Thanksgiving have been a train wreck without Mom. We all miss her and the way she used to make those days perfect —no matter what was going wrong in our lives. Dad hasn't celebrated any of the holidays since she died. It makes me sad for my brothers. I've had holidays at Ellen's to distract me. It hasn't been so bad for me, but what about them? Dad hasn't even put the tree up. He just hands us cards with stacks of cash in them as if that's going to make everything ok.

Next Thanksgiving, I'll make sure it's different. I'm going to teach myself how to cook and try to fill Mom's shoes. I know that's what she would want. I can't replace her or make everyone's sadness go away, but all she ever wanted was for us to be a family. If I can bring some of that back, I'm sure as hell going to try.

The next diary entry I come to is a contradiction to the last one. I was mad at Dad because he had been promising me that he was going to come get me and take me car shopping for the past six months. But then when the weekend would come, he would have some excuse. Ellen was mad that whole time, and I get why. Seeing me upset and disappointed every weekend by my dad really bothered her. But she would never say anything bad about him, no matter how upset it made her.

Dad really is clueless without Mom. I never realized how much she pulled everything together until she was gone. When she died, I think a part of him died, too. Maybe I'm making excuses for him, but he's my dad, and I love him, flaws and all. I know that he will never be the "All-American Dad" I've always dreamed about, but I still feel lucky to have him.

He has definitely broken a lot of promises, but for the most part, he's always there when the going gets really tough. He finally bought me a car when I had to drop out of my first semester in college because I didn't have a ride to school. He was mad that I didn't tell him what was going on before I had to drop out. But why would I? I had given up on the idea that he was going to buy me a car. However, he finally followed through on his word and made sure I had a car before the next semester started.

Since Mom died, he's been saving the social security money once a month and promised me that I would get it when I turned eighteen. I was depending on that money to get me started. When I turned eighteen, I found out that there wasn't anything left of it. I was devastated. I don't think I had ever been so mad at him before. This was not like taking my birthday money when I was a kid and promising to give it back but then never doing it. This was thousands of dollars that was supposed to buy me my freedom. I know he never had to save the money in the first place, but he shouldn't have made a promise he couldn't keep.

I started working full-time as a pizza delivery driver at a small place close to Ellen's. The money I have been able to make has been incredible. I moved in with my friends who introduced me to Greg back when I first started dating him. I was only living there a few weeks before that went bad. Ellen always warned me not to trust that friend. But, like everything else in my life, I had to learn the hard way.

When I was kicked out suddenly without warning, I turned to Dad for help. I had already started accumulating furniture. I found a studio apartment, so I wouldn't need much more, just a few odds and ends. With the money I've made, I've been able to buy myself a bedroom set, a couch, a dining room table, and even my own computer. After trying to convince Dad until I was blue in the face that I could make it on my own, he gave me the $400.00 deposit.

I know in Dad's own dysfunctional way being able to swoop in and save me makes him feel good. Providing has always been his job. When I really need him, I know I can count on him. He may not be able to say it or show it, but in my heart, I know he's proud of me. *I hope.*

I know that going back to Dad's is always an option if I want to or need to. He made it perfectly clear that I can always come home. I think he's worried about me being alone. But in time, he'll see I can do it. I miss them every day, but I'm happy with my life and my freedom. I love my job, and I love going to college. I have so many plans for my future. I don't know the exact path life will lead me down. But I know wherever I end up, someday, I will be helping kids just like me.

I wonder if there is any way I can somehow make a difference in the system. I still doubt myself, but that's something I need to work on. As long as I work hard enough, I know I can do anything. There has to be *something* I can do. The system is broken and I realize that now more than I ever have before.

About a year ago, I ran into my first GAL at church. *Ha! Me, willingly going to church!* I laugh at the thought. He was standing in the doorway, handing out programs as everyone walked through the door. I, of course, recognized him immediately. I said hi and smiled. When I could tell he had no clue who I was, I asked him if he remembered me. Sadly, he didn't. He brushed me off like I must be crazy for thinking I knew him. He said, "God bless," as he handed me the program. And my response to him was, "No, God bless *you*."

It blows my mind to this day that he didn't remember me. I don't know why I am shocked by the revelation. He didn't talk to us one time in four years. I must have been in that courtroom a hundred times. *Why was he in that position if he didn't really want to help us?*

I've heard that he's a top dog defense attorney these days and on his way to becoming a judge. From what I've been told, doing civil service work is a part of working your way up the system. It's nice to know my family, and countless other families, were just a stepping-stone for him to get where he really wanted to be. *Scumbag!*

At the very end, I had the best caseworker I ever had. She was the only one that genuinely cared all of those years. *Figures I wouldn't get her until my time was up.* Everything really does happen for a reason, though. Sometimes, I can see that more clearly than other times. She secretly told me about a program called the Youth in College Program. As long as I'm in college, the state will give me $525 a month to put toward my living expenses. She made me swear I would never tell them who told me about the program because they actually train them not to tell us about it. She was worried she would get suspended or even fired if they knew she told me. *Why is the system so messed up?* They pretend to care about us and say they want us to succeed when we get out, but it's all bullshit. I know how lucky I am to have met her and know about it, but how many other kids don't? I have been blessed to have my father still in my life to help me as much as he has. Most of the kids in the system aren't as fortunate, and they need the help more than I do. The thought of it angers me and sickens me. It may not seem like a lot, but it could make all the difference for someone trying to be on their own. I'm able to pay my entire monthly rent with it and still have money left over. *The system sucks!*

In my almost nine years in the system, I have met far more people who don't care than ones that do. Even some of the ones that I know had the best intentions are clueless and don't know what to do to help. Wouldn't it be nice if everyone who worked for the system knew on a first-hand basis what each kid was going through? Unfortunately, most of the kids who grow up the way I did don't make it through the system with a level head. *Why me, God? There has to be a reason I survived. I promise You that I will not stop trying to do my part; even if I only help one person in the end, it will be worth it.*

As I start to feel sleepy from reading and crying off and on, I put my journal down and go back to the box. "Oh my God!" I say out loud, smiling as I pull out the old *Soul Asylum* tape. I haven't listened to this in years. I still have a tape deck on my radio so I pop it in and hunt for my favorite song.

As it starts to play, I listen intently to the words. I realize I am no longer the "Runaway Train" I used to be, and it makes me smile. I am no longer that angry little girl that just needs someone to love her. I am a strong, independent young woman with her whole life ahead of her. I also realize that I no longer need anyone else's approval as long as I continue to believe in myself. Nothing else matters.

Listening to the song reminds me of when I was little. I always felt different and misunderstood. Those feelings have never gone away, and I know now that it's because I am meant for something greater. I don't know how long it will take me to figure out what it is, but I'm sure that I have many more lessons to learn. I will never lose hope. I will never stop trying. No matter what life brings my way, I will always be who I have always been.

I pick up my journal and write.

Mom,

I will live the life you could only dream about. I will do all the things you could never do. Someday, I will be the mother and the wife that you always wanted to be but couldn't find the strength to become. No matter how hard it is, I make these promises to you and to myself right now. I will not wait for God or the universe to answer all my questions. I will seek the answers for myself, and I will not stop until I find them. I may make mistakes on the way, but I promise to learn from them. I will never give up hope that there is more to my life than all this tragedy. When something knocks me down, I promise you, Mom, that I will continue to do what I have always done because anything else is unacceptable. I will get back up! I promise I will not let anything ever change who I am. And most importantly, I promise you, Mom, I will not let your death be in vain. I will give your life purpose and meaning by walking through the rest of my life striving to make you proud.

The Best Part of You, Heather

Acknowledgments

To My Dad ~

Thank you for never abandoning us no matter how hard life got. There must have been times you wanted to run, and no one could blame you, but you never did, and I love you for that. I learned everything I know about loyalty from you. I hope you find peace in knowing it wasn't all for nothing, and I will keep getting up every single time I fall because that's what you taught me to do. We don't start fights, we finish them, right?

To My Mom ~

Without you, there would be no story to tell, no chance to reach and help others. Even at your weakest points, I was always learning from you. You suffered an immeasurable amount of pain in your lifetime that took me years to understand, but I finally do. Because of you, I have the courage to speak out. Watching you suffer taught me that staying silent will never be an option. Your life had more meaning than you could have ever imagined, and the things you wished for will live on through me and future generations.

To My Big Sis ~

Thank you for riding along with me while I wrote this book. (And for never getting mad at the words spoken and for encouraging me to keep going.) I'm thankful that we were able to get closer during that time and pray to God we continue to grow. No matter how old I get, I'm always going to need my big sister to have my back. I love you!

To My Little Brothers ~

I'm sorry if I ever made you feel abandoned when we were kids. To leave you to fend for yourselves in a world where no kid should fight alone was never what I wanted. I'm always going to be your big sister, and I'm here no matter what. We did it, we survived. I'm thankful that we all have the chance to take this life and the lessons we learned to do what we want with it. Turn it into something great, because that's what Mom would want. I love you both more than words can say.

To the Four Beautiful Souls I Get To Call My Children ~

Thank you for blessing my life in more ways than you could ever know. May you continue to finish what I started and break so many cycles that the generations after you don't even know what pain is. Always remember, because of you, giving up was never an option. All the roads I've traveled were always meant to lead to you. I'd travel them again and again to get here. Without you, my life would be meaningless.

To Grams ~

Thank you for always being my rock, my voice of reason, and my biggest supporter. For always being honest and telling me I was wrong when I needed to hear it, but also making sure I knew how much I was loved and how proud you were of me even when I fell on my face countless times. Thank you for always showing me what true strength really is and how to pull myself up by my bootstraps no matter what life is throwing at me. Most importantly, thank you for teaching me the biggest lesson I could learn in this life: "Don't you ever take no shit from anyone, girl!" Because of you...I won't, I promise!

To Adam ~

My dear friend who helped me with the edits and spent hours upon hours for months and months to get it as close to perfect as we could. You taught me so much during the whole process. Thank you, thank you, thank you!!! Not just for being an amazing teacher, but for being my biggest cheerleader through it all and becoming a close friend in the process. Your kind words and genuine, unconditional support made every single word written possible. And you did it all for nothing...other than the fact that you believed in me and believed in my goals. You helped me turn my wildest dream into reality, and I will be forever indebted to you for it. Thank you for being the amazing person and friend that you are!

To a Few of My Closest Friends ~

Thank you for reading each chapter as I was spitting them out. You know who you are. Your constant encouragement, positivity, and countless hours of listening to me ramble on about it all, kept me going. Without you pushing me, I wouldn't have been able to finish. I love you all and am eternally grateful.

To the Judge I Had All of Those Years ~

Even though I cannot call you out by name, I hope that somehow these words reach you and you know how grateful I am that I had you in my corner. Even when I was undoubtedly a relentless pain in your ass, you never gave up on me. Other judges would have locked me up and thrown away the key. (Not you, though.) Thank you for seeing something in me that I could not see in myself. Your kindness and patience with me helped shape the person I have become. You need to know that even in a severely flawed system, I knew you were one of the ones who actually cared. You made a difference in my life, and I'm sure you did in many others' lives, too. You are a beacon of light in a scary dark world.

To My Last Guardian Ad Litem (GAL) ~

You were a true inspiration to me, and although our time was short, that inspiration to help others the way that you helped me has continued to push me forward.

To the Handful of Caseworkers, Counselors, Mentors, and Foster Parents (there aren't many of you who

genuinely cared about me) ~

You are the only reason the system is not broken completely. Thank you for never giving up on me when I needed you the most. Keep doing what you're doing. Know that even on the hardest days, what you're doing and have done makes all the difference in the world for a kid. It did for me, and I will always love you for it!

To the Best Foster Mother ~

You had so much patience with me during times no one else could have. Thank you for showing me love at a time in my life I needed it most, for guiding me through the darkness, and for showing me that I was worthy. For teaching me how to respect myself more and how to walk away when I wasn't being treated the way I deserved to be treated. For defending me at times when I didn't know how to defend myself and never making me feel like I wasn't wanted. You opened your door and heart back up to me when I would stray off my path. I hope you know how much you meant to me and just how much you helped mold me into the kind of mother I wanted to be someday and have become. Your heart was so big; there was no end to how many you would allow inside of it. You were a true saint, and hundreds of lives have been changed because of your love.

To Brian ~

Thank you for being such a gentle, understandable soul and for never letting me forget my purpose. God put you in my path all those years ago for a reason, my friend. If not for you, I may have let the book collect dust for the rest of my life.

To Kim at KWE Publishing and My Amazing Editor, Maria ~

Thank you for your endless amount of patience and encouragement. Without you, I wouldn't have this opportunity to see my dream through to the end.

Printed in the USA
CPSIA information can be obtained
at www.ICGtesting.com
JSHW011637170524
63145JS00011B/158

9 798986 570549